THE SCOTS' CRISIS
OF
CONFIDENCE

D1428807

Big Thinking:

Big Thinking is an independent agency which seeks to further innovative and inclusive thinking and practice relevant to Scotland and further afield. It engages in a range of activities: publishing, events, seminars, aiming to bring together policy/practice skills, think tank and do tank activities, and work with a range of partners and agencies. Future activities this year include a new edition of Tom Nairn's The Break-Up of Britain, work on the knowledge economy and research on international cities.

Cranhill Arts Project:

The Cranhill Arts Project works in the Greater Easterhouse area of Glasgow. For the past twenty years it has involved local residents in arts projects of various kinds. The photograph on the cover of this book was taken in Cranhill by Margaret Ann Gachagan when she was involved in the Project in 1990. The project leaders are keenly aware that alongside social deprivation there are three main barriers to local people expressing themselves through art: the fear of making mistakes; low self-confidence; and peer group pressure.

Carol Craig

THE SCOTS' CRISIS OF CONFIDENCE

CAROL CRAIG

Big Thinking

First published by Big Thinking, 2003
Reprinted by Big Thinking, 2004

ISBN 0-9544396-0-0

Copyright © 2003 by CAROL CRAIG

Carol Craig has asserted her moral right under the Copyright,
Designs and Patents Act, 1988, to be identified as the author of this work.

All rights reserved. No part of this publication may be
reproduced, stored in a retrieval system, or transmitted,
in any form, or by any means, electronic, mechanical,
photocopying, recording or otherwise, without the prior
permission of Big Thinking, 8 Redford Loan,
Edinburgh EH13 OAX.

For press and publicity enquiries please contact:
07931-177167

Designed by Iain Clark
Printed by Dave Barr Print, Glasgow.

CONTENTS

ACKNOWLEDGEMENTS

I could not have written this book without the support, encouragement and insights of a great many people. I would particularly like to thank the following individuals for taking the time to give me comments on specific chapters of the book: Andrew Bolger, Derek Brown, Robert Crawford, Douglas Gifford, Anne Johnstone, Annette Kuhn, Greg Lucas, Margaret Martin, Mike Russell, John Sangster and Nigel Smith. I am particularly indebted to Jim Greig for his insightful comments on the sections of the book dealing with the impact of religion on Scottish culture. I would also like to express my appreciation to a number of people for devoting time and energy to exploring some ideas with me or supplying me with relevant information: Linda Kinney, Gerry Rice, Frank Martin, Brian Aitcheson, Fran Wasoff, John Laydon, Phil Hanlon, Gill Scott and Sue Innes. Thanks are also due to Dorothy Williamson, Moira Carrick, Pat Davers and Beatrice Wickens for their personal support and encouragement.

Alf Young, my partner for the past twenty-five years, played an important part in the writing of this book. It goes without saying that his newspaper columns on Scottish politics and the Scottish economy have been an important influence on me over the decades and have shaped my thinking on a number of issues. His feedback on some of the early drafts helped me to improve the structure and flow of the argument. In the past two years, as throughout our relationship, Alf has also given me a great deal of emotional, practical and intellectual support, for which I feel indebted. I also want to thank our two sons - Ewan and Jamie Young - for their encouragement and forbearance as their mother became more and more immersed in books and quizzed them repeatedly on their attitudes to all things Scottish. Thanks are also due to my sister Janice, my niece Rhona and my mother and father for the countless discussions we had on these themes.

I am particularly indebted to Gerry Hassan, the Director of Big Thinking, for his unwavering commitment to publish this book. It is very possible that without Gerry's interest, and the support of Big Thinking directors Denis Robertson Sullivan and Chris Warhurst, this book might never have been published. I would also like to thank Rose Pipes for her professional editing and her good humour in dealing with my various literary inconsistencies and foibles. Thanks are also due to Kirsty Wark, not just for reading and commenting on the manuscript and writing the foreword but also for her support and encouragement. I am also grateful to Cath Scott for giving me permission to quote three short poems by her husband, Alexander Scott.

There are three people without whose help, support and encouragement this book would never have been written: my friends Jean Barr and Stewart McIntosh and my sister Marianne Craig. I will ever feel indebted for their patience, understanding and insights. It was to these three people that I turned over the past two years when I needed to talk out some of my ideas. They also helped stiffen my resolve to tackle some of the more contentious issues in the book and provided me with real intellectual and emotional support when I most needed it.

I would also like to thank the thousands of people who have participated in my training courses over the past twelve years. If they had not been prepared to discuss their experiences and share their insights then I do not think I would have been able to understand the blockages in Scotland to the development of real self-confidence. To all of them I want to express my sincere thanks.

Finally, I must add that I alone am responsible for the ideas contained in this book and for any, inevitable, mistakes and errors of judgement.

Henry Drucker

When this book was at the final production stage I learned of the sudden death of Henry Drucker, an American who had lectured in politics at the University of Edinburgh from 1967 to 1986. Henry was an engaging lecturer who inspired a whole generation of politics students. He supervised my Ph.D thesis when I undertook postgraduate studies at Edinburgh University in the 1970s and became a colleague when I joined the staff. Without Henry's encouraging 'can do' philosophy during an important stage of my life, I would not have acquired the intellectual confidence to write this book. I am extremely sad that I will not be able to debate these ideas with him.

To my parents, Mary and Jim Craig
with love and gratitude

Foreword
by Kirsty Wark

I have known Carol Craig for twenty years as a friend and colleague and as someone whose intellect I admire enormously. Each time we meet and talk, our conversation is always, as if by some invisible force, pulled towards Scotland and our complex emotions about our homeland. Scotland is infuriating, judgemental, inspiring and magnificent. We are both utterly thirled to it. Over the years I have watched Carol prepare herself to write this important book. It in she wrestles with the beliefs, attitudes and cultural preferences on which our Scottishness is based and challenges conventional cultural analysis of who we are.

Since the Scottish Parliament was set up there has been a persistent clamour for new thinking. This book provides the tools to do some of that thinking. It is very provocative. Two arguments stand out. First, Scotland does not celebrate difference. Rather than our identity being too weak, Carol argues that ideas of Scottishness are too limiting and prescriptive and that the criticism of 'getting above ourselves' is not just a self deprecating joke, but a deeply corrosive national trait. She includes a wonderful quote from the Scots poet Alexander Scott, satirising the Scots' attitude to equality:

> *Scotch Equality*
> Kaa the feet
> Frae thon big bastard

I thought that should have been the title of her book! I heard another example the other day. Several men were drinking in a Dumbarton pub, and were talking about a local boy who had done well, had built his own construction business and was promoting enterprise. 'Aye,' said one of the group,' but his uncle's an alcoholic.' Her other main argument is that our dependence on logic and rationality, our Calvinist legacy, leads to an extraordinarily critical attitude towards others and at the same time a lack of emotional literacy. She argues that a major fault line running through Scottish society is a lack of respect for individuality, a stultifying culture of conformity. However, this isn't a negative book. It opens the door to new ideas. By highlighting different solutions to Scottish problems, it could help make Scotland a better place. I don't agree with all she has to say, but that's the point. We are allowed to disagree!

This is an eminently readable, stimulating and enjoyable book drawing on everything from the Bible to *The Broons*.

I am very proud of Carol's achievement.

Kirsty Wark
February 2003

Introduction

Robert Louis Stevenson once declared that, despite all the similarities between the Scots and the English, there is 'a very strong Scots accent of the mind'. Time has done little to eradicate, dilute or even smooth out this accent. Indeed for me one of the most striking features of modern Scotland is that the Scots still have a very strong set of attitudes and beliefs. Ask the Scots what these beliefs are and few could tell you. They may say something about Burns, democracy and 'a man's a man' but that is likely to be it, for beliefs are inevitably elusive. They condition and shape the way we see the world but we are often not aware of them. They are so right and natural for us that we do not stop to question them.

Over the years I have sought to understand the forces in people's lives which shape personality, self-confidence and beliefs. I have read a number of books which have helped me understand how being a woman has moulded my attitudes, beliefs and identity. But I cannot think of one non-fiction book about Scotland which has shed a similar intensity of light on what it means to be Scottish. Yet, ironically, there are literally hundreds of books around where the author at some point pontificates about Scottish character and attitudes. Every week, if not every day, the Scottish press contains soul-searching articles on Scottishness and Scottish identity. But such analyses never seem to get very far. And as each attempt to analyse Scotland and the Scots fails to further our understanding, yet another Scottish writer feels prompted to step forward and return to the collective Scottish navel for yet another gaze. How else can we account for the huge and ever-growing word mountain on Scotland and the Scots? Regrettably few of these words help us to understand what it means to be Scottish. Worse still, many simply fuel the fire of Scottish negativity and self-criticism.

A further irony for me is that the Scots are a people with a passionate need to understand. As Scotland is a country with an unusual constitutional status - a nation with no sovereign power

- it is easy to see why the Scots should try so hard to understand themselves and their predicament better. And this leads to something of a Caledonian conundrum: the Scots are a people with a quest to understand but who cannot understand themselves. It is now becoming crucially important that the Scots do begin to understand themselves better. For reasons I set out in a later chapter, in today's world the way we see ourselves, our self-confidence and our predisposition to negative or positive thoughts have huge implications for our personal and economic well-being. The beliefs and attitudes which I uncover in this book have important implications for all of us living and working in Scotland and they affect us both as individuals and as Scottish citizens.

I believe that to build a healthier, wealthier and wiser Scotland we need to change some of our mindset. Before we can do that we first need to understand what shapes our attitudes and our beliefs. While writing this book I have often seen my role as that of an archaeologist who knows something about the culture she is attempting to uncover but whose task is to clear away the sedimentary deposits that have built up over years so that a clearer image of a people and their culture can emerge. To help me undertake this Scottish excavation I have used various tools, insights and experiences in my possession. One such tool is the concept of psychological type derived from the work of the eminent Swiss psychologist Carl G. Jung. These are concepts which I use in my daily employment as a personal development trainer and organisational consultant.

On my courses I also have the opportunity to talk to people living and working in Scotland about their attitudes and beliefs and how they have been shaped by the prevailing culture. And the insights I have derived from these discussions have also been enormously helpful in forming my ideas. However, much of the picture of Scotland which emerges in this book comes from my own personal experience. I was born in Helensburgh in 1951 and have lived all my life, bar a few months here and there, in Scotland - mainly in Milngavie, Edinburgh, Glasgow and now

INTRODUCTION

Stirlingshire. Throughout this book I elaborate a number of Scottish attitudes and views and there is hardly one which I did not personally share for long periods of my life. Many only came to light when I became involved in personal development activities of one type or another. This means that I am not trying to write this book in a supposedly objective, academic way. I do not believe it possible for anyone, no matter how hard they try, to eliminate themselves, their beliefs and experiences from what they are writing about. So throughout this book I give examples from my own life and communicate my opinions where this is relevant. More importantly, many of the types of beliefs and values I discuss are deep-seated, almost unconscious, and so they would not easily be detected by attitude surveys. Indeed I freely admit that while I contend there are significant differences in the way the Scots and the English see the world, some of the recent empirical research shows that there is hardly any divergence between the Scots and the English on a whole range of attitudes.[1] So if you are the type of person who will only be convinced by numbers and 'hard facts' then I suggest you take the book back and get a refund. Of course, I do not simply make assertions and I give different types of evidence to support my views where I can. But ultimately it is up to you as reader to decide if my arguments chime with your own experience and have credibility.

Let me declare at the outset some of my own values and beliefs. I like various aspects of the Scottish belief system and I think they make a positive contribution to Scottish life - for example, the emphasis on principles; the importance of others; the work ethic; and the role of mission and purpose in an individual's life. But I also believe that many of the attitudes and beliefs encouraged by Scottish culture can be self-defeating and prevent us from developing healthy self-esteem, relating well to others or getting together to solve social problems. Indeed one of the recurring arguments in this book is that in Scotland we put far too much emphasis on the nation, the community, the collective and not enough on the individual. But this is not to say that I undervalue the importance of the collective. I simply believe that in Scotland the pendulum has swung too far to the collectivist side and, for balance, we need to understand and respect individuality more. But in arguing for the importance of individuality I am not siding with right-wing individualists, such as Milton Friedman or Michael Forsyth. My concern for individuality is about respect for difference, personal development, self-expression or the process Jung calls 'individuation'. It is not about a smaller state, deregulation or handing over less money in tax.

One of the reasons I am eager to strengthen individuality and difference is that a culture of conformity and mediocrity flourishes in Scottish life and there is a tyranny of public opinion. As a Scot myself I learned early in life that it is dangerous to put your head above the parapet, particularly if you want to say something different. Indeed as I have written some of the more contentious chapters in this book I have had various well-kent phrases such as 'Who does she think she is?' ringing in my ears. In other words, in true Scottish style I have worried about putting my bum out the window. I have persevered because, post-devolution, the Scots need some new angles on themselves. Most typical commentators on Scotland are male and belong to a narrow range of occupations - they tend to be writers, academics or journalists. As I am none of these things, I hope to bring a different perspective.

One of the problems I have encountered in writing this book is that it is extremely difficult to say anything meaningful about a people or a culture as a whole. People are individuals and it is difficult to categorise them as Scots, Italians, Americans and so on. Yet despite this we know from experience that national character does exist. The word 'Italian' conjures up a certain image in people's minds, just as the word 'Japanese' does. But this does not means to say that all Italians we meet fit the national stereotype. Some are quiet, reserved and unemotional. So national character is simply a way of trying to encapsulate the *spirit* and *preferences* of a people. We cannot use it to determine or predict the behaviour of each and every individual from that country. What's more, all human beings, irrespective of culture, share a huge amount in common. We all have emotions, use rational thought, have an instinct to survive, as well as alternating between activity and reflection. This means that when describing a particular people it is unlikely that we will be able to point to much that is unique about them. Every human being, for example, has a face made up of the same basic elements - nose, mouth, ears and so forth. Yet every individual's face is unique and it is the arrangement of these features, the strength of the nose, the set of the eyes, the relationship of the features which make that face distinctive. And etched on the physical structure of a face is that person's experience and emotions. So when I argue that one of the key aspects about Scotland is the love of logical thinking I am aware that the English are also fond of such thought processes. What is different, however, is the primacy of logical thinking in Scotland; the fact it has played such an important role in the evolution of Scottish culture and character. So logical thinking can be likened to a strong, Romanesque nose on the face of Scotland, whereas in England it is a much less noticeable feature. So I freely admit there is hardly a statement I make about Scotland in the course of this book that could not find some resonance in other cultures. What I am much more interested in is the *degree* to which we believe certain things and how these beliefs have shaped the way we see ourselves and the world and become part of how we, often unconsciously, define what it means to be Scottish.

When I started to write this book I had a fairly good idea of the types of attitudes and beliefs which I thought were common in Scotland. What I did not understand were the forces at work within Scottish culture to produce such a world view. Like many Scots I have never had much exposure to Scottish history and so I was not fully aware of some aspects of Scotland's past. It was only when I started to read books on Scottish history that the reasons for some of these Scottish beliefs started to emerge and began to make the picture I was creating much clearer and sharper. For me what has been most startling is the influence the Reformation exerted, and continues to exert, on Scottish life. It is the beliefs of Knox and the Covenanters - albeit in dilute form - which continue to influence the thinking of everyone living in Scotland - Protestant and Catholic, atheist and Muslim. I grew up a Protestant but I am now a confirmed atheist. Since conventional religion leaves me cold, I do not assert the importance of the Reformation to give weight to Protestant ascendancy or to keep Catholics in their place. I simply aim to show how Presbyterianism has made an indelible mark on Scotland and the Scottish people. Many commentators argue that the Reformation in Scotland, and the rise of Calvinism, has been a blight on Scotland and the Scots. But, as far as I am concerned, the Calvinist legacy has been mixed and has led to negative and positive features of Scottish life.

When I began to read many of the books around on Scotland I felt shocked at how negative many of these are. I do not see Scotland as a perfect place. Indeed I was motivated to write this book because I could see many faults and contradictions in Scottish thinking. But the negative images and analyses in many of these books are, to my mind, completely out of proportion. I simply do not recognise the descriptions of the 'schizophrenic', pathological Scot many of them peddle. So the last thing I wanted to do in this book was add my critical comments to this rotting and festering pile. I wanted to clear many of the negative arguments away before laying the foundations for my own analysis. And this I do in Chapter 2. I am aware that I will be charged by more critical readers of attempting to demolish others' arguments and then simply constructing another, equally negative, argument about Scotland. Certainly, there is some overlap between my arguments about the Scots and those advanced by some of the more negative commentators. But the whole tenor of my analysis is different from theirs. I try to show how the Scots' strengths and weaknesses are inextricably linked. I accept we have failings but I do not berate anyone for them. Perfection - being good across the board - is an illusion. This may seem an anodyne point but I believe it is something which many Scots still have to learn, for one of the key Scottish beliefs is that we should all be striving for perfection and that weakness of any kind is completely unacceptable. This is why the feeling of being 'never good enough' pervades Scottish life. So if all that people get from this book is the idea that Scotland is a wee country with good points and bad points then it will be a step forward. We are neither a nation of 'schizophrenics' nor 'the chosen people'. We are much more ordinary than that. Paradoxically, accepting ourselves just as we are is, for me, one of the first things we must do to begin to make life better for ourselves both collectively and individually.

The purpose of the book is quite simple. It aims to come up with a better way to understand Scotland and the Scots - a way which helps us to build Scottish self-confidence, reduce negativity and self-criticism and move on from some of the limiting beliefs of the past. In the following chapters I specifically aim to:

- analyse Scottish culture and the strengths and weaknesses of Scotland and the Scots;
- reveal some deeply held Scottish beliefs and attitudes;
- understand why the Scots lack confidence in themselves and their country.

Some of this book covers fairly intellectual territory but in covering this potentially stony ground I have tried to make the arguments as compelling as possible and I hope that anyone who wishes to understand Scotland and the Scots better will find it an interesting journey. There are many people working in Scotland who on a daily basis have to try and understand what makes the Scots tick; how Scottish attitudes are different from English or American attitudes; and what policies or initiatives would be going with the grain of Scottish culture. And I am thinking here about people working in business development and health education as well as people who are educational psychologists, councillors or MSPs. In fact, anyone who has a policy making role in Scotland.

As the book has a potentially diverse readership and as readers may find some parts of the argument more relevant and interesting than others, I have divided the book into five sections. I have given each section a clear title so it should be easy to navigate your way. I have also tried to make each section fairly self-contained. Section 1 looks in general at the Scottish crisis of confidence. In Section II I use Jung's concept of psychological type to construct an alternative way to view Scotland and the Scots. In these chapters I show how apparently unconnected aspects of Scottish life - such as Scottish country dancing, pulpits and the emphasis on breadth in Scottish education - can be linked and understood better if we have the right conceptual framework. In Section III I continue my search for the roots of Scotland's lack of confidence by examining her history - particularly her Calvinist past. For example, in this section I look at why the idea of equality is so important for the Scots and show how as individuals we may pay a high price for this prevailing value. In this section I also explain why Scotland has developed something of a dependency culture. Section IV is devoted to analysing Scottish identity and some of the conformity and confidence issues which flow from it. It is in this section that I look in depth at my contention that in Scotland it is not our identity as Scots which is in question but our identity as individuals. In Section V I highlight some of the ways in which individual Scots are brought up to have low self-esteem, and in the final chapter I suggest ways to move towards a new, confident Scotland.

As this book is concerned with culture and confidence it could cover every aspect of Scottish life and end up being a huge, unreadable tome. In selecting topics for inclusion I have concentrated on those where I feel I have a contribution to make. It is for this reason that I only make a passing reference to sport. I have also excluded topics, such as the suppression of Gaelic and Scots, where a great deal has already been written on its impact on people's confidence and attitudes. One of my biggest frustrations in writing this book has been on how to cover gender. I have always been interested in women's issues, indeed I was Chair of BBC Scotland's Equal Opportunities Committee for over five years. One of the issues which has interested me is how women are marginalised from mainstream culture. When writing a number of the chapters I was aware that I could have written much more if I had looked properly at gender differences. But, again, I have refrained for two reasons. First because it would have made the book too long and second because in some instances books on specific gender issues have been written. For example, Lesley A. Orr Macdonald's book, *A Unique and Glorious Mission,* is a definitive study of women's role in the Scottish Kirk.[2]

Which leads me conveniently to my penultimate point. I am not trying to write a definitive book on the Scots' crisis of confidence. I simply want to line up some of Scotland's holy cows, poke them to see what they are made of and ask some searching questions. If this process cuts them down to size or illustrates that they are well past their productive life-span, then their demise will create space for some new Scottish thinking.

Finally, at various points I discuss differences between Scotland and England and in one chapter I spend time analysing how the relationship with England may have affected Scottish self-confidence. But I do not address directly whether Scotland needs to become a fully independent country. My own view is probably best summed up in football manager Kenny Dalglish's immortal line 'maybe aye, maybe naw'. What I am clear about, however, is that Scottish independence would *not on its own* be enough to help Scotland become healthier, wealthier and wiser. Whatever the political road forward we need to address some of the confidence issues I raise in this book. And soon.

NOTES

1   See, for example, John Curtice, David McCrone, Alison Park and Lindsay Paterson, *New Scotland, New Society?* (Polygon: Edinburgh, 2001).

2   Lesley A. Orr Macdonald, *A Unique And Glorious Mission: Women and Presbyterianism in Scotland* 1830-1930 (John Donald: Edinburgh, 2000).

SECTION I

THE SCOTS' CRISIS

1
See Us

'See us? We're so pathetically unlucky, so pathologically committed to a horizontal position in the mud, that when the trumpet sounds on that great day when our ship finally comes in - we'll be at the airport.'
W. Gordon Smith, *This is My Country*

One of the consistent observations made by foreign visitors, or by returning Scots émigrés, is that in Scotland there is a palpable lack of confidence. This is why Crawford Beveridge - chief executive of Scottish Enterprise for almost a decade in the 1990s - declared, as he quit the job to return to the United States, that the major issue facing Scotland is a 'lack of self-belief'. People inside Scotland are also beginning to believe it is a big issue for the country. A *Sunday Herald* editorial at the beginning of 2001 even proclaimed 'the biggest barrier' facing Scotland is 'confidence'.

This deficit in self-confidence, self-belief, call it what you will, has wide economic repercussions. For a start it stops us from trumpeting what Scotland has to offer, thus undermining our marketing and tourist strategies. It suppresses the business birth rate and the ambitions of entrepreneurs. And no doubt it also fuels the annual exodus from Scotland. Scotland's migration statistics are truly shocking. At the time of the Union with England Scots made up 20 per cent of the total British population. Soon it will be nearer eight per cent. In the past four decades alone over a million Scots - many of the most talented and educated - have migrated to other lands. Scotland is the only European country where the population is expected to remain the same or decline in the next twenty years. Even Ireland has managed to staunch the haemorrhage of human capital from the country and now attracts people back in impressive numbers. Of course, there are many reasons why people emigrate but one of the most important is the belief that they cannot create a good life for themselves or their families if they stay. In other words they do not have sufficient confidence in their country's future. So

Scotland's record-breaking migration figures and the Scots' lack of belief in their homeland are two sides of the same coin.

The Cringe Factor

The confidence issue also affects Scotland's political culture. The Scots' tendency to criticise Scotland and denigrate the indigenous culture has been dubbed 'the Scottish cringe'. It is a cast of mind based on the belief that anything Scottish must be second-rate. This type of thinking was much in evidence in the devolution referendum campaign of 1979. Opponents of the proposed Scottish Assembly insinuated that, if it were created, it would manifest all the worst features of Scotland - insularity, parochialism and mediocrity. It would be *The Sunday Post* come to life. A glorified 'toon council'. This negative view was much less in evidence during the referendum campaign of 1998 but it was still around. One of my uncles, a former steel worker from Glasgow who made his home in Lincolnshire after the war, pronounced with scorn during a trip to Scotland - 'Devolution? A Parliament in Edinburgh? They'll make a right arse of it'. And this sentiment, albeit expressed in more sophisticated terms, has made its presence felt in newspaper columns and letters penned by anti-devolutionists, not just during the campaign but ever since. For example, in January 2001, a man from Lanarkshire wrote to *The Herald's* letter page to declare 'I hope to God I am not the only person who cringes with embarrassment every time one of that lot opens his/her/their mouths. Monklands Council writ large.'[1] Once Jack McConnell became leader and announced a programme of fairly trivial measures, various commentators even started to complain that the Parliament was 'Monklands writ wee'. So you can see how in this type of climate it is very easy for any falter or set-back in the Parliament to be greeted as evidence of *Scottish* ineptitude.

Before the Parliament was set up it was not uncommon for pro-devolutionists to argue that once Scotland could take responsibility for her own affairs the Scottish people would mature, stop blaming the English for problems, and begin to trust themselves. Political maturity would lead to a growth in Scottish confidence. It is much too early to tell whether these optimists are right. Three years, even ten years, is insufficient time to change a country's attitudes and culture. But given some of the adverse publicity the Parliament and Executive have managed to accrue in the first few years of life, there is a growing number of people who doubt whether devolution can ever be really successful in Scotland. Many of these pessimists are passionately committed to a Parliament in principle, but fear there is something malign at work in Scotland - that there is something bitter and critical in the Scottish psyche which will prevent the tender seedling of devolution from establishing healthy roots. They believe the Parliament will continue but it will be blighted by a toxic press and parties riven by bitter personal conflicts. The ensuing atmosphere will become so noxious, they argue, that talented people will not want to stand for election, thus ensuring that mediocrity will flourish unchecked.

I believe that, since devolution, there has been some rise in national self-confidence; few Scots could have remained unmoved during the opening ceremony for the Parliament when Scotland asserted its belief in egalitarianism; an assertion displayed both in the low-key, yet dignified role assigned to the Queen in the ceremony, and in the choice of song - 'A Man's a Man for a' that'. As a former community councillor, I am also aware that the existence of a democratic decision-making body in Edinburgh has the potential to increase interest and confidence in Scottish public life. But lack of self-confidence is such a challenge for Scotland and Scots I do not believe that the setting up of a Parliament, or additional powers, will eliminate the problem.

Wha's Like Us?

The Scots' lack of confidence is not confined to business and politics. It also manifests itself in that vitally important part of Scottish life - football. According to Scottish novelist and Hollywood script writer, Alan Sharp, this is not simply about whether Scotland can score enough goals to qualify for the World Cup but is about something much deeper than that:

> Football is the process which takes all those diverse elements of Scottishness which, in their real form, involve psychology and history and sociology, and it nutshells them, so when you see a Scottish football team play they play exactly like Scotsmen. They've not just got blue jerseys on, they've got all that complex inferiority/superiority thing going, they play in a certain kind of very fragile, arrogant, aesthetic way, and you realise that you're looking at your own image when you see a Scottish football team playing with all its defects and its enormous richness as well. To that extent it is ... a very pungent reminder, of your origins.[2]

It is not uncommon for commentators to argue, as Sharp does, that the Scots' lack of confidence can sometimes manifest itself as a defensive arrogance - an inferiority/superiority complex. And this notion of a vacillation between these two positions is common in what people write about Scotland. For example, a year or so after the Parliament was set up, the journalist and novelist Allan Massie wrote of his hopes that Scots' confidence was on the rise, saying that:

> In the past when we have not been wallowing in misery ('can we no dae anything right?') we have had an absurd blustering pride ('Wha's like us? Bloody few an' they're a' deid!'). Neither attitude smacks of maturity or sound mental health.[3]

The Individual Dimension

Self-confidence is not just an issue facing the Scots as a nation, it is an issue confronting many individual Scots. For example, in the mid 1990s the World Health Organisation undertook research which looked, amongst other things, at the self-esteem of fifteen year olds in twenty five countries. It found that Scottish teenagers were third bottom of the list on feelings of self-confidence. Only teenagers from Estonia and Slovakia ranked lower. Psychologists working in Scotland with young people are not surprised by such findings, saying that Scottish culture is designed to cut people down to size and that sarcasm, negative comments and put-downs are as common as wet days.

Health education professionals believe that lack of self-esteem lies behind many of Scotland's appalling health statistics. Why should people give up smoking, take exercise or generally look after themselves if they do not think they are worthwhile people? Poor self-esteem, they also believe, lies behind many of Scotland's atrocious mental health statistics, particularly the levels of depression and the fact that Scotland's suicide rate for young men is now twice that of England's. No doubt some readers will think this is not an esteem issue - that people would feel better about themselves if they lived in better areas, had money, jobs and opportunities - and I am not for a moment denying the importance of such factors in how people feel about themselves. But there is a chicken and egg problem here as well. Lack of ambition, feelings of worthlessness and general lack of self-confidence act as barriers which prevent people from taking up the opportunities which often do exist. This is the point that Chris Warhurst and others make in research they undertook in Glasgow.[4] They show how Glasgow's employment base has shifted from heavy industry to what they call 'the style market' - upmarket shops, hotels and restaurants. These new employers want employees who are presentable and self-confident and who possess good inter-personal skills. Many of these new service sector jobs are not being filled by unemployed people living in Glasgow's poorer areas but by people, often middle-class students, commuting into the city from places like Bearsden. In short, disadvantaged Glaswegians are not able to take advantage of the opportunities which do exist because they often lack inter-personal skills or confidence.

Confidence Matters

My own interest in confidence issues came to the fore about twelve years ago when I was working at the BBC as an education officer. Wanting a change in career and direction I trained to become an assertiveness trainer. Shortly thereafter I left the BBC to embark on a career as a training consultant running a wide variety of courses. Most of these courses have been in Scotland and have given me the opportunity to discuss with thousands of people living, working or studying in Scotland, their attitudes to self-confidence and how they see themselves, as well as how these attitudes can be traced back to their parents' beliefs. What began to concern me is that Scottish society as a whole, and many Scots individually, are deficient in self-confidence at a time when that very quality is soaring in importance. Change is now a constant feature of all our lives and most people in work have to learn a variety of new skills. Those who cope best with such changes are people who feel most confident. Indeed many employers no longer want to employ staff who need to be told what to do and who feel fearful or resistant to change. They want staff who can solve immediate problems themselves, who can work creatively on their own initiative, who embrace learning and who are good with people - either customers or fellow workers. This means that many of the people who are in demand are those who excel at what many male economic analysts dismissively call 'soft skills'. Even in high tech industries, managers are not as interested as you might think in hiring people with good technical skills and are often intent on recruiting self-confident people with good social skills, and the 'right' personality to fit into their company culture. The Scottish manager of a Japanese computer company told me recently that they were increasingly aware that they could teach new employees the technical skills they needed to work there; what they could not easily instil in employees were new attitudes or self-confidence.

The Scottish psychiatrist Alex Yellowlees argues that a whole range of studies have shown that good self-esteem also correlates with the ability to maintain good, positive relationships with others. It also is a major contributor to people's mental and physical health. And, like me, Dr Yellowlees believes that the fact that Scots are not brought up to feel confident in themselves is acutely worrying. Quite simply, if Scotland fails to do something about its confidence crisis it will increasingly affect our economic and social well-being as well as our intimate personal relationships, our attitudes to learning and our mental and physical health. Indeed confidence is now such an important quality in a people that in the future it may become something of a determinant of economic and social development, just as the existence of natural resources was a determinant in previous centuries. The politician in Scotland who most seems to understand this trend is Henry McLeish. When he was First Minister of the Scottish Parliament he tried to make an increase in confidence one of his main priorities. During his brief tenure in office, McLeish was fond of arguing that there are three keys to Scotland's success - 'competitiveness, compassion and confidence.' Indeed Henry McLeish spoke so much about the importance of increasing confidence that *The Sunday Herald* argued that 'if Henry McLeish has a "Big Idea" then it is "confidence"'.

The Elements of Confidence
Self-confidence results from an individual's basic belief that he or she is a worthwhile person who has the ability to act in the world in a way that is commensurate with his or her intentions. Self-confidence is thus a subtle interplay of two factors - self-acceptance (feeling worthwhile) and self-efficacy (feeling confident about being effective). Self-esteem is similar to self-confidence but gives more weight to feelings of self-worth than to self-efficacy. Self-confidence so defined obviously has significant implications for the effectiveness and creativity of individuals in their daily lives as well as for their personal relationships. If we lack self-confidence and feel we are useless, hopeless people then we may succumb to a victim mentality or we may over-compensate - try to 'prove' ourselves by acting in an arrogant or bullying fashion. In either case it is no foundation for good relationships with others. This lack of confidence can make us very negative or jealous of others' achievements. Henry McLeish described such a phenomenon when he said about the Scots 'we don't like success', adding, 'if success is paraded we knock that down'.[5] Other commentators on Scotland home in on the

problem with 'self-efficacy' - the sense of being able to make an effective and successful impact on the world. For example, sports writer Hugh McIlvanney once argued 'If there is ever a World Cup for self-destructiveness, few nations will have the nerve to challenge the Scots. It seems astonishing that the race has never produced a kamikaze pilot'.[6] In an oft-quoted passage in *Trainspotting*, one of Irvine Welsh's characters continues this idea of the Scots' inability to get anything right: 'It's nae good blaming it oan the English for colonizing us. Ah don't hate the English. They're just wankers. We can't even pick a decent, healthy culture to be colonized by.' And this thought then leads to the extremely self-critical conclusion that the Scots are 'the scum of the earth. The most wretched, servile, miserable, pathetic trash that was ever shat intae creation.'[7]

Self-acceptance - the sense of being at heart a decent human being - is another building block of self-confidence and, if Welsh and other Scottish commentators are anything to go by, the Scots are short of that as well: 'The typical Scot ... is a loser and he knows it,' writes Alan Bold. 'He is forever trying to cover up the pathological cracks in his character.'[8] Political columnist Iain Macwhirter believes that negativity is so much part of Scottish life that 'the Scots never miss an opportunity to soil their own nests'.[9] As self-acceptance is an important ingredient of self-esteem this constant fault-finding and criticism must play an important part in undermining the Scots' confidence in themselves and their country.

It is, however, true to say that running alongside this negative current about Scotland and the Scots there is also a great deal of pride. For example, it is impossible to read the recently published volume *Being Scottish*, in which one hundred people write about what Scottishness means to them, and not be struck by the strength of patriotic feeling. For many this manifests itself in an intense love of the Scottish landscape. But, as the editors Tom Devine and Paddy Logue point out in the Postscript, 'A deep pride in Scottish values and achievement also comes through in this book.'[10] The celebrated Scots documentary-maker John Grierson once argued that at the very 'heart of our national philosophy' is an 'obligation to work and aspire for the common good'.[11] And this view of the Scots as an unpretentious hard-working people, who believe in equality, is the bedrock for most of the positive statements about Scotland and the Scottish people.

Ironically the fierce pride many Scots take in Scottish values and principles fuels much of Scottish negativity about the country and undermines collective confidence. As I will show in Chapter 10 there is a strong Utopian streak in Scottish culture. It is common for Scots to want Scotland to become a truly humane, egalitarian society where everyone has opportunities in life and engages in productive debate and action to improve the world. When Scots' idealism encounters the harsh realities of life in modern Scotland - the stark inequalities, the prejudice, the in-fighting and the pettiness - it usually propels them to the other end of the scale and they feel bitter and frustrated. Mel Young, who founded *The Big Issue* in Scotland, encapsulates such simultaneously positive and negative feelings about his homeland in his opening statement in *Being Scottish:* Being Scottish for me', writes Young 'is a contradiction. On the one hand I am fiercely proud of being Scottish, on the other it makes me feel wretched, embarrassed and sick'.[12] Fellow contributor Owen Campbell writes that, in Scotland 'Failure is not the killer; we are used to that. It's the hope that gets you every time'.[13]

So confidence is an issue which affects the Scots at both an individual and a collective level and it takes many forms. If we are to grow real self-confidence in Scotland we have to find what stunts its growth and saps its strength for it is impossible to come up with revitalising solutions unless we have more insight into the precise nature and origins of the problem.

Before embarking on my own analysis of Scotland's confidence problem I first want to present some of the conventional views on Scottish culture. It is here that we can see most clearly the Scots' tendency to self-criticism and exaggerated, rhetorical language. I do not go into the intricacies of these arguments and theories but simply try to encapsulate some of the dominant, and negative, images which the Scots themselves have come up with when writing about the Scottish people.

NOTES

1 Letter to *The Herald*, 21 January 2001.

2 Quoted in W. Gordon Smith, *This is my Country: A Personal Blend of the Purest Scotch* (Souvenir Press: London, 1976), p. 251.

3 Allan Massie, *Scotland on Sunday*, 3 September 2000.

4 Chris Warhurst, Dennis Nickson, Anne Witz and Anne Marie Cullen, 'Aesthetic Labour in Interactive Service Work: Some Case Study Evidence from the "New" Glasgow', *The Service Industries Journal*, vol. 20, no. 3, 2000, pp. 1-18.

5 Quoted in *The Sunday Herald*, 15 November 2000.

6 Hugh McIlvanney, *The Observer*, 11 June 1978.

7 Irvine Welsh, *Trainspotting* (Mandarin Paperbacks: London, 1996), p. 78.

8 Alan Bold, 'An Open Letter on the Closed Mind' in *Chapman* No 35-36, July 1983.

9 Iain Macwhirter, *The Sunday Herald*, 17 January 2001.

10 Tom Devine and Paddy Logue (eds), *Being Scottish* (Polygon: Edinburgh, 2002), p. 299.

11 John Grierson, 'The Salt of the Earth' in Forsyth Hardy (ed.), *John Grierson's Scotland* (The Ramsay Head Press: Edinburgh, 1979), p. 32.

12 Mel Young in Tom Devine and Paddy Logue (eds), *Being Scottish*, p. 293.

13 Owen Campbell in Tom Devine and Paddy Logue (eds), *Being Scottish*, p. 51.

2
Through a Glass Darkly

'In Scotland our cultural analysis has been obsessed with images of our self-hate.'

Cairns Craig, *Out of History*

Jekyll and Hyde

One of the strongest themes to emerge from books on Scotland is that there is a deep division within both the Scottish psyche and the culture Scots create. According to many writers, it is only right and fitting that Jekyll and Hyde, the most potent symbol of a divided self, was created by Robert Louis Stevenson - a Scotsman. 'We are a country of paradoxes, ' writes John Grierson. 'We have John Knox on the one side and Mary Queen of Scots on the other. We divide our loyalties with great ease between what is highly proper and what is thoroughly improper.'[1] Moray McLaren, a prolific writer on Scotland, maintains the Scots are '... about as confusing a collection of opposites as you are likely to meet anywhere in the world. They have more internal differences of character and opinion than almost any other nation.'[2] The novelist John Buchan talks about 'two master elements in the Scottish character - hard-headedness on the one hand and romance on the other: common sense and sentiment: practicality and poetry: business and idealism.' Buchan maintains that everybody has a little bit of both in their make-up but the 'peculiarity of the Scottish race is that it has both in a high degree.'[3]

The notion of a division within the Scots character has led a number of commentators to observe how difficult it is to say anything about the Scottish people - as soon as you make a pronouncement, you are aware of a contradiction. 'Pinning down our national character', writes W. Gordon Smith, 'is like trying to trap mercury with a bent fork'.[4] Given the large number of words produced on the subject, the difficulty has clearly not put them off.

At times writers simply attribute the split within the Scottish character to the geographical divide within Scotland. They tell us that Highlanders by nature are romantic and sentimental while Lowlanders are more rational and down to earth characters. Many writers also point up the division of Scotland into historical Edinburgh and industrial Glasgow. Another common contrast is between the Scottish Sabbath and the raucous Saturday night. It may seem harmless enough but in much of the literature the 'peculiar, divided Scot' is attributed to a deep split within the Scottish psyche itself.

The idea of a deep division within the Scot can be traced back to a book written in 1919 by the literary critic G. Gregory Smith. Smith's rather innocuous idea is that Scotland's literature is extremely varied and closer inspection shows a 'combination of opposites'. Smith famously terms these two moods 'the Caledonian antisyzygy'.[5] Smith's diagnosis was eagerly seized on by Scotland's famous poet Hugh MacDiarmid who aimed to encourage a greater expression of what he termed 'Scottish psychology' in Scots literature. In the 1920s Scotland had gone through a substantial process of Anglicisation, so the problem was how to define the essence of Scottishness. Smith's thesis furnished MacDiarmid with an answer - the Scots were essentially an eccentric, contrary people. It also provided MacDiarmid with the inspiration for his great work of poetic genius - 'A Drunk Man Looks at the Thistle'. The poem's power and energy comes from MacDiarmid's use of opposites and sudden changes in tone - the commonplace and the metaphysical, the satirical and the lyrical. Few would doubt the genius of this poem or deny it a place at the pinnacle of Scottish literature, but MacDiarmid's idea of the Scot as an extreme and divided character has provided inspiration and sustenance for some truly bizarre notions of Scotland and the Scots. Edwin Muir, another great Scots literary figure, also took up the idea of the Caledonian antisyzygy but, unlike MacDiarmid, he argued it is a negative, unhealthy aspect of Scotland.[6]

From MacDiarmid and Muir on, it became commonplace for writers to portray Scotland and the Scots as peculiarly and unhealthily divided. In tune with society's increasing interest in mental illness, more recent commentators have talked about Scotland's 'schizophrenia'. This is best seen in the work of Scotland's celebrated political theorist Tom Nairn. In an essay first published in 1968, 'The Three Dreams of Scottish Nationalism', Nairn writes of 'the chronic laceration of the Scots mind' and makes the customary reference to Jekyll and Hyde. The work is liberally seasoned with reference to the Scots', or particular Scottish groups', 'masochism', 'sadism', 'authoritarianism' and 'narcissism'.[7] Five years later, in an essay in *The Red Paper on Scotland* (edited by Gordon Brown, the current Chancellor of the Exchequer), Nairn had evidently warmed to the theme. Now, alongside 'schizophrenia', Nairn diagnoses 'neurosis'.[8] He also maintains that Scotland is a country which has a deep and 'freakish' division between its sentimental Scottish heart and its rationalist British head. Two years later, by the time Nairn's highly successful book *The Break-up of Britain* had been published, the patient's condition has worsened even further: sanity has been lost and Scotland is now described as an 'asylum', with Nairn even prepared to admit to his role as psychoanalyst:

> The subjectivity of nationalism must itself be approached with the utmost effort of objectivity. It should be treated as a psychoanalyst does the outpourings of a patient. Where - as is not infrequently the case with nationalism - the patient is a roaring drunk into the bargain, even greater patience is called for. [9]

In his latest book, *After Britain,* published in 2000, Nairn's Scottish patient has been 'partly lobotomised and partly placed in cold storage'.[10] But, thankfully, in this later work Nairn drops much of the medical terminology and adopts a more moderate tone. One of the chapters is based on a speech he gave to the SNP to mark its seventieth anniversary. In it he refers to Scotland's 'famously split personality' and consciously desists from rehearsing the arguments again.

Tom Nairn's terminology and analysis of Scotland may seem far-fetched and contrived but his work has had, and continues to have, a huge impact on Scotland's intellectual community. Shortly after the publication of *The Break up of Britain* the editors of the *Scottish Government Yearbook* for 1981, Henry and Nancy Drucker, hailed Nairn's work as 'the most thoughtful book about contemporary Scotland'. And they are so taken by his diagnosis of the 'Jekyll and Hyde physiognomy of Scottishness' they borrow his white coat: 'Scots still do not know how to fulfil their political instincts', they write, 'mostly they are suppressed behind Dr Jekyll's respectable façade - but occasionally they erupt within Mr Hyde'.[11] And then, bizarrely, they treat us to a Jekyll and Hyde diagnosis of Scottish electoral politics.

The idea of division in Scotland and the Scots is still reproduced in contemporary academic works. Scottish sociologist David McCrone hails Nairn's work as 'the most perceptive and critical account we have' on Scotland. He goes on to argue that Nairn's characterisation of Scottish culture as split, divided or deformed in some way (the 'Caledonian antisyzygy') is 'perhaps the most common characterisation of Scotland'. McCrone also argues: 'This sense of separation, of fragmentation, runs throughout much intellectual analysis of Scotland.'[12] In other words, thanks in large part to Nairn, there is a pervasive notion in the academic debate on Scotland that Scottish identity itself is deeply problematic if not pathological.

As devolution was often seen as a panacea to solve Scotland's problems, the question is - has the notion of Scottish 'schizophrenia' disappeared with the advent of a Scottish Parliament and a brave new Scottish world? Unfortunately it has not. The dreaded, but ubiquitous, Jekyll and Hyde make a star appearance in a book designed to celebrate 'the new Scottish politics' exactly a year after the Parliament was set up. They are the guests of the highly respected political correspondent Iain Macwhirter who even calls the first section of his article 'The Jekyll and Hyde Parliament'.[13] The editors also give great weight to the idea of Scotland's 'cultural schizophrenia'. The notion of splits and divisions is also rife within recent literary and journalistic analyses of Scotland.

Over the years a few Scottish commentators have deliberately avoided using the notion of a division. Douglas Dunn, for example, writes: 'a better image of Scottishness might be the kaleidoscope ... It seems more positive and at the same time more complicated than the idea of Scottish personality as "double" or "divided"'.[14] But Dunn and company have as much chance of being heard as a horse whisperer in a force ten gale, for the idea of the Scots as a peculiarly divided people could be likened, not to a wee rolling stone kicking up stoor and momentum as it travels through time, but to a huge boulder crashing its way into almost every theory on Scotland and the Scots advanced by Scottish intellectuals. Moving from the mountainside to the loch, we can also liken the 'Caledonian antisyzygy' to the fish that got away, for the idea of the 'schizophrenic' Scot has become larger and more monstrous with each retelling. If we look for real, hard evidence to support the idea of the Scot as a Jekyll and Hyde figure - a sick, pathological and divided character - we shall be disappointed. But this lack of evidence has not prevented our analysts from swearing they have caught sight of him and from elaborating on all the pathological things he is up to. Indeed in true fisherman fashion they compete with one another to tell the tallest story. But what they have spotted is simply a normal human being - not a 'schizophrenic'. Philosophers from the beginning of time - both East and West - have argued that human beings and the cultures they create are fundamentally divided. So it would be odd if we could not find conflicts and divisions in Scotland and the Scots. In his great work 'A Drunk Man Looks at the Thistle', Hugh MacDiarmid wants to advance the idea of the Caledonian antizysygy ('to pit in a concrete abstraction/My country's contrair qualities') but what makes this a great poem is the universal significance of the opposites he deals with: life and death; past and future; humankind and God; masculine and feminine; flesh and spirit; high and low.[15] Of course, some of the symbolism of division in the poem is particularly Scottish but it would be a queer country indeed that could not come up with its own version of the divided nature of human experience.

Arthur Herman makes a similar point in his recent, and refreshing, book *The Scottish Enlightenment.* Herman is an American academic with no Scottish connections and he was motivated to write about Scotland because he believes that the Scots have literally shaped the 'modern world'. Herman has read widely on Scotland and his last chapter is on modern Scotland so he is familiar with all the arguments about dichotomies and divisions. And he simply tries to present it positively, as an insight which Scots, like Sir Walter Scott, had into human experience:

> Scott was aware of ... divisions in himself - between the romantic poet and the historical scholar, between the lover of nature and the student of science, between the sentimental Jacobite and the hardheaded lawyer, between the staunch Tory and the admirer of progress ... And he was aware of the same split in Scottish culture ... The credit for defining the artist as a person who can hold two inconsistent ideas at once goes to F. Scott Fitzgerald. The credit for realising that that is precisely what all modern men can do - indeed, must be able to do, belongs to Sir Walter Scott.[16]

As for Jekyll and Hyde, it simply does not make sense to argue that this has some exclusively Scottish meaning. Not only did Stevenson set the novel in London, he wrote it in 1885 during the height of Queen Victoria's reign - a period well known for its hypocrisy and the corrosive division between an outer show of public virtue and private acts of immorality. Undoubtedly, the book was inspired partly by Stevenson's personal experience of Edinburgh, and the character of Deacon Brodie, but he could have found such inspiration in every other city in the British Isles, so deep was the hypocrisy of Victorian Britain. In his book *The English* Jeremy Paxman devotes considerable space to charting the extent of male hypocrisy in Victorian times. Women were instructed to be chaste and 'respectable' while men went to prostitutes and were obsessed by 'foreign sexuality'. 'The sheer hypocrisy of many Englishmen, pretending morality, while debauching themselves,' writes Paxman, 'takes some believing'.[17] But Paxman does not then go on to argue that there must be something pathological about England or the English as a result of this behaviour.

In Scotland the notion of the Scots as a 'schizophrenic', pathologically divided people is a rather tired and inadequate analysis hammered home by many of our literati because they do not have alternative ways to diagnose or describe some of the problems they perceive. And, as we have just seen, they often attempt to analyse supposedly *Scottish* problems when there is not even a particularly Scottish problem to discuss. Joep Leerssen has made a study of national identity and national stereotypes and he argues that 'countries are always contradictory in a specific way: their most characteristic attribute always involves its own opposite.' He also argues that 'the ultimate cliché that can be said of virtually any country is that it is "full of contrasts"'.[18]

If we examine the notion of a fatal division between head and heart, the core of Nairn's analysis of Scotland and the essence of Muir's idea of a split between thought and feeling, then we shall see there is nothing particularly Scottish about it. Indeed the term 'disassociation', much used by cultural analysts to describe the notion of division in Scottish literature, was first used by T.S. Eliot to describe a trend he perceived in English poetry. The head/heart divide - often portrayed as a split between masculine reason and feminine emotion - haunts all Western societies. It is present every time a voter enters a polling booth and feels torn between idealism and realism; public good versus immediate private interest. It is at play in our private lives when we opt for the security of a loveless marriage or a well-paid job rather than act on our deepest feelings and desires. The heart/head division is a deep, fundamental conflict which often manifests itself in our dreams. Whatever way we look at the divided Scot, whatever definition we use, one thing remains clear: there is nothing particularly Scottish about division of this type. We are not dealing with pathological monsters or 'schizophrenics', simply ordinary human beings.

The Scots are not any more divided than other people but they do tend to think in either/or terms. And it is this, rather than the divisions themselves, which leads to an important insight about Scottish consciousness which I will return to in Chapter 13.

The 'Blight' of Calvinism

A similarly simplistic and polarising discussion underpins analysts' depictions of the influence of Calvinism on the Scots. As a Scot I am aware that there are certain traits in the Scottish character which can be attributed to a Scottish upbringing, such as a strong belief in the importance of principles, a highly developed work ethic and a sense of duty and social responsibility. All these qualities are part of Scotland's Calvinist legacy. Of course, these qualities can be overdone and have a negative side - a diminished interest in pleasure and a heightened sense of guilt, for example. But for me, and for many Scots, these are still positive features of the Scottish character. This is not the view taken by many Scottish analysts, many of whom lay at the door of Knox and Calvin everything they believe to be wrong with Scotland and the Scots.

A common theme in the literature is that the Scots have been contorted in some way by the religious fanaticism of the past. George Blake talks about Scotland being 'infected' by Calvinism and the notion that the Reformation ushered in some kind of disease of the mind is commonplace. For example, W. Gordon Smith writes:

> Four hundred years of bloody bigotry bitten deep into the bone. Centuries of self-righteousness and extreme unctuousness. Slavering hypocrisy and unrepenting smugness. The rape of logic and the murder of reason. Blindness, deafness, and beggared imagination ... To think that in this age of penicillin and streptomycin there's no anti-biotic to cure such a pox of the mind.[19]

Willa Muir, the novelist and critic, maintains that 'the Reformation was a kind of spiritual strychnine of which Scotland took an overdose.'[20] Another common charge against Calvinism is that it made the Scots a guilt-ridden, joyless people, with few social graces. Continual quibbling over religious meaning also turned us apparently into a nation of 'nit pickers' and 'pedants'. According to many commentators, the ministers snuffed out art and culture of every kind. Edwin Muir, who was very influential on the literati's views of Scotland, was a stern critic of Knox and the Reformation. Indeed Muir saw John Knox and Andrew Melville's Reformation as largely responsible for Scotland's spiritual and artistic 'desolation'. In his poem 'Scotland 1941' Muir writes about this desolation crushing 'the poet with the iron text'.[21] Art critic Cordelia Oliver even blames Calvinism for the 'rusty bedsprings', 'gin bottles' and the general 'ugly mess' that 'disfigures the natural beauty of so much of the west coast of Scotland and the Highlands'.[22] And Tom Nairn's most famous soundbite is that Scotland could only be 'reborn the day the last minister is strangled with the last copy of *The Sunday Post*'.[23]

The link between various aspects of Scottish society and Calvinism, the positive and the negative, are charted in the more scholarly works on Scotland, but many modern writers attribute everything - rusty bedsprings, pedantry, dourness or the lack of an indigenous dramatic tradition in Scotland - to the 'terrible' course Scottish history took following the Reformation. In other words, Calvinism is portrayed as having only a negative and disfiguring effect on Scottish culture and the Scottish people and heightens the notion of the Scots as deranged and 'schizophrenic'. It is little wonder then that Harry Reid in his independent and provocative book on the Church of Scotland - *Outside Verdict* - maintains that the Kirk in Scotland is ashamed of its past and particularly keen to distance itself from John Knox. Reid believes that if the Church of Scotland is ever to regain its confidence and build support it will have to embrace the past rather than feel embarrassed by it. And the past he is referring to is the early days when much of the foundation of modern Scotland was laid by figures like Knox.

Sentimental Scots

Another well-worn theme is that the Scots are particularly, and embarrassingly, sentimental. The novelist John Buchan claimed he liked the emotion and sentimentality of the Scots but he is almost alone for most share George Blake's diagnosis of the 'chronic Scots disease of nostalgia'.[24] Neil MacCallum speaks for a whole raft of analysts when he writes: 'The Scot in tears is an appalling piece of human wreckage.'[25] Iain Finlayson argues that the Scots are 'deeply emotional' but they deny it with 'passion'. 'They don't much care for the heart freely bleeding on the sleeve', writes Finlayson, 'but have an insatiable taste for the artificial heart strapped to the forearm and made to beat by means of a rubber bulb, hidden in the pocket, pumping air into it so it palpates madly and inexhaustibly.'[26]

Commentators who decry the sentimental side of Scottish character also disparage the culture which, they say, it creates. They argue that Scots sentimentality has led to a national fascination with the Highlands and much of the iconography of Scottish culture - bens and glens, but and bens, mystic mountains, Bonnie Prince Charlie and ferries to Skye. Much of our analytical literature paints the Scots as ridiculously sentimental about their supposed Highland past. Our literati repeatedly portray the Scots sniffing back the tears, maudlin', nostalgic, talking about their 'ane folk', remembering their 'granny's hielan' hame' or breaking into yet another verse of 'Roamin' in the Gloamin'.

One school of thinkers argues that Scottish sentimentality is unhealthy and sick because it shows the Scots, one of the most urbanised and industrialised people in the world, obsessed by a romantic Highland past which has no bearing on their current reality. Here are the Scots, they say, living in some of the ugliest slums in the world and in some of the most desperate conditions but instead of facing up to the reality of their conditions they escape into drink and sentimental fantasies about kilts and heather. Such nostalgia and sentimentality could be seen compassionately as an understandable 'opium' of a city-based people plagued by social problems and deprived of nature. But

Scottish analysts are much more likely to castigate poor, sentimental city dwellers for their failings than to show them any empathy or compassion.

In reality there is nothing pathological or odd about the Scottish tendency to be sentimental. As I shall show later, the Scots are first and foremost logical people and the development of logic in a person's character is inevitably at the expense of a mature and controlled expression of feelings and emotions. In other words, one downside of being logical is that it means you can easily become sentimental. I am fully aware that this argument means the Scots have definite weaknesses and are imperfect beings, but that's life. There is nothing specifically Scottish about being flawed and imperfect.

The Kailyard

The criticism that much of Scottish culture is 'rancid with false sentiment' also extends to that particularly unloved child of Scottish literature - the Kailyard. This is the name originally given to a genre of nineteenth-century Scottish novels which show Scotland as a land of idealised communities and couthy natives. Our analysts argue that these books are completely devoid of literary merit and only became popular in Scotland because they were nostalgic and sentimental. The Kailyard is now a term of abuse intellectuals use to cover anything of this ilk produced in Scotland - *Dr Finlay's Casebook, Take the High Road, The People's Friend, The Broons* and the Alexander Brothers. Anything which can be labelled 'Kailyard' is deemed worthless and is used as further evidence of Scotland as a cultural backwater where the natives have become sick on too much 'sugarally' water. In the words of one critic, literature of this sort is 'not so much drama as diabetes.'[27]

The Kailyard analysis also reinforces another negative image of the Scots - as an inward-looking people. Recently I attended a lecture in Glasgow given by a senior official of the World Bank who was putting forward proposals on how people from all round the world could come together to solve problems which can only be tackled globally. A senior official from Scotland's economic development community then got to his feet to give an initial response from a Scottish perspective. The speaker has the reputation for being lively, open and optimistic but on this occasion he began by saying how depressed he felt by the lecture as there was a genre of literature in Scotland, called the Kailyard, which highlighted how inward-looking the Scots are and how they do not see beyond their own cabbage patch ... But is this really true? The Scots have always been an adventurous, outward-looking people who explored the world. Before the Union, the Scots were much more international in outlook than the English or the Chinese, for example, whose insularity is well-known. Currently, Scotland is a small country within a bigger partnership and she does not have the same need to enter into dialogue with other countries that she would if she were an independent state. But this does not make the Scots an insular people uninterested in what is going on outside their borders. Countless Scots still travel the world as migrants and tourists. The same cannot be said of that truly inward-looking nation - the United States. What I found most depressing at the lecture was that our Scotsman's first response was to be negative about the Scots when it would have been very easy to be positive and upbeat. He could have argued that the Scots were obvious candidates for involvement in global issues forums because we believe passionately in social responsibility.

Tom Devine believes the Kailyard has attracted such criticism because the original writers of Kailyard novels had 'committed the unforgivable sin of being hugely successful'. But I think there is something else at work here - male pride.[28] As I shall argue later, most of the analysis on Scotland has been written by men and it is shot through with a male view of the world. Men tend to be more egotistical than women. A man will often over-react if he thinks his ego is being dented in some way, and when it comes to the Kailyard this appears to be the problem for some of our male literary critics. According to Blake - the man who first led the charge - the Kailyard writers 'held up their fellow countrymen as comic characters for the amusement of the foreigner'. Later he complains of a 'betrayal of national dignity.'[29] And this finds echoes in Tom Nairn's work many years later when he brings up the rearguard action. With the passage of time Nairn has more Kailyard targets to hit. He sets his sights on *Doctor Finlay's Casebook* and its ilk rather than *A Window in Thrums* but the point is generally the same. Nairn wholeheartedly agrees that the producers of such works are guilty of 'holding up our fellow-countrymen ... to the ridicule and contempt of all sane and judicious human beings'.[30] Given Nairn's views on Scots pathology, I suppose 'the sane' beings to which he refers means people living outside Scotland. Personally, I would rather be portrayed to the world as the bright and brisk Janet in *Doctor Finlay's Casebook,* than Nairn's 'schizophrenic' inmate of a lunatic asylum.

As the idea of the Kailyard has been a major supporting pillar in the notion of Scotland and the Scots as culturally backward, insular and pathological, I am pleased to report it is beginning to be attacked from within the intellectual community itself; the edifice is starting to crumble. For example, Tom Devine in his much acclaimed history of Scotland points out that the three writers most accused of peddling crude, sentimental images of Scotland in their Kailyard novels - S. R. Crockett, Ian Maclaren and J.M. Barrie - only wrote 'a dozen books in a single decade' and sold most of them to the upper middle classes in Scotland, England and abroad. This means two things: first that the significance of the Kailyard novels to Scottish literature is greatly overdone. Quite simply it was no big deal. And second there was nothing particularly *Scottish* about the appetite for such sugary and unhealthy fare.

Authoritarianism

The Scots pride themselves on being democratic, yet another common theme to emerge from the literature is that the Scots are a people with strongly authoritarian tendencies. The Scots schoolmaster, or dominie, is commonly portrayed as a cruel and authoritarian figure. So too are the ministers and elders of earlier times who, we are told, took great delight in humiliating and punishing sinners for their misdemeanours. If we believe our analysts, no area of Scottish life escaped the icy blast of Scottish authoritarianism. In the nineteenth century, Robert Louis Stevenson gave the Scots a sense of the authoritarian personality in *The Weir of Hermiston,* but the idea that the Scots have a particularly callous and authoritarian streak muscled its way into the Scots' notion of themselves following the publication of *The House with the Green Shutters* by George Douglas Brown in 1901. The novel revolves round the twisted, callous, authoritarian personality of the central male character - John Gourlay. As the illegitimate son of a farmer, Douglas Brown felt he was a victim of a small Scottish community. He loathed the false portrait Barrie and others had painted in their works so his novel was designed as a deliberate 'counterblast' to the Kailyard. He too set his novel in a rural community and he adopted elements of the genre, but there the similarity ends. In place of couthy sentimentality we have what was once called the 'Scot malignant'. His novel is a pessimistic and melodramatic tale of Scottish village life. It is about malicious gossip, spite, weakness, pride and self-interest. John Gourlay, and his family, are ultimately destroyed by his authoritarian ways, his arrogance and his pride.

All the characters in *The House with the Green Shutters* are uniformly black. There is no white, or even shades of grey in them. Indeed George Douglas Brown's work is as much a caricature of Scottish life as are the Kailyard novels. This is not a well-rounded picture of Scottish characters and communities - the good alongside the bad. He has simply gone to the other end of the spectrum to find the material for his characters and story. Yet even on publication a *Glasgow Herald* reviewer described it as 'True to the verge of being merciless ... Overdrawn, but grimly true, and full of promise.'[31] The novel was greatly admired by commentators and intellectuals who saw it as 'compelling', an important rebuttal of the Kailyard and an insightful commentary on Scotland. It was highly praised by many well-known Scottish writers. Poet and intellectual Hugh MacDiarmid believed *The House with the Green Shutters* to be 'distinctively Scottish in the deepest sense', and it is still seen as an important landmark in Scottish literature.[32]

The character of John Gourlay himself has lived on in the minds of our intellectuals and commentators as the man who epitomises an extremely harsh and authoritarian side of the Scottish character. Tom Nairn writes: 'We all have a vital bit of John Gourlay inside us ...' Nairn's belief that authoritarianism is bred in the bone of 'bourgeois' Scots leads him to argue that if the SNP ever came to power in Scotland they would be a 'junta of corporal punishers'.[33] Yet again we see this tendency in Nairn and others to pounce on any negative characteristics displayed by Scots and then claim them either as particularly Scottish or as more pronounced in Scotland. This is why Nairn comes up with the view that there is 'no Stalinist like a Scottish Stalinist'[34] when quite simply no Scottish Stalinist has ever been in the same league as the original Russian Stalinist.

Nonetheless it is true to say that the Scots are rather troubled by authority - simultaneously attracted to and repelled by it (an idea I shall explore more fully in Chapter 10). But it simply is not true to say that the Scots are particularly authoritarian. Throughout the world we can see examples of the authoritarianism, and potential sadism which easily flow from patriarchy and male power. Often it is institutionalised in religion - not just in Calvinism but in Catholicism and Muslim fundamentalism. The priests depicted in many an Irish novel are as capable of tyranny and preaching 'hell fire and damnation' as their Scottish Protestant counterparts. And John Gourlay and his ilk are nothing in comparison to some of the world's Ayatollahs. Nairn may sneer about the possibility of a 'junta' but the Scots as a people have never flirted with fascism or been attracted to political dictatorship of any kind. By contrast much of the world has physically suffered under the hands of *real*, not imaginary, tyrants - Germany, Spain, Italy, Chile, Argentina, Korea, Afghanistan, South Africa - the list is enormous.

John Gourlay was a fictional tyrant who lorded it over his family, his workers and anyone else he could bully but there is nothing particularly Scottish in the male authoritarian figure who rules the roost. He is the Yorkshire mill owner of many a novel, or Citizen Kane. Nor is there anything distinctly Scottish about the cruel husband or father who physically or mentally abuses his wife and children. English novelist D. H. Lawrence suffered cruelly at his father's hands, so did Beethoven. The Irish singer Sinead O'Conner has talked openly of the abuse she suffered as a child. So too has Brian Wilson of the Beach Boys.

Most authoritarian characters are male, as women rarely need to shore up their egos in this way. But women are not immune and some recent cases have shown that women as mothers, or as nuns, are capable of authoritarian cruelty. Most authoritarian figures, male and female, are very similar to John Gourlay - they are insecure and arrogant, they detest weakness in any form, and they have to be right. They cruelly use and abuse their physical and economic power. There is nothing particularly Scottish about John Gourlay's malevolent spirit - sadly, it haunts the world. We may regret its existence, but we have no reason to brand it *Scottish*.

The 'Tartan Monster'

It was Tom Nairn who coined the phrase, much loved by our analysts, the 'tartan monster'. They extend the term 'tartanry' to cover any Scottish knick-knacks or particularly Scottish type of gathering. This could include the Edinburgh military tattoo or a Murrayfield Rugby International replete with kilts and pipers. And they hate it all. Some are particularly critical of 'tartanry' because it shows the Lowland Scots (the vast majority of the Scottish population) stealing the Highlander's kilt and other symbolism and using them to establish their own identity - an act of cultural theft which, they claim, is particularly reprehensible since Lowlanders used to denounce Highlanders as savage and barbaric. When I read the literature, however, I cannot help feeling that more than anything else it is the 'vulgarity' of it all our that analysts particularly detest. For example, the journalist Neal Ascherson writes about 'the fringe of glaring tartanry on sale along Princes Street ... the joke cards about shooting haggis, lifting kilts and tickling sporrans', and adds, 'nobody selling this stuff would be seen dead with it at home'.[35] But all that Ascherson is saying is that Scottish knick-knacks are 'Kitsch' -

cheap, plastic goods made for the tourist market. And Kitsch can be found all round the world - it isn't the monopoly of Scotland. Nairn acknowledges this fact but still can't resist giving the Scots first prize. 'How intolerably vulgar! What unbearable crass, mindless philistinism!' writes Nairn, 'One knows that Kitsch is a large constituent of mass popular culture in every land: but this is ridiculous!'[36]

Yet again we see the formulation at work - Scotland = the worst. And once more the idea of the Scots as 'the worst' cannot be justified. If you have travelled at all you will have seen hideous Kitsch everywhere - day-glo holy water bottles in Lourdes which play a tune, leaning tower bookends in Pisa. Right round the world local people have 'commodified' their culture, inventing or embellishing where necessary, and then selling the resultant Kitsch goods to tourists to make money. I personally do not like Kitsch, but I don't consider Scottish Kitsch more vulgar and ridiculous than what is produced in most other countries. In fact, some Scottish Kitsch is less offensive than what's produced elsewhere. Like it or not, tartan is a very sophisticated branding and marketing tool for Scotland and throughout Europe tartan is seen as attractive and 'chic'. Garishness is in the eye of the beholder.

One of the problems I perceive in the analyses of Scotland and the Scots is that they have mainly been undertaken by academics, literary specialists or by writers of one type or another who have simply exaggerated the negative and undermining effects of Scottish popular culture. Not only have they blown out of all proportion the real significance of the Kailyard, they have also exaggerated the negative effect of tartan. I grew up in a working-class household in the west of Scotland in the 1950s and 60s - we watched *The White Heather Club,* and *Doctor Finlay's Casebook,* and read *The Sunday Post.* We watched *Brigadoon* and *Whisky Galore.* We ate shortbread at New Year. We took tartan gifts down to England if we went to visit relatives. My dad occasionally played Scottish tunes on the accordion and has been known to break into a chorus of 'Nobody's Child'. We all knew this was not a complete, well-rounded picture of 'real Scotland'.

Even if there was a strain of sentimentality, it did not make us either mad, pathologically divided people or social inadequates.

If I reflect on the beliefs and attitudes which I have learned in Scotland; examine the messages which I imbibed from an early age and then try to rank them in order of importance - tartanry, sentimentality and a modern version of the Kailyard would not even register on the scale. As Scotland is a small place it has been very easy for these literary types to exert a great influence on one another. Indeed there is something of a greenhouse effect at work. An idea germinates and then, in the confined and intensive world of literary Scotland, it is quickly able to take hold and then scatter its seed widely. Before you know what is happening rhetorical rashes are springing up in all sorts of different places.

Men to a Man
And finally, as you have no doubt noticed, there is another striking feature of the Scottish character, as described by our analysts - it is unquestionably male. 'You and I are Scotsmen, members of a famous race,'[37] writes John Buchan, and no modern woman reader can fail to notice that she is excluded from this early literary discussion on Scotland. Much of what was written on Scotland by Scots, up to the 1980s at least, was written by men for men. Unless they specifically state they are talking about women, all the symbols, the topics, and the language these men use to talk about Scotland and the Scots are masculine. Everything is seen from a man's point of view - whole areas of life have simply been omitted or hardly mentioned. There is little about childhood or family relationships, nothing about maternity, almost nothing on sexual relations or sexuality. In fact there is hardly anything about personal relationships of any kind. However, there is nothing particularly Scottish about such myopia. The fate of women in every culture dominated by men is that they are either ignored, forgotten about, or mentioned as an afterthought.

There is little doubt that some of Scotland's 'great men', most notably Hugh MacDiarmid, were happy to keep women in their place:

> Now, I am not a misogynist by any means. I simply
> believe there is a time and a place for everything ...
> And like a high proportion of my country's regular
> and purposive drinkers I greatly prefer a complete
> absence of women on occasions of libation ... *no one*
> wants to be distracted from that absorbing business
> by music, women, glaring lights, chromium fittings
> ...[38]

The entire thrust of MacDiarmid's views is quite simple -
women's experiences and opinions don't count. We are no more
than distractions from the serious business of drinking!

If women had contributed to the analysis of Scotland there
might have been a more well-rounded portrayal. This point is
exemplified by Catherine Carswell, the woman most often
mentioned as part of the Scottish Renaissance of the 1920s and
30s. She was a successful novelist who wrote an acclaimed
biography of Robert Burns. In the introduction to this book she
makes some general comments about Scottish history and in
these few pages she displays more warmth and willingness to
understand the full impact of Calvinism, the good and the bad,
than many of her male colleagues manage in entire volumes. In
short, she is not out to attribute blame and she displays an
abundance of empathy and compassion. For example, she
dutifully charts the clergy's suppression of culture and talks about
'brutal persecution' but at the end of a section on Scottish poverty
she writes: 'Through the darkest years the Scottish ministers, with
all their faults, had truly been the leaders of the people, and they
had done much to preserve and fortify the soul of the nation'. She
is able simultaneously to tell us about the 'fulmination' and fear
preached from the pulpit and then remind us that 'other voices
with more of pleasantness and peace in them were calling to the
people of Scotland. For not all the ministers were stern
evangelicals.'[39] Sadly Carswell did not make many general
comments about Scotland and the Scots and this type of
compassionate voice is missing in much of the diagnosis we get
from male analysts.

So at the end of this romp through some of the literature dedicated to the analysis of Scotland and the Scots how can we best summarise what we have seen? One thing is certain, it is not a pretty sight; the archetypal Scot routinely portrayed in much of the literature by fellow Scots is a grotesque, inward-looking Harry Lauder figure dressed in a kilt, suffering from 'schizophrenia' and a Calvinist pox of the mind, simultaneously nasty and authoritarian and pathetically emotional and sentimental. I should, of course, add that our 'typical Scotsman' isn't feeling too good about himself. He has something of an inferiority complex. He lacks self-confidence. Surprising, isn't it?

Such views of Scotland and the Scots are now being routinely challenged by intellectuals themselves. In 1989 Craig Beveridge and Ronald Turnbull published a highly influential and ground-breaking book called *The Eclipse of Scottish Culture*.[40] Drawing on Frantz Fanon's *The Wretched of the Earth,* they argue it is 'inferiorism', the type of mindset third world peoples develop as a result of colonisation, which leads some commentators to disparage Scottish culture and represent it as deformed or pathological. The Scottish literary expert Cairns Craig has undermined many of the negative arguments in his insightful book *The Modern Scottish Novel* [41] and the sociologist David McCrone has also tried to normalise the debate about Scotland. Even Tom Nairn has toned down his language. But it is quite wrong to believe that this type of negative portrayal of Scotland is history. It constitutes a significant part of the debate on Scotland in the literature - pick up a few Scottish volumes and you cannot help but see Scotland through this dark, negative glass. What's more, many of those who studied aspects of Scottish politics or culture at university at the height of the negativity in the 1970s and 80s are now teaching children in schools, writing for Scottish newspapers or are involved one way or another in Scottish public life. And this may be one of the reasons why negative views of Scotland continually seep into the Scottish press. So the intellectuals themselves may no longer indulge in this extremely negative discussion, but Scotland may well suffer from the consequences of such analytical self-criticism for some time to come.

Moreover, from a confidence point of view I do not think that some of the counter arguments are necessarily that helpful. Take Beveridge and Turnbull's argument about the Scots having a colonial mindset. I think there is some truth in this view but believe the argument can easily be overdone. The Scots, outside the Highlands, have never been colonised in a way that is similar to third world peoples. In fact, the Scots were enthusiastic partners in the British Empire and were often the colonisers to which Turnbull and Beveridge refer. The Scottish political theorist, Tom Nairn, has always been scathing about any attempt to liken Scotland to a colony but in his speech to the seventieth anniversary conference of the SNP he nonetheless put forward arguments which give some credence to the theory of inferiorism. He argued that a central issue in the history of the Scottish nation is 'shame' and attributed some of his 'frankly nihilistic excesses about strangling Kirk ministers' to the shame and feelings of hopelessness inspired by the Union and the political and cultural climate it engendered. He argued that for ordinary people these feelings often led to migration but that for the intellectual community, of which he himself is part, it meant trying to become someone else, or 'adopting and displaying a superior persona'.[42]

The problem with arguing that Scottish negativity about Scotland is essentially about shame, or a colonial mindset, is that it puts the Scots in the position of hapless, helpless victims of English imperialism. 'It isn't our fault. They've done it to us and we didn't have the power to stop them.' Or it bounces back in Irvine Welsh's notion that we must be pathetic people to have allowed this to happen to ourselves. And psychologically neither stance helps us to start building Scottish self-confidence. It also leads to the idea that the solution to Scotland's confidence and negativity problem is simple - liberation from England. Nationalists as a whole tend to argue that any problems with Scottish confidence, the Scottish Parliament, or anything Scottish for that matter, could be changed almost overnight if Scotland won independence. According to them, any faults in the Scottish psyche lie not with the Scots themselves, but are a direct result of the inferior position Scotland occupies in the United Kingdom. For them, a free Scotland would inevitably be a confident Scotland.

But for me the problems of Scottish confidence are much more complex than this. Of course, a substantial shift in political power is likely to boost Scottish self-confidence but I do not believe it would be enough to eliminate the confidence issues facing the Scots. A great deal of the Scots' negativity about Scotland, and lack of confidence, cannot simply be blamed on our political state or on the English - they arise from a particularly *Scottish* way of looking at the world.

NOTES

1 John Grierson, 'The Salt of the Earth' in Forsyth Hardy (ed.), *John Grierson's Scotland* (The Ramsay Head Press: Edinburgh, 1979), p. 32.

2 Moray McLaren, *Understanding the Scots: A Guide for South Britons and Other Foreigners* (Frederick Muller: London, 1956), p. 8.

3 John Buchan 'Some Scottish Characteristics' in W.A. Craigie, John Buchan, Peter Giles & J. M. Bulloch, *The Scottish Tongue* (Cassell & Company: London, 1924), p. 58.

4 W. Gordon Smith, *This is my Country: A Personal Blend of the Purest Scotch* (Souvenir Press: London, 1976), p. 29.

5 G. Gregory Smith, *Scottish Literature: Character & Influence* (Macmillan: London, 1919).

6 Edwin Muir, *Scott and Scotland* (George Routledge and Sons: London, 1936).

7 Tom Nairn, 'The Three Dreams of Scottish Nationalism' in Karl Miller (ed.), *Memoirs of a Modern Scotland* (Faber and Faber: London, 1970), p. 35.

8 Tom Nairn, 'Old Nationalism and New Nationalism' in Gordon Brown (ed.), *The Red Paper on Scotland* (EUSPB: Edinburgh, 1975).

9 Tom Nairn, *The Break-up of Britain* (Verso: London, 1981), p. 93.

10 Tom Nairn, *After Britain* (Granta Publications: London, 2000), p. 101.

11 H.M. Drucker & N. L. Drucker, *The Scottish Government Yearbook 1981* (Paul Harris: Edinburgh, 1980), p. 1.

12 David McCrone, *Understanding Scotland: The Sociology of a Stateless Nation* (Routledge: London, 1992), pp. 175-6.

13 Iain Macwhirter, 'Scotland Year Zero' in Gerry Hassan and Chris Warhurst (eds), *The New Scottish Politics: The First Year of the Scottish Parliament and Beyond* (The Stationery Office: London 2000).

14 Douglas Dunn, *Scotland: An Anthology* (Harper Collins: London, 1991), pp. 5-6.

15 Hugh MacDiarmid, *A Drunk Man Looks at the Thistle* (Caledonian Press: Glasgow 1953) p. 71.

16 Arthur Herman, *The Scottish Enlightenment: The Scots' Invention of the Modern World* (Fourth Estate: London, 2002), pp. 263-4.

17 Jeremy Paxman, *The English: A Portrait of a People* (Penguin Books: London, 1999), p. 212.

18 Joep Leerssen, internet document 'National Identity and National Stereotype', www.hum.uva.nl.

19 W. Gordon Smith, *This is my Country*, p. 262.

20 Willa Muir, *Mrs Grundy in Scotland* (George Routledge: London, 1936), p. 165.

NOTES

21 Edwin Muir, *Collected Poems* (Faber and Faber: London, 1960), p. 97.

22 Cordelia Oliver, 'The Visual Arts in Scotland' in Duncan Glen, *Whither Scotland? A Prejudiced Look at the Future of a Nation* (Victor Gollancz: London, 1971), p. 220.

23 Tom Nairn, 'The Three Dreams of Scottish Nationalism', p. 54.

24 George Blake, *Barrie and the Kailyard School* (Arthur Barker: London, 1951), p. 18.

25 Neil McCallum, *It's an Old Scottish Custom,* (Dennis Dobson: London) p. 180.

26 Iain Finlayson, *The Scots* (Oxford University Press: Oxford, 1988), p. 231.

27 G. M. Thomson, *Caledonia: Or The Future of the Scots* (Kegan Paul, Trench, Trubner: London), p. 65.

28 I have undertaken too much equality work in organisations to be unaware of the dangers of gender stereotyping but I think it is safe to say that men's egos are more highly developed than women's. The socio-longuist, Deborah Tannen, has written a number of books based on her research into differences in male and female speech. She uses this empirical evidence to support her thesis that generally women see the world as a web of connections whereas men see it as a hierarchy where they are either 'one up or one down'. Men are therefore more likely than women to scan their outer environment to see where they are placed in the pecking order.

29 George Blake, *Barrie and the Kailyard School,* pp. 16-75.

30 Tom Nairn, *The Break-up of Britain,* p. 158.

31 Quoted in George Blake, *Barrie and the Kailyard School,* p. 93.

32 See Beth Dickson 'Foundations of the Modern Scottish Novel' in Cairns Craig (ed.), *The History of Scottish Literature Volume 4* (AUP: Aberdeen, 1989), p. 51.

33 Tom Nairn, 'The Three Dreams of Scottish Nationalism', pp. 49-51.

34 Ibid., p. 44.

35 Quoted in David McCrone, Angela Morris & Richard Kiely, *Scotland - the Brand: The Making of Scottish Heritage* (Polygon: Edinburgh, 1999), p. 56.

36 Tom Nairn, *The Break-up of Britain,* p. 162.

37 John Buchan, 'Some Scottish Characteristics', p. 49.

38 Hugh MacDiarmid 'The Dour Drinkers of Glasgow' in Hugh MacDiarmid, *The Uncanny Scot: A Selection of Prose* (MacGibbon & Kee: London, 1968), pp. 93-94. My emphasis.

39 Catherine Carswell, *The Life of Robert Burns* (Chatto & Windus: London 1951), pp. 9-10.

NOTES

40 Craig Beveridge & Ronald Turnbull, *The Eclipse of Scottish Culture* (Polygon: Edinburgh, 1989).

41 Cairns Craig, *The Modern Scottish Novel: Narrative and the National Imagination* (Edinburgh University Press: Edinburgh, 1999).

42 Tom Nairn, *After Britain*, p. 104.

SECTION II

RETHINKING
SCOTLAND

3
A Way with Words

'To understand the character of a particular people we must examine the objects of its love.'

St Augustine, *The City of God*

One of the aims of this book is to establish an alternative way to understand Scotland and the Scots better - a way which encourages self-acceptance and builds genuine self-confidence. And it is only possible to do this if we can undertake a realistic assessment of national strengths and weaknesses.

This is a difficult and complex task but I believe it is possible if we utilise conceptual tools set out by the eminent Swiss psychologist C. G. Jung in his groundbreaking book, *Psychological Types.*[1] In everyday life we can see that people have different personalities. They are motivated by different things, they see the world differently and have different strengths and weaknesses. But most of the time we cannot explain why - we cannot come up with plausible explanations for why individuals differ from one another. Ancient philosophers used various schemes to classify people into different personality types but Jung was the first modern thinker to attempt such a task. Jung's theory primarily explains differences between individuals but we can use his concepts to help us understand organisations and national cultures

Over eighty years ago, Carl Jung came up with the terms 'introvert' and 'extravert' to describe a basic difference between people and it is these terms which help us to grasp an essential feature of Scotland. 'Extravert' and 'introvert' have entered our everyday vocabulary, but we now tend to use these terms to mean something other than Jung intended. We use 'extravert' only to describe someone who likes to be the centre of attention or is the life and soul of the party. The term 'introvert', by comparison, is used to describe people who are shy, and rather anti-social. But on both counts, the Jungian definition is much more subtle and complex. In the following exposition I shall not confine myself to Jung's precise definition of these terms but will also draw on the work of Katharine Briggs and her daughter Isabel Briggs Myers who used Jung's concepts to devise a questionnaire called the Myers-Briggs Type Indicator™. This instrument, which aims to help people understand their type preferences, was the first of its kind and is now used by millions of people throughout the world. I have used the MBTI™ with literally thousands of people in Scotland and so I shall also utilise my own experience when elaborating ideas about type differences.[2]

Introversion and Extraversion

The simplest way to grasp introversion and extraversion is to understand that as human beings we constantly move between two distinct and separate worlds. One is the extravert world, which exists outside ourselves - it is the world of people, things and activity. When we speak, communicate, act, and pursue many interests or hobbies we are in extravert mode. In fact we are directing our attention outwards - extraverting as opposed to introverting - every time our attention is drawn to the outer world. The introvert world is the world which exists inside our heads. It is a world of inner reflection. Here we process thoughts, make decisions, mull over our experiences or whatever in a solitary manner. Our attention is drawn inwards.

Jung acknowledges that all individuals introvert and extravert and so the issue is which of the two worlds each of us prefers. For Jung an essential difference between introverts and extraverts is how they gather and use energy. Extraverts are energised, literally turned on, by action and interaction. They are stimulated by talking, doing and being with other people. They allow their energy to flow into the external world. So extraverts are energised in the extravert world and expend most of their energy there. Introverts derive their energy from internal sources. They can easily feel drained by involvement with the external world and have to turn inwards to recharge their batteries. Introverts are people who reflect deeply on life, but as they often have no real need to communicate these thoughts to others, this depth is often hinted at but not fully revealed. The term, 'still waters run deep' was certainly coined to describe introverts.

Like individuals, cultures can and do exhibit a preference for extraversion or introversion - the outer world or the inner world. This is not about numbers in the population who prefer one or the other; it is about which preference has come to dominate within public life and which encapsulates the spirit of the people and their culture. So what is the preference in Scotland? The most obvious thing to say is introversion. After all the Scots are often thought to be a dour, quiet, rather expressionless people and that seems more in tune with introversion than extraversion. So too does the fact that a frequent and continuing complaint the Scots make about the English is that they talk too loudly in public and too freely. (The Scots generally do not approve of idle chatter on topics of little consequence.) And, of course, the Scots are often portrayed either as an inarticulate people or as a people who prefer to keep their own counsel. I do not personally recognise the inarticulate Scot who has been much written about, but I am fully aware of Scottish reticence. Indeed the Scots are often shy and do not want to draw attention to themselves (more of this later) but that does not mean to say they have a preference for introversion. In fact, I believe the opposite to be true - Scottish culture exhibits a profound preference for extraversion and this preference helps us to understand an essential feature about Scotland.

An Active, Outward-looking People

The Scots have always been an outward-looking people greatly drawn to explore foreign lands. Even in medieval times the Scots were precocious sailors and traders and many Scots established themselves as military advisers to foreign governments. Many became teachers in foreign universities. Before the Union with England, Scotland had great ties to other European nations. For example, thousands of Scots studied at universities in France and the Low Countries. Indeed it is estimated that in the sixteenth century three thousand Scots studied at the University of Leyden alone. The historian and journalist Michael Fry argues that the

Scots were the first 'global traders': tobacco, textiles, tea - these and other goods were carried around the world in Scottish ships. In fact, Fry argues that all 'the great Victorian shipping lines' - including Cunard and P&O - had Scottish origins.[3]

Exploring the external world has held such huge appeal to Scots that it seems appropriate that the famous explorer, David Livingstone, was a Scotsman, and the missionary, Mary Slessor, a Scotswoman. And of course the first man to set foot on the moon, Neil Armstrong, is an American Scot. Many of the books on Scotland portray the Scots as wanderers and adventurers and at some point feature some variation on the story of a Scotsman going to the ends of the earth - a Himalayan mountain top, the back streets of Calcutta, a survival hut in the North pole - only to discover that some bloke from Possilpark or Mallaig had not only got there first but had been there so long he was practically a native.

If you read books on Scottish history you will soon see that the Scots traditionally have been 'men of action' (I use such a sexist term deliberately as these books concentrate almost exclusively on men). Of course, we have produced our reflective philosophers, scientists and theologians, but Scotland's past demonstrates that the Scots have primarily been great activists. Fighting, exploring, colonising, inventing, engineering, building, preaching, shipbuilding, coal mining - for centuries these have been some of the main types of roles Scots have played in the world. As many of our analysts point out, not only have the Scots been great 'doers' they have also been 'out and about' types.

An 'Energetic' culture

A preference for introversion or extraversion can also be seen in a nation's culture. Nations which prefer introversion, such as Japan, manifest a cultural preference for calm, quiet and solitude. They like things to happen slowly and gracefully. Think about traditional Japanese music and drama (or even their flower arranging) and you will see what I mean. Now compare this with Scotland's traditional music and dance which have a real energy, enthusiasm and vitality about them. As someone once remarked 'the best way to torture the Scots is to nail their feet to the floor and play a Jimmy Shand record'. Scottish music and dance is exciting - it demands from us an energetic, physical response. In its blend of formal structure, sociability and sheer extraverted energy it captures something fundamental about the Scottish spirit. This energy and sociability is also present in Highland Games, fiddlers' rallies, choirs and pipe bands. The only counterpoint I can think of to all this outward display of energy is the solitary piper and the pibroch, and even in the most extremely extraverted cultures there is still going to be some expression of, and a hankering after, introversion.

The Love of Speech

One of the paradoxical things about Scotland is that, despite these obvious extravert tendencies, the Scots have a reputation for being reticent and inarticulate. Screeds have been written over the years about how the loss of the old Scots tongue and the imposition of English has created a people who are unable to express themselves well, yet, in reality, the Scots are not only drawn to expressing themselves in speech, they are good at it. Preaching, discussing, debating, arguing, declaiming, entertaining - all are ways of communicating that the Scots find deeply attractive and at which they can excel. Over the years we have produced some of the United Kingdom's most gifted talkers in the shape of people like the theologian and lecturer William Barclay, the comedian Billy Connolly, the barrister Helena Kennedy, or any of the numerous orators from the days of Scotland's militant past: John Maclean, Jimmy Maxton or Jimmy Reid. Indeed it is said of Maxton that he addressed more political meetings than any other person in the world. In nineteenth-century Scotland there were also impressive numbers of women orators such as Helen Lockhart Gibson, Jessie Macfarlane, Agnes Walker and A. S. Hamilton. In the present Westminster Parliament some of the finest speakers are either Scots or have Scottish connections - Gordon Brown, Tony Blair, Robin Cook, Menzies Campbell, Charles Kennedy and Liam Fox. And in the UK's broadcast media, where people have to talk for a living, many of the most successful figures are Scottish - Kirsty Wark, Sheena MacDonald, Jim Naughtie, Muriel Gray, Kirsty Young, Alan Little, Andrew Neil, Kay Adams, Lorraine Kelly and Nicky Campbell.

The Scots also have a strong oral tradition. Scotland is reputed to have the finest tradition of 'work songs' in Western Europe and both Highland and Lowland cultures have a rich history of folk-song and ballads. This is how James Hogg, the Ettrick Shepherd, described the importance of song when he grew up in the Borders in the late eighteenth century:

> In my young days, we had singing matches almost every night ... with the exception of Wads, and a little kissing and toying in consequence, song, and song alone, was the sole amusement. I never heard any music that thrilled my heart half so much as when these nymphs joined their voices, all in one key, and sung a slow Scottish melody.[4]

Later in the same article Hogg explains how 'these songs (which) had floated down on the stream of oral tradition' were 'inflicted' a 'deadening blow' when Walter Scott, who, ironically, was trying to preserve them for posterity, collected these songs in written form. Hogg recounts how his parents were 'highly offended' and maintained that the songs had been changed and ruined in the process of being captured on paper.[5]

The Knoxian Presbyterian tradition, with its emphasis on formal education, encouraged the Scots to respect books and reading but it also played an important part in encouraging the Scots to love the spoken word. The Scottish reformers abolished the ceremonies and displays of the Catholic Church and put 'the word of God' at the centre of religious worship. In the 1930s one churchman argued that this meant the Calvinists had difficulty in creating a religious service:

> Lacking in stately ceremonial, without the glory of the mighty utterances which the spirit of worship

had fashioned, divested of impressive ritual and
without the dramatic movement of the soul's ascent,
without the poetry of devotion ... It makes its appeal
exclusively to the hearing ear ... [6]

The sermon, which could often be up to three hours long,
became the centrepiece of the new Kirk service. Churches were
redesigned - in place of an altar was a centrally positioned pulpit
where the 'hearers', as the congregation was often called, could
listen to God's word. (Pulpits were only moved off centre in the
late nineteenth century.) In the past, ministers were expected to
extemporise and reading from a manuscript was greatly frowned
on. It is commonplace for historians to portray Scottish
worshippers as under the thumb of authoritarian ministers, but
many a minister in Scotland felt tyrannised by his congregation's
demand that he preach off the cuff for hours - notes of any kind
were forbidden. In an article on Scottish preaching, David Read
argues that the Scots' 'passion for expounding the Word' won
them an international reputation as preachers. He also argues that
in America, where this reputation is most strong, Scottish
preachers struggle to retain 'the lilt and cadence of their native
tongue'. According to Read a preacher's Scottish origins
'immediately raise the expectation of powerful preaching'.[7] This
tradition has largely been lost but it was once an important part
of Scotland's Presbyterian heritage.

In Jungian terms, speech is the preferred mode of
communication for extraverts. Introverts do not have the same
need to communicate what is going on in the inner world and if
they do decide to communicate many choose to write rather than
speak. But in Scotland the extravert impulse is so strong that it
even permeates the written word. In a fascinating article on this
theme the literary expert Roderick Watson argues that, from the
early eighteenth century on, Scottish literature shows the Scots'
'national preference for the speech act ... over the written text,
even if that speech is paradoxically written down.'[8] Watson gives
numerous examples of how many Scottish literary works heavily
rely on vernacular speech and also points out how many Scottish

novels use narrators and are essentially speech based. For example, a number of Robert Louis Stevenson's novels are narrated (*Dr Jekyll and Mr Hyde, Kidnapped, Catriona,* and *Treasure Island*) as well as other Scottish classics such as James Hogg's *Confessions of a Justified Sinner* and John Galt's *Annals of the Parish.* Many of Burns's poems are addresses and a 'speaking voice' is also much in evidence in some of his famous works such as 'Tam o'Shanter' and 'Holy Willie's Prayer'. Hugh MacDiarmid's great Scottish classic 'A Drunk Man Looks at the Thistle' is also written in the first person. And that quintessentially Scottish novel, *Sunset Song* by Lewis Grassic Gibbon, intertwines the 'speak o'Kinraddie' with Chris Guthrie's interior monologue. Watson notes that the speaking voice is also a device used by contemporary Scottish novelists and poets, such as James Kelman and Tom Leonard. Carl MacDougall in his recent book *Painting the Forth Bridge: A Search for Scottish Identity* also gives prominent place in his analysis to the role of 'voice' in Scottish culture. He argues that 'the first person narrative is the dominant feature of Scottish writing.'[9]

Watson argues that 'place', a subtle interplay of geography and history, also suffuses the works of Scottish literature. And again we could interpret this to mean that the works connect to the outer, extravert world more than to the inner world of the author's individual imagination. In Watson's view much of the character of Scots literature comes from its *energy* - an energy derived in part from place and in part from 'the speed, flexibility and passion of spoken discourse (with its roots in vernacular Scots), as opposed to the more formal registers of written English.'[10] Watson also argues that this 'oral energy' is even to be found in some of the more formal English texts written by Scots writers such as James Boswell and Thomas Carlyle.

Enlightening Conversations

If we turn to the philosophical types involved in the Scottish Enlightenment we find this same attraction to speech. The Scottish Enlightenment is a period in Scottish history from the Act of Union to the 1830s when Scotland had so many first-rate thinkers and intellectuals it was as if 'giants walked the land'. Even the great French philosopher Voltaire remarked that 'it is to Edinburgh that we look for our ideas'. The roll-call of scholars was certainly impressive and included such weighty figures as the philosopher David Hume; the author of the highly influential book *The Wealth of Nations*, Adam Smith; Adam Ferguson, the father of sociology; James Hutton the founder of geology; the eminent chemist Joseph Black; and the medical pioneer William Cullen, to name only a few. Many of these scholars came up with groundbreaking ideas but they were not rarefied intellectuals cloistered in ivory towers. When historians write about Enlightenment Scotland they describe it as a period characterised by *discourse, discussion, debate* and *conversation*. To use modern terminology, we could say that these men (and they were all men) were part of a self-conscious network - they flocked together to talk and learn from one another. And the purpose of this knowledge was not simply to understand the world but to improve on it. David Hume wanted to see philosophy conducted as 'conversation' - as an activity carried out with other people. He placed communication between people as the strongest of all social bonds. This is why Hume declares 'Be a philosopher: but amidst all your philosophy, be still a man.'[11] Indeed Hume and other Scottish Enlightenment figures believed it unwise for intellectuals to abandon the social world and spend too much time in solitary, introverted, reflection.

George Davie, in his book *The Democratic Intellect,* outlines Scotland's distinctive intellectual tradition and shows how, from the late nineteenth century on, the Scottish universities were forced to reorganise themselves along English lines. The Scottish university tradition emphasised the importance of a number of interrelated beliefs. Most relevant here is the belief in the efficacy of a general, rather than a specialist, education. Another is the importance of speech and face-to-face communication. It was the lecture, not individual research or study, which was therefore the keystone of Scotland's traditional universities. The lecture was augmented by 'examination hours' where the professor questioned and debated with students. Indeed Davie maintains that 'the catechising system', based on question and answer, was a central feature of the whole system. And it is for reasons such as these that Davie argues that the 'pedagogical tradition' in Scotland was 'full of energy and vitality.'[12]

All of this was in complete contrast to the values of learning inculcated in the traditional English universities. According to Roger Scruton, the English idea of 'scholarship ... saw knowledge as a way of life detached from the arena of action'. Indeed Scruton even states that 'The further the subject seemed from the day-to-day concerns of the student, the more worthy of study was it held to be'.[13] Over the years Scottish universities have come under increasing pressure to specialise and adopt an English model but vestiges of Scotland's old beliefs still remain. For example, the Scots' emphasis on the importance of generalism means that Scottish school pupils still follow a broader curriculum than those in England - hence the greater number of subjects studied at Higher level in Scotland than at A-level in England. And in the old Scottish universities it is still possible to take a general degree.

The Voice of Scotland

Donald Dewar, Scotland's first First Minister, was a man very much in this generalist tradition and a great admirer of the Scottish Enlightenment. Dewar was well known to be something of a scholar and had a great respect for books but he was a typical Scot in that he paid much more attention to the outer, extravert world than to the inner world. He was an extremely sociable man who loved nothing better than the opportunity to be actively and energetically engaged with others. A man who, on a good day, could be a fine orator. Happily for Scotland, one of the best days for Donald Dewar's oratory was on 1 July 1999 - the opening of the Scottish Parliament. In his role as First Minister, Dewar spoke for the Scottish people and in some passages of his address he encapsulated, as no-one has ever done before, the importance of speech to the Scots:

> This is about more than our politics and our laws.
> This is about who we are, how we carry ourselves.

There is a new voice in the land, the voice of a
democratic Parliament. A voice to shape Scotland as
surely as the echoes of our past:
the shout of the welder in the great Clyde shipyards;
the speak of the Mearns, with its soul in the land; the
discourse of the Enlightenment, when Edinburgh
and Glasgow were a light held to the intellectual life
of Europe;
the wild cry of the Great Pipes;
and back to the distant cries of the battles of Bruce
and Wallace.

Despite his position as a public figure, Donald Dewar was a
reserved man. He did not like fuss or being in the limelight unless
there was a good reason. Nor did he like talking in public unless
he had something worthwhile to say. He was a shy, contained
extravert and, in this respect, he admirably epitomises this aspect
of the Scottish character. Unfortunately, many commentators
have seized on this shy, reticent quality in the Scots and labelled
them introverts. In the process they have failed to grasp an
essential features of Scottishness - the importance of the external
world, the sociability and the love of activity and speech.
Sometimes our commentators have noted the reserve and the
sociability and then used this as evidence of Scottish
'schizophrenia.' In Chapter 6 I shall explain why the Scots tend
to be reserved, so all I want to say here is that it is slightly unusual
and quirky for extraverts to eschew the limelight in the way the
Scots often do, but there is certainly nothing pathological or
'schizophrenic' about it.

A Calvinist Legacy
Writing this book has taught me one simple lesson about
Scotland - it is almost impossible to say anything about Scottish
culture or character without making constant reference to the
influence of the Kirk. And it is difficult not to conclude that the
extravert nature of Scottish life is to a large extent the product of
Presbyterianism. Some religions, most notably eastern religions

like Buddhism, encourage individuals to turn inwards - they believe that individuals must look within themselves to find God. This is why isolation and prolonged periods of meditation are part of the religious practices of most eastern religions and why these cultures often have a profoundly reflective quality. Christianity is a religion which encourages its followers to look outwards to find God. In this scheme, God is in every fibre of the external world. Some versions of Christianity stress that God also lies within all of us, but Calvinism, believing as it does in the monstrous nature of human beings, does not make much of the notion that God is to be found in the human heart (or any other part of the vile, loathsome body we all inhabit). Indeed Calvinism, the religious belief system which most influenced the Scottish way of Christianity, believes that it is dangerous for people to spend time idly for 'the Devil makes work for idle hands and idle minds'. So Scotland's religion is not simply a religion which stresses the importance of hearing God's word, it also incites its believers to action.

Strengths and Weaknesses

Scottish culture's preference for the extravert rather than the introvert world has led to some distinctive features and to marked strengths and weaknesses. As we have already observed, the essential characteristics of Scotland's culture are the strong oral tradition, the love of debate and discussion, and sociability. The Scots at their best are energetic, lively people who want to act on the world. By nature they are 'doers' rather than observers. The downside of this activity and attention to the outer world is that there is little about Scotland or the Scots which you could describe as 'deep'. The Scots are not a people noted for acute sensitivity; creative or imaginative thinking; spirituality; or literary insight. Such skills are more likely to be acquired by people who prefer to spend time in the inner, introvert realm - a world which the Scots, as a result of the cultural preference for extraversion, are not encouraged to inhabit. Of course, many individual Scots have a preference for introversion and some have given to the world the insights from their inner reflections - Hugh

MacDiarmid and Edwin Muir are undoubtedly two such examples - but somehow they are going against the grain of Scottish life, as Scottish beliefs and culture encourage activity and speech rather than deep reflection. One day I spotted a book in a second-hand bookshop called *Scotland's Inner Man*. I pounced on it enthusiastically hoping it would help me understand the reflective Scot, only to discover that it was about food and food production.

A Balancing Act

Jung's theory of types is complex because he argues it is important for the psyche to balance itself. Extraversion and introversion are essential aspects of human life. Extraverts will still be drawn to introvert, though they will not do it as often, and introverts will still want to extravert. We can see this balancing mechanism at work in Japan - a culture with a pronounced preference for introversion. Japanese culture encourages its people to cultivate their inner world and to hold back on communication with others. For example, the Japanese believe that it is childlike for someone to make his or her wishes known directly in speech and they greatly favour indirect, subtle, non-verbal forms of communication. Japanese culture in this and other ways makes a virtue of privacy. Japan also encourages people not to draw attention to themselves. But, according to Jung, the impulse to extravert cannot be repressed too much and it will find an outlet. In Japan one of the bizarre ways Japanese extraversion is expressed is in Karaoke bars, where normally quiet and reserved people make an exhibition of themselves.

So what is the equivalent of Karaoke for the Scots? There appear to be three main avenues of introvert expression in Scotland. One is what Sir Compton McKenzie once called 'the Lone Shieling complex' - the urban Scot's fascination with remote crofts, misty mountains and solitary pipers. A second avenue is the Scots' predilection for secrets. In the present permissive age this is less apparent than formerly, but countless commentators have remarked that the Scots, despite their outward principles and piety, were a nation of secret drinkers and fornicators. Secrets are still at the root of that other great and enduring Scottish pastime - guilt. For Catholics, these guilty secrets can be expunged in the privacy of the confessional box, but for Presbyterians and atheists in Scotland there is no obvious outlet for them and they can be likened to a stagnant river which makes its presence felt on the edge of Scottish life, seeping here and there into literature.

And finally, there is Sabbatarianism. Historically, Presbyterians in Scotland believed that nothing should be done on a Sunday other than reading the Bible or worshipping the Lord. Sabbatarian practices are still to be seen in parts of Scotland, most notably in some areas of the Highlands and Islands, where even the ferries do not set sail on a Sunday. Sabbatarian beliefs were not part of the first phase of Scotland's Reformation but when they did arrive they gripped the country with a vengeance. Silence and stillness descended across most areas of the country. Even young children were stopped from playing. Although there is nothing exclusively Scottish about Sabbatarianism - the English, under the Puritan Oliver Cromwell, were strict observers of the Sabbath - it is true to say that Sabbatarianism gripped Scotland as a country tighter, and for longer, than other Protestant nations. One possible explanation for this vice-like grip is that the reformers realised that their religion of action was going against the grain of human life; that reflection, stillness, even idleness, were essential human needs and that the fulfilment of these needs should not be left to individuals but had to be controlled by the church. So the Kirk dictated to the Scottish people that they should spend time one day a week in quiet contemplation and reflection.

Introvert and Extravert Nations

Most Western cultures display a preference for extraversion and most Eastern cultures a preference for introversion. This is why Western cultures believe that self-confident, well-adjusted individuals should be assertive and good communicators. So is my claim that Scotland is an extravert culture little more than the obvious statement that she is part of Western culture? I believe I am saying something substantially more than that for one simple reason - nations, like individual extraverts themselves, vary in their strength of preference. Some extraverts are indeed the life and soul of the party; they talk a lot, and spend almost all their time with people. But there are others extraverts whose preference is far less marked and who try to maintain more balance in their lives. Italy and the Republic of Ireland are two countries where the preference for extraversion is a significant feature of the culture. A cultural preference for extraversion is less obvious in France as the French are much more reserved and laconic. So what about the English? It is, I concede, difficult to talk about England in introvert/extravert terms as she is a country with considerable regional and class variation. Nonetheless it is still illuminating to compare Scotland and England in this way.

In 1998 the television presenter Jeremy Paxman published a highly acclaimed book called *The English - Portrait of a People*. Paxman never uses the word 'introvert' when describing the English but on almost every page the portrait he paints is of a people with a strong preference for introversion. Not only does he point out, as many commentators before him, 'the insularity' of the English, he also argues that historically they were 'inclined to see the rest of Europe as nothing but trouble'.[14] Paxman also describes the English as having a 'natural reticence' and being a 'diffident' and 'reserved' people with a 'curious reluctance to engage with one another'.[15] The critic Roger Scruton makes similar points in his book about England claiming that traditionally 'English society was a society of strangers, who kept each other at a distance'.[16] Both writers argue that 'privacy' is very important to the English. Paxman quotes many foreigners' views on the English and claims that most believe the English are 'impossible to get to know'. For example a nineteenth-century visitor to England maintained:

> If you remark to an Englishman, in a smoking compartment, that he has dropped some cigar-ash on his trousers, he will probably answer: 'For the past ten minutes I have seen a box of matches on fire in your back coat pocket, but I did not interfere with you for that.'[17]

Throughout his book, Paxman makes little distinction between North and South or between classes when discussing the English character. And I am not that convinced that the need for privacy and lack of social interaction is as strong an English phenomenon as Paxman makes out. Other commentators on England, such as Beryl Bainbridge, have also noted what Paxman describes but believe it to be a characteristic of southern England. As Bainbridge writes in her book *Forever England:* 'You could move into a street in the South and nobody would even glance in your direction until you grew old and were carried out in a coffin'.[18] The reticence which Paxman describes is also much more evident in the 'home counties' as many of those from the North - Geordies and Liverpudlians, for example - seem positively garrulous and are much friendlier than Paxman allows. However, the fact that the spirit and character of England has been defined largely by the upper classes in the South means that Paxman is right - there is a prevailing sense in England that somehow it is vulgar and common to be over friendly.

There is also little doubt that for all that the Scots berate the English for talking too loudly and too publicly, the English do not share the Scots' cultural fascination with talk and speech. Paxman and Scruton argue that the English are obsessed by 'the word' but it is the written word they mean, not the spoken word. In that quintessential English institution - the Civil Service - people will sit feet away from one another yet still prefer to communicate by memo, or nowadays by email, rather than speak. Nor does English culture have the active, energetic quality that Scots culture has. Compare traditional English and Scottish weddings and you will soon see what I mean. And the descriptions of the English advanced by critics such as Paxman and Scruton are of a rather dull, inactive people enthralled by peace and tranquillity. It is a land of Elgar and Vaughan Williams rather than Jimmy Shand and pipe bands. What's more, the images the English use of their own country are of a quiet, reflective land. 'Somehow the English mind', writes Paxman 'kept alive the idea that the soul of England lay in the countryside'.[19] John Major, the former Conservative Prime Minister, defined

England as 'the country of long shadows on county grounds, warm beer, invincible green suburbs, dog lovers, and - as George Orwell said - old maids bicycling to holy communion through the morning mist. And ... Shakespeare ... '[20] Major was in fact trying to define Britain in these terms, not just England, but there is no way that any Scot could identify with such a picture. Given how douce Major's definition is, it is tempting to speculate if football hooliganism could be England's equivalent of Karaoke! In his book on England, former editor of *The Herald,* Harry Reid, makes a similar point. He reports that many English people he spoke to could only describe England as a 'green landscape and lovely villages' and he wonders if the riots which happen from time to time in England and the types of anti-social behaviour some young English people indulge in 'represents a release from the vegetation which seems to characterise much of modern English life'.[21]

I am not seriously arguing that England is an introverted culture along the lines of Eastern countries like Japan, but I believe there is a moderate preference for introversion in England. Comparing Scotland and England in this way brings into focus an important truth about Scotland - she is a nation with a strong preference for the outer, extravert world.

It is important to realise that the application of the concept of introversion and extraversion to Scotland or any other nation is not about numbers of people in the population with that preference. It is about whether one of these preferences has, for whatever reason, come to be expressed more within that nation's culture. It is about the spirit and character of a people as a whole. And we can see that the spirit and character of Scotland and her southerly neighbour could not, in this respect, be more different.

In the introduction I argued that over the years Scottish writers have engaged in a prodigious amount of navel gazing. As a result of this continual self-analysis the Scots are often thought to be an introspective people. So how does this fit with my claim that Scottish culture is essentially extraverted? Introversion and introspection are often used interchangeably but they refer to different processes. Introspection means to reflect on one's own self and consciousness. It is about becoming self-aware. This activity is not the preserve of introverts as introverted reflection does not usually lead the introvert to reflect on him or herself as such but on inner ideas, logical thought processes, values, facts, experiences and so forth. Introspection, by contrast, is something which people do when they want to become more fully aware of themselves and their motives, and such people can either be introverts or extraverts. The Scots as individuals are not particularly introspective, self-aware types of people. But the penchant for collective introspection - the tendency to gaze inwards at Scotland as a whole - is something of a Scottish pastime. And it seems to spring from a fusion of the need to understand with the Scots' lack of concepts to understand themselves better. Almost like the torture of Sisyphus, as each attempt to understand ourselves fails, we try again. And again.

NOTES

1 C. G. Jung, *Psychological Types* (Routledge: London, 1991).

2 The Myers-Briggs Type Indicator instrument and the MBTI are registered trademarks of Consulting Psychologists Press in the USA and Oxford Psychologists Press in the UK. The best introductory text on the relationship of the MBTI to Jung's concept of psychological type can be found in Isabel Briggs Myers *Gifts Differing* (Consulting Psychologists Press: Palo Alto, 1980).

3 Michael Fry, *The Scottish Empire* (Tuckwell Press and Birlinn: Edinburgh, 2001).

4 James Hogg 'On the Changes and Habits, Amusements and Conditions of the Scottish Peasantry' in Judy Steel (ed.), *A Shepherd's Delight: A James Hogg Anthology* (Canongate Publishing: Edinburgh, 1985), p. 41.

5 Ibid., p. 42.

6 Quoted in 'Worship Since 1920' in Duncan Forrester and Douglas Murray (eds.), *Studies in the History of Worship in Scotland* (T. & T. Clark: Edinburgh, 1984), p.157.

7 David Read, 'The Scottish Tradition in Preaching' in Duncan Forrester and Douglas Murray (eds.), *Studies in the History of Worship in Scotland,* p. 132.

8 Roderick Watson, 'Dialects of "Voice" and "Place": Literature in Scots and English from 1700' in Paul H. Scott, *Scotland: A Concise Cultural History* (Mainstream Publishing: Edinburgh, 1993), p. 99.

9 Carl MacDougall, *Painting the Forth Bridge: A Search for Scottish Identity* (Aurum Press: London, 2001), p. 27.

10 Roderick Watson 'Dialects of "Voice" and "Place"', p. 104.

11 David Hume, *An Enquiry Concerning Human Understanding,* p.1.

12 George Davie, *The Democratic Intellect* (Edinburgh University Press: Edinburgh, 1961), p. 19.

13 Roger Scruton, *England: An Elegy* (Pimlico: London, 2001), p. 168.

14 Jeremy Paxman, *The English: A Portrait of a People* (Penguin Books: London), p. 31.

15 Ibid., p. 116.

16 Roger Scruton, *England: An Elegy,* p. 54.

17 Quoted in Jeremy Paxman, *The English: A Portrait of a People,* p. 116.

18 Beryl Bainbridge, *Forever England* (Duckworth/BBC Books: London, 1987), p. 14.

19 Jeremy Paxman, *The English,* p. 147.

20 Speech to the Conservative Group for Europe, 22 April 1993. Quoted in David McCrone, Angela Morris & Richard Kiely, *Scotland - the Brand: The Making of Scottish Heritage* (Polygon: Edinburgh, 1999), pp. 23-24.

21 Harry Reid, *Dear Country: A Quest for England* (Mainstream Publishing Company: Edinburgh, 1992), p. 204.

4
Sceptical Scots

'A nation has a development: the things which happen to it possess a logic in which is concentrated ... its national spirit.'
Edwin Muir, *Scottish Journey*

Moray McLaren tells the story of a young couple who went to visit an old uncle on their return from honeymoon, taking with them a photograph album which they had carefully produced. The old man looked through the album without saying anything and then he slowly went through the pictures again. 'The young couple', writes McLaren, 'a trifle dampened by his silence, awaited his verdict. At length it came. Putting a broad spatulate finger upon one picture he uttered the words, "That's the worst"'.[1]

I am sure every single person living and working in Scotland will be aware that the Scots find it much easier to be critical than appreciative; negative rather than positive. In the first two chapters we saw just how negative and critical the Scots can be about themselves, but the Scots' tendency to be critical is not confined to self-criticism. The Scots have a highly developed critical faculty, and if we return to Jung, and his concept of psychological type, it is not difficult to see why.

Defining National Character
In *Psychological Types* Jung argues that human beings use four mental functions. He calls these *sensing, intuition, thinking* and *feeling*. Sensing and intuition are the functions which structure how we take in information, whereas thinking and feeling are two different ways to evaluate. Individuals have the capacity to use all four functions, and do use them in their everyday lives, but they do not tend to use them equally. An individual's psychological type is defined by the way they prefer to use these functions and whether they prefer to use them in the introvert or extravert world. All four mental functions that Jung describes can help us to understand not just individuals but cultural preferences better.

In this chapter I shall concentrate on the thinking/feeling dimension as it is 'thinking judgement' (see later in this chapter) which helps us to understand Scotland and the Scottish people better. Again, for the purpose of this exposition, I shall not confine myself to Jung's original concepts but will elaborate from my own experience of the types.

Let us imagine there are two countries - near neighbours - who have certain cultural characteristics in common such as a similar language, a shared music tradition and a reputation for being friendly people with a strong belief in equality. Both our imaginary countries have citizens with individual preferences for thinking and feeling, but at a cultural level there is national respect and encouragement for one of the processes rather than the other. So our two countries differ. One has a national preference for feeling judgement and one for thinking judgement.

Types that prefer feeling judgement use their personal values to evaluate and make decisions and usually place great emphasis on harmony and appreciation. So the nation that prefers feeling judgement has an international reputation for being warm and friendly; its people smile a lot, their hospitality is legendary, and they are adept at seeing the best in things and being appreciative. For example, they may say 'it's a fine morning' even though it is raining. They have extremely good social skills and can be very persuasive and charming. Their way with words, their insight into their own and other people's feelings, and their general sensitivity, means they can be gifted writers. In fact, this nation has a world-wide reputation for its poets, playwrights and novelists. To these undoubted strengths we must add a few weaknesses. This nation is not noted for logic - it boasts few gifted philosophers and scientists, for example. The emphasis on personal values means it has been difficult for this nation to maintain standards in public life and it has been rocked by a few scandals involving brown envelopes. As this is a nation which encourages harmony, caring and compliance rather than independent-mindedness and questioning, the Church has dominated society and its abuse of power has also emerged belatedly in a number of scandals. Finally, the charm of its people is almost without equal but this charm can be overdone and when this happens they can come across as manipulative and insincere.

As thinking types use objective logic to evaluate, the people in the thinking culture, by contrast, have developed good analytical skills. They are quick to see the flaws in anything and their questioning, sceptical minds mean they are not easily taken in by others. They care deeply about principles and standards in all areas of life and they have an international reputation for honesty and integrity. In short, people from other nations trust what they say. This thinking nation has made a huge contribution to intellectual endeavour of all kinds - philosophy, science, social science and technology. A number of important inventions have been made by these people. Again, this country has undoubted weaknesses. These people are not very clued-up on feelings - their own or others'. Over the centuries this country has produced a few literary giants but is not now noted for the quality of its literary output. The tendency to criticise rather than appreciate has also created a cultural environment which is rather negative and intimidating.

By now, many of you will have realised that I am not describing two fictitious nations. The nation which prefers feeling judgement is, of course, the Republic of Ireland and its thinking neighbour is Scotland - two nations where the indigenous culture has encouraged the development of distinctly different personality types, as pithily captured by the English poet Ewart Gavin:

> The Irish are great talkers
> Persuasive and disarming
> You can say lots and lots
> Against the Scots
> But at least they're never charming.

The Scots are not inclined to be 'charming' for they are too busy being critical, sceptical and logical. In other words, their attention tends to be taken up using the mental function Jung defines as 'thinking'.

Thinking Judgement

In everyday language we use the term 'thinking' to cover any kind of reflection or inner thought processes, but in Jungian psychology the term is confined to mental activity of a particular type. Thinking refers to the mental process which involves evaluating, drawing conclusions or prioritising on the basis of objective logic. Thinking therefore involves making a judgement or evaluation and making it as objectively as possible. Most thinking decisions involve the application of logical 'if ... then' reasoning. As thinkers try to reach a conclusion objectively and logically based on the available evidence, they usually believe that any other reasonable person in their position would come to the same conclusion because it is 'right'. In Jung's scheme, the alternative way to evaluate is to use feeling judgement. This is also a rational way to evaluate, but instead of objectivity and logic, the feeling type uses his/her subjective value system to reach a conclusion. When a person uses 'feeling' he/she is not being 'emotional' for it is a *mental* process just as 'thinking' is. The difference is that when individuals use feeling judgement they evaluate on the basis of personal values and relationships. Everyone has the capacity to use both mental functions and will use both but it is impossible to use the two processes simultaneously. We are only able to use one and then the other, as we cannot be subjective and objective at the same time. Most individuals have a preference for one of the two ways to evaluate and use it more frequently. Repeated use then shapes the individual's personality and determines some of their strengths and weaknesses.

When assessing the evidence I present in the following pages to support my contention that Scottish culture heavily endorses the use of logical thinking, please remember that I am not arguing that individual Scots *all* prefer logical thinking. Many have an individual preference for feeling judgement but, in a culture which encourages the use of logical thinking, they are aware of being 'out on a limb'. For example, Scottish feeling types do not feel as confident as their Irish counterparts in expressing their values or in being openly appreciative. Even though feeling judgement is a mental process - a way of analysing and deciding on the basis of values and relationships - and not simply an emotional response, feeling types often berate themselves for being 'weak' and will often try hard to see the world through thinkers' eyes. In this way feeling judgement has been driven almost underground and logical thinking has been allowed to flourish. As thinking judgement plays down the importance of subjective values, emotions and relationships it is much more in tune with a conventionally 'male' way of looking at the world and so the dominance of this preference helps to account for the distinctly masculine character of Scottish culture - a theme I shall return to in Chapter 8. Scotland is not the only country where thinking judgement dominates in this way; we can see a similar pattern in Germany, for example.

A Very Logical People

Over the years various commentators have noted the Scots' liking for logic. For example, the author of a nineteenth-century book entitled *Scottish Characteristics* argues that 'One of the most essential attributes of the Scottish mind is its orderly, methodical, in a word its logical character'.[2] Many also point out how much the Scots love words like 'partly, nevertheless and outwith' - words that help to structure the thinking process. Given this love of logic it is no coincidence that the great master of solving problems by the application of logical reasoning, Sherlock Holmes, was created by Sir Arthur Conan Doyle who was born and brought up in Edinburgh. What's more, Doyle modelled Holmes on the eminent surgeon Dr Joseph Bell who taught him forensic science at Edinburgh University.

In the literature on Scotland there are countless examples of Scots who, despite their humble origins, were able to make a huge contribution to knowledge as a result of their ability to employ logical reasoning. One man sums this up. He is James Ferguson, a self-taught shepherd boy who eventually became a fellow of the Royal Society. He was a celebrated astronomical instrument maker and theoretician yet he had only three months of formal schooling in his whole life. While still a boy, he looked after sheep by day and studied the stars at night, and despite having no knowledge of elementary maths was nevertheless determined to explain the nature of the universe: 'Even before his voice had broken he devised a string threaded with beads. With this device ... he went to the fields at night, and - lying on the ground - he laid his beads across the firmament'.[3]

Gazing at the stars can inspire human beings to all sorts of things; it may encourage them to dream, to write poetry, to feel spiritual, to contemplate God, or to speculate on the possibilities of life on other planets. It has inspired humans to ponder the effect of the heavens on their own personal lives, thus giving rise to astrology. Star-gazing led James Ferguson, and other Scots, to elaborate the principles of astronomy and to devise the instruments necessary for understanding the heavens.

A leading specialist on psychological type, Lenore Thomson, argues that all human societies, even underdeveloped ones, have to make sense of what is happening in their external world by relating their 'experiences to principles they can count on'.[4] So they use the thinking process to try to order the universe. The principles people devise are not always scientifically accurate but this does not matter, argues Thomson, for the function of thinking is to ensure that these 'principles are reliable enough to use as consensual bench-marks, thereby freeing us from the dictates of immediate experience'.[5] So it does not matter if other cultures use a different way of measuring time, for example, because what counts is that people in any given social group have an agreed, impersonal way of defining it.

From the seventeenth century on there was increasing pressure in the Western world not only to ensure that these organising principles were applied to more and more areas of life but also, where possible, for these principles to correspond with scientific fact. Much of this pressure came from Scotland and so did much of the groundbreaking work. Interestingly, the American academic, Arthur Herman, uses the subtitle *The Scots' Invention of the Modern World* for his book *The Scottish Enlightenment*. Scholars of this period showed how human beings were 'ultimately creatures of their environment' and that the changes which alter human beings' behaviour and character are not 'arbitrary or chaotic. They rest on fundamental principles and discernible patterns'. But, as Herman also points out, the Scottish Enlightenment project was much more than the creation of a proper study of history or the 'science of man', for it:

> ...embarked on nothing less than a massive reordering of human knowledge. It sought to transform every branch of learning - literature and the arts; the social sciences; biology, chemistry, geology, and the other physical and natural sciences - into a series of organised disciplines that could be taught and passed on to posterity.[6]

The period known as the Scottish Enlightenment spanned more than a century and involved people from many different spheres - philosophers, lawyers, scientists, engineers, historians, poets, architects and artists. It would be wrong of me to portray it as a movement where objective logical thinking reigned in splendid isolation. Thinking was not the only one of Jung's four mental functions to feature in this great period of Scottish intellectual life. As we shall see in the next chapter, speculative ideas (intuition) played a large part in the Scottish Enlightenment and even feeling judgement had its place. Indeed the mental process Jung defines as 'feeling' had a central role in the early part of the movement thanks to the influence of the man generally credited as its father - Francis Hutcheson. Hutcheson was an Ulster Scot and his intellectual work sprang, not from a desire to codify or understand, but from his personal conviction that human beings are essentially good, altruistic beings. Hutcheson was a hugely compassionate man and, according to Herman, his mission was to get the Presbyterian church 'to take on a more humane, comforting face'.[7] Hutcheson was, by all accounts, a brilliant lecturer who inspired a generation of students with his ideas. One of these students was Adam Smith, who talked about his mentor as 'the unforgettable Hutcheson'. And we can detect the influence of Hutcheson's ideas in the role Smith assigns to sympathy in his moral philosophy, as well as in the works of some of the other great Enlightenment figures, such as Adam Ferguson, who also appears to have been a compassionate man whose work is animated by his deeply-held values. But more commonly, feeling judgement made its presence felt in this movement, not as a sophisticated grown-up, but as a rather gauche teenager. Indeed the great sentimental work of this period, Henry MacKenzie's novel *The Man of Feeling*, was, in the words of Bruce Lenman, a 'lamentable tear-jerker'.[8]

There is little doubt, however, that the lasting legacy of these great Scottish intellectuals was their ability to using objective, logical thinking. Over the years many analysts and visitors to Scotland have passed comment on the Scots' ability to use thinking skills. For example, the nineteenth-century English political theorist, Walter Bagehot, maintained that 'There appears in the genius of the Scottish people ... a power of reducing human actions to formulas or principles'.[9] The Scottish Enlightenment era was one in which Scottish intellectual achievement was at its height, but even after this high-water mark had been reached, Scotland continued to produce some truly great scientists and thinkers such as the physicists Lord Kelvin and James Clerk Maxwell. Scottish science is still a credit to the nation and, per head of the population, Scotland ranks third in the world for the publication of science research papers.

As Bagehot pointed out, many Scottish scientists and intellectuals were particularly concerned to develop arguments and theories based on 'first principles'. And we can see that throughout history principles have mattered greatly to the Scots. Given the Scots' preference for objective thinking this makes sense - thinking types are greatly attracted to principles as they are derived from logic and founded on notions of universal truth. So it is hardly surprising that it is difficult to escape the word 'principle' in the evolution of Scottish intellectual life and institutions. For example, Scottish law is founded on Roman law and is concerned with establishing first principles. This is unlike the English and American legal systems, for example, where law is essentially judge-made and based on precedent. As we shall see later, fundamental principles also underlie the work of the new Scottish Parliament.

The Historical Legacy

The love of the mental process Jung defines as thinking is so strong and pervasive in Scotland that we can see its presence even in traditional song. Scotland was once noted for its rich ballad tradition - a ballad being simply defined as a folksong which tells the story of a 'crucial situation' by 'letting the action unfold itself in event and speech' and where the story is told 'objectively with little comment or intrusion of personal bias'.[10] In other words, the singer does not impose his or her personal values or morality on the tale.

The American historian Wallace Notestein, in his historical study of the development of this Scots characteristic, maintains that even in medieval times foreigners, like Erasmus, noted the Scots' love of logic and the 'dialectic'.[11] Alexander Broadie, currently Professor of Logic and Rhetoric at the University of Glasgow, has written numerous books and articles which illustrate that a strong and distinct philosophical tradition has existed in Scotland from the days of the philosopher John Duns Scotus in the thirteenth century.[12] Many other writers on Scotland have observed that it was the Scots' inclination towards logical thought which led them to support the Reformation with such enthusiasm. In England Protestantism had its beginnings in Henry VIII's desire to divorce his Queen, but in Scotland the roots of the Reformation were essentially ideological.

Life for the average Scot in the sixteenth century was fairly tough. Many lived in back-breaking poverty and no doubt resented the wealth of the Church. It is calculated that the unreformed Church in Scotland had control of about half of the country's revenues. Many of the most educated and powerful in Scottish society despised the Catholic Church as it had become increasingly degenerate and corrupt and churchmen were notoriously ignorant. A growing number of Scots were also critical of the Church because they believed its 'mumbo jumbo' and religious ritual were obscuring the word of God.

Calvinism is an intensely rational religion and so it held great appeal for the logical Scots. John Knox and his followers fashioned out of Calvinist dogma a religion for the Scottish people which stressed the importance of *understanding.* The key to this new religion was education: the ordinary parishioners in Scotland were to be taught not only how to read the Bible but also how to understand its meaning so that they could enter into debate on the scriptures. The scheme to transform the Scots into a people capable of such understanding was set out in the *First Book of Discipline* written by a commission appointed by the General Assembly in 1560 and led by John Knox. The Book stated that all children in Scotland, no matter how poor, should receive an education. It also set out a scheme for the development of the Scottish universities. Provisions were made for children to be publicly examined on the Catechism and every year the ministers and elders were to examine each parishioner publicly on the chief points of the Bible. The scheme envisaged by the Books of Discipline was never formally instituted, partly because of lack of funds, but Knox and his followers did ensure that for hundreds of years Scotland educated her people along these lines. In the centuries that followed, visitors to Scotland were amazed that even the poorest peasants could not only read but also debate arcane points of religion. As Campbell Maclean, a Church of Scotland minister, points out in an article on the Scots' way of religion, Knox's vision for education 'produced the most knowledgeable and articulate lay theologians in the history of the Christian church'.[13]

Obviously this emphasis on understanding and debate has had huge implications both for the Scottish Presbyterian church and for Scots culture and character. As many commentators have remarked, in Scotland 'God is an intellectual'. The core of the Scottish service is the sermon - the singing, prayers and communion are mere appendages. The bareness of the Presbyterian service and the lack of ritual, candles, kneeling and so forth, obviously appealed to the reformers' taste for logic and understanding but inevitably they created a religion which caters for the mind at the expense of the emotions: there is little beauty in Scottish Presbyterianism - little balm for the soul.

More importantly, for the Kirk itself, by emphasising the importance of independence of mind - of each parishioner being able to debate the finer points of theology - it sowed the seeds of its own destruction. It would have been well nigh impossible for there to have been one single Church in Scotland given the disputatious nature of the Scots. The fact that the Scottish Kirk survived intact for almost two hundred years is indeed remarkable. Infighting and disputes did become commonplace leading ultimately to the Great Disruption of 1843 when Thomas Chalmers and four hundred others walked out en masse from the General Assembly. As Campbell Maclean points out:

> It is true that many of the departures from the established church were undertaken more in a spirit of sorrow than anger and always with a high-minded disregard for the subsequent loss of privilege and property of the dissenters. But inevitably, once the flood began, it gave rise to a spate of self-indulgent sectarianism so farcically delicate of conscience that it could only be satisfied by every Presbyterian having a kirk to himself.[14]

Ultimately a church which encouraged people to think for themselves was also paving the way for agnosticism and atheism and this is precisely what happened in Scotland. In urban areas, even by the nineteenth century, many Scots took the view that religion was a matter of personal belief and conscience.

Earlier I argued that many popular commentators on Scotland only portray the Reformation and Knox's legacy as a huge blight on Scotland. They will often hold this view while simultaneously praising the thinkers of the Scottish Enlightenment. But historians generally believe that *the intellectual and economic activity of this period in Scotland would not have happened without the Reformation and the Presbyterian emphasis on education, independence of mind and logical thinking.* Indeed Tom Devine argues that by the eighteenth century Calvinism had developed into a set of religious beliefs which stimulated 'an interest in moral, philosophical and scientific questions'.[15] Likewise Herman argues that it is impossible to understand 'the story of the Scots' place in modern civilisation' without 'an appreciation of Scotland's Presbyterian legacy'.[16]

Philosophy

In the last chapter we saw how the Scots and English education systems differ in their approach, with the Scots being more in favour of generalism. But, traditionally, there was another key difference between the Scots and English education systems and it could be summed up in one word - philosophy. The Scots believed that to be properly educated a student had to have a good grasp of philosophy. Before the Scottish universities were forced to adopt the English system, Scottish students started at university at the age of fifteen or sixteen - at least two years before English students - and were then given a general classical and scientific education in which philosophy was given pride of place. The Scots abhorred the idea of specialising too early and believed that it was better for students to get a broad, philosophical education in their first few years at university and then go on to specialise, in law or science, for example, at a later date. The Scottish approach was in line with what happened on the continent but it was out of step with the English tradition. Nevertheless, as George Davie charts in his book *The Democratic Intellect,* the Scots were still forced to introduce specialised first degree courses along English lines. These changes meant that Scotland lost touch with an important part of her intellectual tradition - a tradition which had, at one point, led her to be one of the great intellectual centres of the world. There is little doubt that over the years Scotland has made a major contribution to philosophy. Not only is David Hume reckoned to be the most important philosopher to write in English but Scotland has produced a score of significant, albeit less well-known, philosophers such as the father of the Common Sense school, Thomas Reid, and the moralist John Macmurray, who influenced Tony Blair. Indeed Blair argues that anyone wanting to understand what drives his politics simply has to do one thing - read the Scottish philosopher John Macmurray.

A Nation of Logical Thinkers

Philosophy as such has dimmed within Scottish cultural life but logical thinking has not. Indeed the love of logical thinking is so ingrained within the Presbyterian tradition in Scotland it would have taken more than a change in university practices to eliminate it. Quite simply, the Jungian thinking process is still common currency within Scotland. It is the mental process we are expected to use. And this is true not just for Presbyterian Scots but for Catholics, atheists and Asian Scots as well, for the prevailing culture in Scotland encourages everyone to adopt this type of thinking.

Logical thinking still holds sway in contemporary Scotland. Viscount Stair enunciated the principles underlying Scottish law in the seventeenth century and three centuries later the Scots are still intent on putting principles at the heart of Scottish public life. The Scotland Act legislated for the establishment of a Scottish Parliament but its ethos and working practices were defined by the Consultative Steering Group - an all-party group established by Donald Dewar. And this group determined that the Parliament's activities should be anchored by four guiding *principles* - power-sharing, accountability, openness and participation/equal opportunities.

Nowadays the Scots can still be described as an independent-minded, opinionated and sceptical people. As Cliff Hanley once remarked, if Scotland were to have a slogan it should be 'aye that'll be right'. (For the sake of foreign readers, I should point out that these words sarcastically convey disagreement, not agreement!). Even when the Scots appear outwardly to respect authority, few will accept others' opinions and views at face-value. As I know very well as a trainer, many Scots turn up to courses feeling very sceptical and often sit, arms folded, waiting to be convinced. This need to be convinced, to see the logic and rationale behind something, means the Scots are more likely to be questioning rather than accommodating. However, many Scots do not want to draw attention to themselves (a theme I shall return to later) and this often stops them from being argumentative in formal or on public occasions. In more relaxed, informal surroundings like pubs, they are often extremely opinionated and argumentative. Stand at the bar in many a busy pub and you will soon be in no doubt that the Scots love exchanging opinions and arguing about football, politics or even the meaning of life. And they will often argue their point of view even in the face of higher authorities. John Buchan recounts a story which illustrates this well: 'I remember an old shoemaker in Fife who was a great theologian,' writes Buchan; 'He was always discussing points of theology, and on one occasion his opponent quoted St. Paul against him. 'True,' said the old man, 'but that's just where me and Paul differs'''.[17]

The Scots' love of logical thinking also means they have a highly developed critical faculty and are much more aware of what they think is wrong with something than what is right. And it is this trait which can lead to the impression that Scotland is a 'can't do' or an 'ah ... but' culture. As John Buchan once pointed out, there is also a tendency in Scotland to delight in 'pricking other people's bubbles' - to see others' enthusiasm as something to be dampened rather than encouraged. The predisposition for logical thinking also means that praise and appreciation tend to be squeezed out. Indeed anyone who lives in Scotland will be aware that if they want to criticise someone or put them down they have a veritable treasure chest of Scottish expressions to choose from. (Terms such as glaikit, hackit, sleekit and greetin-faced immediately spring to mind.) The Scot who wants to appreciate, compliment or praise has fewer expressions to convey positive thoughts and will also tend to ca' canny on compliments because he or she knows from experience that saying positive things to people in Scotland, outside the immediate family at least, easily causes embarrassment. So stinting can the Scots be with praise, that not being criticised is a bonus. Campbell Maclean maintains that any minister overhearing a parishioner saying of his sermon 'I've heard worse' should feel that his 'time was not wasted'. He also tells a very believable story of an English summer visitor of the evangelical tradition visiting a country church service in Scotland. After some very enthusiastic singing he started to:

punctuate the sombre-toned sermon with cries of 'Hallelujah! Praise the Lord!' At last, an aged worthy, unable to abide these intrusions any longer rose from his seat and addressed him in a cold, emphatic voice: 'We dinna praise the Lord here!'[18]

Traditionally, if the Scots wanted to show affection or liking in every day life they simply said 'wee' or stuck the letters ie on the end of words and talked about 'lassies', 'laddies' or 'beasties'. This is a theme pursued in a fascinating article on the Scots' liberal use of diminutives published in the 1920s in which Miss Symon, a Scottish poet from Dufftown, is quoted as saying:

> Diminutives are our only emotional outlets. We have practically no endearments. The southerner spreads himself out on 'dears', 'darlings', 'beloveds' and such-like saccharinities. The tidal wave of passion swamps the Scot. Even the mildest of ordinary, everyday loves remain unexpressed either directly or indirectly because there is no vocabulary for them ... In a vague, unformulated fashion we consider tenderness a weakness, very nearly an indecency. At any rate we fight shy of it. We *are* shy of it. "Love but dinna lat on" about sums up all the erotic philosophy of the hill plaid and the sleeved weskit. So in our soft moments - no dithyrambics, no little urbanities, or amiabilities. We just drop into diminutives.[19]

Of course, the advent of the mass media, and some would say the Anglicisation of Scottish life, means that terms of endearment are now used more routinely in Scotland. Nonetheless it is apparent that the Scots feel on more familiar terrain if they are criticising or pointing out what is wrong with something, rather than praising it or showing affection.

The logical thinkers' tendency to home in on what is wrong with something rather than to appreciate what is good about it was very much in evidence in the delicate bedding-in period post-devolution. Almost overnight many of the Scottish media corps went from being keen on the idea in principle to becoming the staunchest critics of the new Parliament. The Presiding Officer, David Steel, issued a public rebuke and even took *The Daily Record* to task for 'bitch journalism'. Newspaper columnist and television presenter Iain Macwhirter broke ranks to attack his colleagues for churning out such critical copy, yet in the process he simply added to the sense of despair and negativity by peddling well-worn images of Scottish deformity: 'The assault on the Parliament probably has something to do with latent philistinism and cretinism in the Scottish character', writes Macwhirter.[20]

Criticising the Critical Scots

Commentators on Scotland have not had the conceptual tools to allow them to see that the Scots have a penchant for what Jung defines as thinking, but they have been aware of the weaknesses which can easily flow from the use of this mental function. Edwin Muir laments what he calls a 'thoroughness in the Scottish character' due to the inability to compromise and the desire to take things to their logical conclusion. Sir Iain Moncrieffe likewise maintains it is independent-mindedness which means the Scots find it practically impossible to agree with one another on anything 'except Rabbie Burns'. 'The snag is', writes Moncrieffe, ' having thought for themselves, they tend to carry things to their logical conclusion ad absurdum: so that they tend to be pretty intolerant of those who disagree with them'.[21] George Blake believes that in 'the Scottish nature' there is 'a tendency to niggle over shades of meaning, the hesitation to accept large generalisations and make easy agreements'. Indeed Blake believes there is a great 'capacity' in Scotland 'to slice metaphysical sausages into the finest slivers'.[22] In a judgmental, critical culture which holds every individual to account those who feel called to express themselves artistically are often most fearful of exposing themselves or of not getting it 'right'. Various artists in Scotland have referred to such fears. According to film-maker Bill Forsyth, 'You are only allowed one chance in Scotland, and if you blow it, that's your lot'.[23] The poet Alan Bold once said 'Anyone who has the temerity to set up shop as a writer in Scotland is bound to attract hostility'.[24] Others just feel oppressed or ground down. 'The skin of a man of letters is peculiarly sensitive to the bite of the critical mosquito,' claimed Alexander Smith, a nineteenth-century Glasgow poet, adding 'and he lives in a climate in which such mosquitoes swarm. He is seldom stabbed to the heart - he is often killed by pinpricks'.[25] And more recently the novelist Alasdair Gray asserted:

> The curse of Scotland is these wee hard men. I used to blame the English for our mediocrity. I thought they had colonised us by sheer cunning. They aren't very cunning. They've got more confidence and money than we have, so they can afford to lean back and smile while our own wee hard men hammer Scotland down to the same dull level as themselves.[26]

The problem for artists in Scotland is not just the prevalence of a judgmental critical atmosphere, and people thinking their opinions are superior to others, but also, as Jung himself points out, extraverted thinking types are often poor in 'aesthetic activities, taste, artistic sense'.[27] In other words, logic can easily suppress imagination as well as feeling and so weaken literary expression - a process which may help account for why, in the words of Scottish literary expert David Craig, an '"all-round" literature' did not emerge in modern Scotland.[28]

As this type of thinking can sometimes repress passion it can easily lead to the unenthusiastic, dour Scot. As logical thinkers do not routinely consult their feelings to make decisions, they can also become emotionally illiterate. In fact thinking types often fear emotions and believe that feelings, their own and others', get in the way of good (i.e. logical) decisions. This means that a logical thinker's feeling side often remains childlike and undeveloped. Thinking types usually like to believe that their tender side, their feelings, can be kept at bay, but inevitably, as human beings, they are not able to do this. Logical thinkers need to pay attention to their feelings and values and when they do they can easily become sentimental - attracted to cheap and easy expressions of emotion.

The Other Side

Which leads me to the one potential flaw in my argument about Scotland's great penchant for logical thinking and hence the critical and unappreciative Scot - Robert Burns. Burns is the most celebrated and famous Scot not only within his own country but also abroad and it would be impossible to describe him as critical, unappreciative, or unprepared to engage with his emotional, feeling side. Of course, Burns was a gifted intellectual, but his reasoning took place, not on the basis of objective logic, but on his personal values. Burns was aware of this himself and talked about being governed not by his 'head' but his 'heart'. Even when Burns was critical, for example in his bitingly satirical poems, his criticism rarely sprang from a cool, principled opposition but from deep feeling. Burns also differs from the typical Scot in that not only was he comfortable expressing emotion, he also passionately wanted to understand himself and his personal responses.

Accepting that Burns is a feeling type does not, however, undermine my argument about the importance of Jungian thinking in Scotland. It strengthens it. Jung argues that all human beings have the capacity to use both the thinking and the feeling processes. They cannot completely ignore one and concentrate on the other. Through use one will become preferred and developed, thus colouring the individual's personality, but the undeveloped process will still demand some expression. It will still make its presence felt in the individual's life. In the last chapter we saw this process at work in the outlet the introverted Japanese find in Karaoke or the extraverted Scots found in Sabbatarianism. Burns is so important to Scotland because he encourages the otherwise logical, critical Scots to celebrate and appreciate what is important to them in their everyday lives - daisies, mice, simple family ways, a smile, a sweetheart. Since Burns's poetry is heartfelt but not deep it is easy for the Scots, enthralled as they are by the outer world, to understand. Burns was undoubtedly a highly energetic extravert, not a deep, reflective type. Indeed those who knew Burns often said that he was even more gifted as a speaker than a writer, which may account for why much of his poetry is written as speech. When Burns writes with feeling in his poems these feelings have arisen, not from deep introspection, but from everyday encounters. In other words, he writes mainly about how he feels about people and events. So the difficulties most Scots have in understanding Burns spring from his use of language or the historical period he is responding to and not because the poems themselves require much deconstruction. Nor do they require us to search deeply within ourselves to find resonance.

Burns's capacity to redress an important imbalance in the Scottish character and Scottish life is best seen on Burns night. At Burns suppers, men who in normal life would never dream of expressing emotion in public, stand in front of an audience and declare 'my love is like a red, red rose'. They make all sorts of enthusiastic, positive statements about things they like - whisky, lassies, lines from Burns's poems, haggis. They talk in passionate terms about their homeland. The toast known as 'the Immortal Memory' is also known as 'the Appreciation' and the one rule a speaker must observe is that it must be positive about Burns, Scotland and humankind in general. Any speaker who is critical or accusatory strikes the wrong note. Indeed my *Burns Supper Companion* tells me that one of the key ingredients of this speech is its 'warmth'. Fairly tedious, predictable criticism is permitted in the 'Toast to the Lassies' and 'the Reply'. But even then, my *Companion* informs me, both should end on a 'conciliatory note'.[29]

There are few occasions in Scottish life where these are the terms of engagement - even the Kirk does not function like that. The Scots are much more likely to be argumentative than conciliatory. They are critical rather than appreciative. The Scots do not openly talk about love, relationships or emotions. Except on Burns night. Earlier I asserted that Scotland possesses a 'masculine culture' and it is interesting to note that even the emotional, feeling side of life in Scotland is carried by Robert Burns - a Scotsman.

There is hardly a commentator on Scotland who has not tried to fathom why Burns should be celebrated by the Scots to the extent he is; why Burns is not just an important national poet, but a demigod with a cult following. Some argue that Burns's popularity is intrinsically tied up with Scotland's relationship with England and how he galvanised nationalist sentiment. Others show how Burns carries important Scottish values. Another common argument is that Burns was a chameleon who could easily be 'all things to all men'. I have no doubt there is much merit in all these arguments. All I am saying is that there is another reason as well: Burns encourages a very logical, unemotional people to get in touch with their tender side. Remove Burns from Scottish life and it would be greatly impoverished. Without Burns to encourage us to consider our hearts, not just our heads, the Scots would be more aware of living in a world dominated by cold, impersonal logic. A world where scepticism reigns and where it is more acceptable to criticise than appreciate. Where it is very easy for us to lose sight of what is important in life.

One-sided Development

As I wrote the last few pages, I could not help hearing in my mind's ear a few gleeful guffaws and a chorus of 'we tell't ye, we tell't ye' for have I not more-or-less confirmed the images of the Scots I decried in Chapter 2? Do my words not conjure up the image of the Scot as a divided self - logical and prone to thinking they are right on the one hand and with a tendency to gross sentimentality on the other? Yes, to some extent they do. But it is simplistic and unhelpful for commentators and analysts to rage against what they perceive as Scottish weaknesses and not simultaneously see such weaknesses as a consequence of positive qualities which they may like about Scotland and the Scots - for example, the principles, the intellectual skills and the independent-mindedness. For me the most liberating and life-enhancing insight to be gained from Jungian typology is the understanding that development is inevitably one-sided; that strengths and weaknesses are inextricably linked. To understand why, we have to know a little more about Jung's typology.

Jung's concept of psychological type is fairly complex. At this stage all that readers have to grasp is that thinking and feeling are *opposite* processes. We use either one or the other. For example, thinking is a process of judging or deciding which requires us to stand back and try to make evaluations objectively. It requires us to try to take ourselves out of the decision-making by being impersonal. Whereas feeling is a process where we consciously put ourselves at the heart of the decision and evaluate subjectively in relation to our own personal values. We can move from using thinking to using feeling judgement but we cannot use the two functions simultaneously. This means that someone who prefers objective thinking will, as a result of using this function, develop the strengths associated with it, but inevitably it also means that he or she will have less time and energy to devote to developing the opposite side - in this case feeling. So logical thinking is cultivated *at the expense* of feeling judgement and vice versa.

For reasons I'll explain in later chapters, there is in Scotland a very common belief that we should all strive to be good across the board; that if we do anything it should be perfect. Of course, we know that perfection is unattainable but somehow we think it should be attainable and that imperfections of any kind are fatal flaws - something to berate ourselves or others for. But what Jung teaches us above all else is that being good at something means you are not good at something else. Time and attention put into one function means time and attention not devoted to another function. As Jung himself writes, humankind 'always develops qualities at the expense of others, and wholeness is never attained.'[30] Certainly there are individuals who do not have a clear preference for either thinking or feeling and who move constantly between the two, but there is no great advantage in doing this. If we use handedness as an analogy we can see that it is better for an individual to have one really strong, skilful hand and one poor hand, than two hands of average ability. One-sided development is thus the route to excellence. In an individual, and in a country or organisation, indistinct preferences can mean blandness and mediocrity. However, it is also the case that a preference for any of the four mental functions can be so exaggerated that this strength becomes a liability. We can detect such exaggeration at work in some Scottish attitudes - the tendency to be overly critical, for example, but again it is not helpful to use this as proof of Scots' pathology or deformity as the development of this type of weakness is all too human. Indeed, when some of our analysts come out with extremely negative and critical theories about Scotland, ironically all they do is highlight, in their own work, some of the tendencies they deplore in other Scots.

NOTES

1 Moray McLaren, *Understanding the Scots: A Guide for South Britons* and *Other Foreigners* (Frederick Muller: London, 1956), p. 27.

2 Quoted in W. Gordon Smith, *This is my Country: A Personal Blend of the Purest Scotch* (Souvenir Press: London, 1976), p. 188.

3 Neil McCallum, *A Small Country* (James Thin: Edinburgh, 1983), p. 128.

4 Lenore Thomson, *Personality Type: An Owner's Manual* (Shambhala: Boston, 1998), p. 257.

5 Ibid., p. 258.

6 Arthur Herman, *The Scottish Enlightenment: The Scots' Invention of the Modern World* (Fourth Estate: London, 2002), page 54.

7 Ibid., p. 68.

8 Bruce P. Lenman, 'From the Union of 1707 to the Franchise Reform of 1832' in R. A. Houston & W. W. J. Knox (eds), *The New Penguin History of Scotland: From the Earliest Times to the Present Day* (Penguin Books: London, 2001), p. 345.

9 Quoted in Christopher Harvie, *Scotland and Nationalism: Scottish Society and Politics, 1707-1977* (George Allen & Unwin: London, 1977), p. 130.

10 Quoted in Douglas Gifford, *James Hogg* (The Ramsay Head Press: Edinburgh, 1976), p. 11.

11 Wallace Notestein, *The Scot in History: A Study of the Interplay of Character and History* (Yale University Press: United States, 1947).

12 See, for example, Alexander Broadie, *Why Scottish Philosophy Matters* (The Saltire Society: Edinburgh, 2000).

13 Campbell Mclean 'Who is Their God?' in Alastair M. Dunnett (ed.), *Alistair MacLean Introduces Scotland* (Andre Deutsch: London, 1972), p. 196.

14 Ibid., p. 202.

15 T. M. Devine, *The Scottish Nation* 1700-2000 (Penguin Books: London, 1999), p. 69.

16 Arthur Herman, *The Scottish Enlightenment,* page 10.

17 John Buchan 'Some Scottish Characteristics' in W.A. Craigie, John Buchan, Peter Giles & J. M. Bulloch, *The Scottish Tongue* (Cassell & Company: London, 1924), p. 63.

18 Campbell Mclean, 'Who is Their God?', p. 207.

19 Quoted in J. M. Bulloch 'The Delight of the Doric in the Diminutive' in W.A. Craigie, John Buchan, Peter Giles & J. M. Bulloch, *The Scottish Tongue* (Cassell & Company: London, 1924), pp. 143-144.

NOTES

20 Iain Macwhirter, *The Sunday Herald,* 5 September 1999.

21 Sir Iain Moncrieff, 'The Long Story - to Queen Victoria' in Alastair M. Dunnett (ed.), *Alistair MacLean Introduces Scotland* (Andre Deutsch: London, 1972), p. 77.

22 George Blake, *The Heart of Scotland* (B. T. Batsford: London, 1934), p. 69.

23 Quoted in Angela Cran & James Robertson, *Dictionary of Scottish Quotations* (Mainstream Publishing: Edinburgh, 1996), p. 134.

24 Alan Bold, 'Dr Grieve and Mr MacDiarmid' in P. H. Scott & A. C Davis (eds), *The Age of MacDiarmid* (Mainstream Publishing: Edinburgh, 1980), p. 38.

25 Alexander Smith, *Dreamthorp* (1863).

26 Quoted in Angela Cran & James Robertson, *Dictionary of Scottish Quotations* (Mainstream Publishing Company: Edinburgh, 1996), p. 150.

27 C. G. Jung, *Psychological Types* (Routledge: London, 1991), p. 348.

28 David Craig, *Scottish Literature and the Scottish People 1680-1830* (Chatto & Windus: London, 1961), p. 14.

29 Nancy Marshall, *Burns Supper Companion* (HarperCollins: Glasgow 2002).

30 C. G. Jung, *Psychological Types,* p. 540.

5

The Pull of Possibilities

'Speculative hard-headedness unites in the national character with a sublime and lofty enthusiasm concerning things altogether remote and intangible.'

Paxton Hood, *Scottish Characteristics*

It is impossible to read Scottish history and not be struck by the fact that for centuries the Scots have been discontented with the status quo. John Buchan believed this 'unsettlement' to be one of the most important aspects of Scottish history. In recent times Kirsty Wark highlighted the Scots' unsettlement in her TV series on Scottish politics, 'Restless Nation'.

For centuries the Scots have dreamed of change and possibilities and have responded to a vision of a different future. A good example of this is the Scottish Covenant of 1949. This document was the brainchild of John MacCormick, a Scottish lawyer, who was instrumental in the formation of the SNP. MacCormick went on to set up the first Scottish Convention - an all-party group designed to exert pressure for 'reform of Scottish Government'. It held a 'Scottish National Assembly' in 1947 and over six hundred delegates from all walks of Scottish life attended. Ultimately this organisation supervised the creation of a Scottish Covenant to allow the Scottish people simultaneously to swear their loyalty to the United Kingdom and their commitment to the creation of a Scottish parliament. The document was unveiled at a crowded national assembly meeting in the General Assembly building on the Mound in Edinburgh in October 1949. Over twelve hundred people attended what seemed at the time like a momentous Scottish occasion. John MacCormick recorded the event in the following terms:

> Unknown district councillors rubbed shoulders and joined in pledges with the men whose titles had sounded through all the history of Scotland.

Working men from the docks of Glasgow or the pits of Fife spoke with the same voice as the portly business-men in pin-striped trousers. It was such a demonstration of national unity as the Scots might never hope to see, and when, finally, the scroll upon which the Covenant was inscribed was unveiled for signature every person in the hall joined patiently in the queue to sign it.[1]

As with earlier Scottish Covenants, copies were distributed around Scotland - in colleges, shops and cafés. Although two million people eventually signed, Westminster ignored the Covenant and a Scottish Government did not materialise. The vision remained unfulfilled until 1999 and the inauguration of the Scottish Parliament.

Other examples of vision playing a major role in Scottish life include the original Scottish Covenant of 1638, which I discuss more fully below, when 300,000 signatures were collected in support of Scottish religious independence. Another is the founding of an ill-fated Scottish trading colony at Darien in the late seventeenth century. On that occasion Scots did not simply sign their name in support of a vision but gave money to support a trading venture. Indeed it is estimated that a third of all Scotland's liquid assets were sunk into the proposal. On other occasions, particular sections of the Scottish community were involved in the furtherance of a vision: the nobles in the Declaration of Arbroath or the workers in Glasgow during the period known as Red Clydeside. And no doubt many of the millions who have chosen voluntarily to leave Scotland over the centuries did so animated by their own personal vision of a new life for themselves and their families.

One possible reason for the Scots' responsiveness to vision is that historically they have been unhappy with their lot. Lacking opportunities at home they have packed up and gone elsewhere. What's more, because Scotland is the junior partner in an incorporating union, and an ancient state without sovereignty, the Scots are bound to feel discontented with the situation in which they find themselves. So the Scots may well be attracted to the vision of a different future because they do not care too much for the status quo. But I believe there is another reason as well. The Scots are much more responsive to visionary ideas than the English, for example, not simply because they have a constitutional position they dislike, but because they are fairly comfortable with abstract ideas and are more open to the idea of change. Of course, there is a distinct backward-looking strain within Scottish culture. But such a strain is apparent in any modern society. The nostalgic longings of millions of Scottish émigrés have also strengthened 'the Lone Shieling' complex. And no doubt Scotland's proclivity for sentimentality, which I explained in the last chapter, has also encouraged the tendency to romanticise aspects of the past. But none of this gainsays the fact that there is a strong, progressive current within Scottish thought. In the last chapter I argued that the Scots are logical thinkers, but there is much more to it than that. Traditionally the Scots have also been bold, speculative thinkers who are comfortable with theories and abstractions. Vision, speculation, abstraction and theories may not seem linked but we can easily appreciate the connection if we return to Jung's tool box and borrow the two remaining mental processes he describes - sensing and intuition.

Sensing and Intuition

In everyday life we can see that some people are 'big picture' types whilst others are interested in 'detail'. We can also see that some people like change and innovation whilst others are conservative and prefer the known to the unknown. But while we can see these differences we cannot account for them. We have no idea why people vary in this way. Jung provides an explanation by describing the underlying mental processes.

Sensing is a way of taking in information from the five senses. When individuals use the mental process Jung defines as sensing, they pay high quality attention to real, concrete information. In short, they live in the moment, with their feet on the ground, noticing what is going on round about them, or they tap into their memory banks to access information based on real, lived experiences. Obviously, everyone has to pay attention to some sensory information, but the difference between sensing types and intuitive types is that the former *prefer* this kind of information. They concentrate their attention to what is real and to what they know from experience to be true. People who prefer sensing information also respect facts and care about practicalities and details.

People who prefer intuition, by contrast, are not motivated by what *is* but by *what could be* - they are pulled by what Jung calls 'possibilities'. So intuitives do not pay much attention to real, concrete information; they pay more attention to a vast array of information gleaned from their unconscious mind. Intuitives often describe this type of information as a 'hunch'. What this means is that the intuitive instinctively 'knows' something even though he/she cannot support it with concrete facts. So intuitives favour a type of information gathering which looks beyond or behind what is really there. The intuitive process encourages individuals to do a variety of different things, such as ask questions about meaning, construct theories, speculate, associate, or visualise a different future.

So sensing is a process which respects concrete facts and prefers to confine its attention to the real and the known, whereas intuition is more concerned with an abstract world of possibilities, theories and ideas. Each individual uses both processes to some extent in life and will move from one to the other, but one of the processes is usually preferred, and its use seems right and natural, just as when we use our dominant hand.

Again a preference for one of these two functions leads to significant personality differences in individuals. People who prefer sensing are down-to-earth, practical, realistic, good on detail and are motivated by facts and personal experience, whereas intuitives get bored easily and look for new possibilities and opportunities to theorise or innovate. Another key difference between people who prefer sensing and those who prefer intuition is that the former tend to be conservative, valuing the known to the unknown, whereas intuitives stress the importance of possibilities and vision and are drawn to change.

It is important to understand that intuitives do not completely disregard facts or believe they are unimportant; but their preferences often lead them to devise a theory based on their hunches and then work backwards to see how the facts fit.

The Scots' Intellectual Method

If we examine the work of those involved in the Scottish Enlightenment we shall see just how strong the preference for intuition was during the heydey of Scots' intellectual endeavour. In fact, the Scottish Enlightenment project, with its particular focus on 'progress', 'improvement', radical, social, economic and scientific change, was undoubtedly a movement dominated by intuitive thinkers. Of all the types it is those who combine thinking and intuition who are most intent on changing the world through new ways of thinking and conceptualising. In a nutshell this is what the Scottish Enlightenment was all about. It is tempting simply to say that as many intellectuals and radical thinkers have a preference for intuition then there was nothing special about the Scottish Enlightenment thinkers, but the English historian Henry Buckle helps us see that Scottish intellectuals, in the past at least, did differ from their English counterparts.

Buckle was a historian of ideas. Although his book is called *The History of Civilization in England,* Buckle died before writing specifically about England. But he did write a general introduction to his history, a study of Spain and a full history of Scottish ideas. In this volume, entitled *On Scotland and the Scotch Intellect,* Buckle compares the intellectual method preferred in England and Scotland. He argues that, following Bacon, English scientists and intellectuals used 'inductive reasoning'. By that Buckle means reasoning which takes place on the basis of concrete facts and that English intellectuals reason from the particular to the general. 'The inductive philosopher', writes Buckle, 'is naturally cautious, patient and somewhat creeping'.[2] According to Buckle, 'deductive reasoning', which the Scots intelligentsia preferred in the eighteenth and nineteenth centuries at least, proceeds from 'generals to particulars and from the ideas to the senses'.[3] Buckle's thesis does not fit precisely with Jungian definitions of sensing and intuition but it seems legitimate to argue Buckle uses concepts which overlap with three of Jung's four mental functions. Buckle maintains that the English, following scientific method laid down by Bacon, proceed from facts - that is, sensing - whereas the Scots either reason from first principle - thinking or from abstract ideas - intuition. In either case, the Scots in their preferred intellectual method relegate sensing, e.g. paying attention to concrete facts, to second if not third place. Presumably this is one of the reasons why the Scottish universities traditionally gave weight to philosophy and were less concerned to engage in practical research.

Buckle gives many examples of the Scots' penchant for the deductive method. For example, he writes:

> *The Wealth of Nations* ... is entirely deductive, since in it Smith generalises the laws of wealth, not from the phenomenon of wealth, not from statistical statements, but from the phenomenon of selfishness; thus making a deductive application of one set of mental principles to the whole set of economical facts. The illustrations with which his great book abounds are no part of the real argument: they are subsequent to the conception; and if they were all omitted, the work, though less interesting, and perhaps less influential, would, from a scientific point of view, be equally valuable.[4]

Buckle is critical of the Scottish deductive method yet a great admirer of Scottish thinkers such as Adam Smith. He not only praises the bold sweep of the book and the 'prodigious' work Smith undertook, he also claims it to be 'the most important book ever written'.[5] He also maintains that Smith realised that 'an inductive investigation (i.e. one based on facts) was impossible, because it would require the labour of many lives even to assemble the materials from which the generalisation was to be made'.[6] According to Buckle, Smith was influenced 'by the intellectual habits which prevailed around him' and argued on the basis of hypothesis and the 'intentional suppression of facts'.[7]

Buckle asserts that even the great empiricist Hume, in works such as *The Natural History of Religion,* used a deductive method for he established principles to support his arguments without the use of facts and observation and then simply used facts as illustrations. 'In him a contempt for facts', writes Buckle 'was merely the exaggerated result of a devotion to ideas'.[8] Again Buckle claims that 'If Hume had followed the Baconian scheme, of always rising from particulars to generals, and from each generalisation to that above it, he would hardly have written one of his works'.[9] Buckle also maintains that the Scots used deductive reasoning in the natural sciences. According to Buckle, Professor Joseph Black, who was famous for his theory of latent heat, 'began to speculate concerning heat', and taught his theory a number of years before the necessary experiments were undertaken to prove it. Buckle claims that Hutton, whose theory on the evolution of the earth earned him the title 'father of geology', likewise proceeded from ideas and not from facts when coming up with his *Theory of the Earth:*

> It ... appears that one of the chief parts of the Huttonian Theory, and certainly its most successful part, was conceived in opposition to all preceding evidence; that it presupposed a combination of events which no one had ever observed, and the mere possibility of which nothing but artificial experiment could prove; and finally, that Hutton was so confident of the validity of his own method of inquiry, that he disdained to make the experiment himself, but left to another mind that empirical branch of the investigation which he deemed of little moment, but which we, in England, are taught to believe is the only safe foundation of physical research.[10]

I have little doubt that Buckle is right - speculative ideas and theories have played an important part in the work of great

Scottish thinkers throughout history and into our own time. One of the great strengths of the Enlightenment thinkers and other great intellectual Scots such as James Clerk Maxwell or Sir James Frazer who wrote *The Golden Bough,* a groundbreaking work on anthropology, is that the Scots are not content to study detail and confine themselves to facts. They are good at seeing the patterns in a mass of information and then coming up with new theories to explain what is happening. This does not mean that Enlightenment thinkers did not have a respect for inductive reasoning and use it where relevant, but that they were not constrained or limited by it.

Buckle's book on Scotland's preferred intellectual method is the only work I know which shows in detail how, if we look beneath the Scots' love of logical thinking, we often find attraction to abstract ideas and intuitive hunches. He helps us to see that the success of many Scots thinkers is that they had the courage and confidence to build grand theories or take great intellectual leaps of faith. But this does not mean, as Buckle argues, that the Scots underrate the importance of concrete reality, facts or experience. As we have already seen, Scots intellectuals have always been drawn to the external, extravert world and want their ideas to be relevant to that domain. Scots rarely fit the description of ivory-tower intellectuals who do not think it important to ground their theories in the real world. Scots intellectuals and inventors have been intent on coming up with theories and ideas and then working backwards to see how they could be supported by facts and made to work in the real world. James Watt is a good example of this. A gifted instrument maker and good with his hands, he ultimately devised a steam engine which revolutionised production and transport, ushering in the technological age. Watt's invention did not result from inductive reasoning and observation in a laboratory or workshop. Watt's big idea for a separate condenser, which solved the limitations of the Newcomen engine, occurred to him one Sunday morning when he was walking across Glasgow Green. He was later to say that he 'had not walked further than the golf-course when the whole thing was arranged in my mind'. Neil McCallum writes of Watt:

After devising the separate condenser, there were years of work, of laborious make-shifts with imperfect materials. His ideas leaped ahead of the ability to translate them into mechanism. There was a succession of models, always amended and improved on paper before they were completed. But his essential idea was so sound, and Watt so persistently fertile with secondary ideas, that the harnessing of power to industry followed with logical certainty.[11]

What McCallum describes is the working in tandem of the two mental processes Jung defines as intuition and thinking. And Watt was not the only Scot to excel at generating ideas and then, mainly through the application of logical reasoning, make them practical. The Scots have come up with a number of hugely important inventions - the steam engine, the telephone, television, chloroform, penicillin, modern surgical methods, the commercialisation of gas lighting, tyres, tarmac, various agricultural improvements, ultra-sound scans and countless more. And there is little doubt that many of them came upon their new idea not by cautious, creeping observation but through an intuitive leap. Once they had the idea they not only worked backwards to see how it may work in real life but they also had the technical abilities and know-how to make it practical.

So it is not difficult to see why the British social scientist Havelock Ellis, who conducted an objective study of British genius, concluded that over the centuries, in proportion to their numbers, that Scotland has produced more productive geniuses of the highest talent than the rest of the United Kingdom.

Buckle was simply wrong to argue that the English inductive method is superior to the Scots approach - science is a much messier process than he describes. Most great scientists, inventors and theoreticians, such as Einstein, follow their intuition - they make huge leaps - they do not simply observe concrete reality. They are not the cautious observers of fact that Buckle describes. Indeed the science he describes is the science of the school room.

It is not the science that makes great discoveries and changes the world. As Jung himself observes, 'even physics, the strictest of all the applied sciences, depends to an astonishing degree upon intuition, which works by way of the unconscious'.[12] Though he adds that 'afterwards' it is possible to go back and demonstrate 'the logical procedures' that would have led to the same result.

Buckle's work was very influential in its day, throughout Europe. It was much quoted in Russia, for example, and in the UK George Bernard Shaw rated Buckle's influence on him and his generation as great as Karl Marx.[13] George Davie argues that Buckle's criticisms of the Scottish intellectual method gave impetus to those who wanted to restructure the Scottish universities along English lines. Yet Davie, in his celebrated book on the philosophy of Scottish education, writes little about the substance of Buckle's theory though he does claim that the book is 'lively and authoritative'.[14] In contemporary Scotland you are hard pressed to find in books on Scottish history and culture a mention of Buckle, let alone any proper examination of his thesis. Even McCallum, in his detailed portraits of Scottish Enlightenment figures, does not mention Buckle's argument. And the only explanation I can find for this failure to see anything interesting in Buckle's claims is that Buckle used his argument to say some very unflattering things about Scotland and the Scots. Indeed Buckle's motivation to write the volume on Scotland largely came from his anti-clericism. Having witnessed the spectacle of the Great Disruption of the Church of Scotland in 1843, he believed that religious thinking and the Kirk played a hugely important part in Scottish life and that as a result 'there runs through the entire country a sour and fanatical spirit'.[15] As he also believed 'there is no country which possesses a more original, inquisitive and innovative literature than Scotland does',[16] he wanted to provide an explanation for this apparent contradiction.

The nub of Buckle's ensuing argument is that ordinary people are more likely to understand the inductive method (reasoning from observable facts) because it is similar to the way they view the world. So where this method predominates, as it did in

England, a rift does not open up between intellectuals and ordinary citizens. Science and other types of intellectual endeavour can therefore have an impact on everyday life and lead to the development of a generally civilised and prosperous country. According to Buckle, in countries where deductive reasoning predominates, intellectuals 'consider things at too high an altitude' and so they are unable to 'influence the body of the people'.[17] This is what Buckle thinks has happened not just in Scotland, but in ancient Greece and nineteenth-century Germany. According to Buckle, Scotland may have had brilliant intellectual thinkers but their ideas were so removed from the lives of ordinary people that they did little for economic prosperity and hardly dented religious fanaticism. In Scotland during the eighteenth century 'superstition and science', writes Buckle:

> ... the most irreconcilable of all enemies, flourished side by side, unable to weaken each other and unable to come up into collision. ... The two forces kept apart, and the result was, that, while the Scotch thinkers were creating a noble and most enlightened literature, the Scotch people, refusing to listen to those great masters of wisdom which their country possessed, remained in darkness, leaving the blind to follow the blind, and no one there to help them.[18]

And it is these views which lead Buckle on to some of his most vehemently anti-Scottish statements.

But Buckle is misguided here too. Scottish thinkers were, as I argued earlier, no ivory tower intellectuals, far removed from reality. They cared about everyday life and were immersed in it. They also wanted to come up with ways to improve society and did come up with groundbreaking ideas and inventions. The Scottish intellectuals Buckle analyses *did* challenge superstitious religious thinking and managed to found 'the Common Sense School' of philosophy as well as the academic disciplines we now call 'social science'. And they did not just win over the Scottish mind in the process - they ultimately influenced the world.

Buckle was also wrong, for another reason, to maintain that the intellectual method in Scotland created a rift between the educated elite and ordinary people. For centuries Scottish culture has encouraged everyone to be much more open to speculation, theories and possibilities than they are south of the border. There is much more willingness in Scotland for people, even those who are not intellectuals, to speculate on the meaning of life; to construct pet theories and to think about possibilities for the future. In the words of William McIlvanney, Scotland is an 'intense talking shop' where 'the Ancient Mariner haunts many pubs and Socrates sometimes wears a bunnet, and women at bus-stops say serious things about the world'.[19] The English writer Charles Jennings, in his recent book on Scotland, *Faintheart,* also remarked that, despite the constant swearing, there is a higher level of chat in pubs than is the case down South.[20] Indeed one of the things that irritates many Scots about the English is that they are happy to chatter on about topics of no consequence. And in modern Scottish culture we can still find the existence of what George Davie calls 'metaphysical Scotland' in unexpected places. Pick up a copy of *Trainspotting,* for example, and you will find the junkie 'Rent Boy' explaining to the magistrate that he stole a volume by Kierkegaard because he is interested in the philosopher's 'concepts of subjectivity and truth'.[21]

The Conservatives Next Door
Clearly it is difficult to reduce the character of whole peoples to a few lines and to say the English are like this and the Scots like that, as there is scope for huge individual variation. However Jung's concepts of sensing and intuition can help us better to understand not just the Scottish intellectual method but some of the key differences between Scottish and English culture. Take the practice of law. Arthur Herman, when writing about the eighteenth century, encapsulates some of the differences in the legal system north and south of the border:

> Scottish advocates had been practising before the bar
> since the thirteenth century, and had formed their

own guild, the Faculty of Advocates, in the sixteenth. The rules for admission had been increasingly strict, even scholarly. The Faculty required from its members a full course of study of philosophy and law at a university for at least two years, in lieu of formal experience for seven.

The contrast with England was striking. The English barrister received no formal academic training at all. Instead, he learned his trade at the Inns of Court in London entirely in the old medieval style of hands-on apprenticeship. Like his solicitor counterparts, the young English barrister learned to play follow-the-leader, and to obey the dictates of precedent, because there was no practical alternative.

But his Scottish counterpart was as much the product of rigorous scholarly erudition as of practical skills. Two years of overseas study, at universities in Holland or even in France, gave the Scottish bar a cosmopolitan air the English never achieved. [22]

So in law, as in intellectual life, the Scots appreciated the importance of practicality and observation but they did not revere this approach so much that they down-graded the importance of intellectual rigour or ideas. In contrast, it is commonplace for commentators on England to point out that the preference for the known and the practical in England has, over the centuries, led to a certain hostility to new ideas. And this hostility is not confined to the legal and academic worlds but permeates English culture. The Irishman Edmund Burke, for example, was a keen observer on English life. When he wrote his famous *Reflections on the Revolution in France* in 1790 he had lived in England for the best part of forty years and deeply identified with their world-view. And in page after page of this book Burke describes the English as a deeply conservative people who dislike ideas:

> Thanks to our sullen resistance to innovation, thanks to the cold sluggishness of our character, we still bear

the stamp of our forefathers ... We are not the converts of Rousseau; we are not the disciples of Voltaire; ... We know that we have made no discoveries; and we think that no discoveries are to be made, in morality; nor many in the great principles of government, nor in the ideas of liberty ... In this enlightened age I am bold enough to confess ... that instead of casting away all our old prejudices, we cherish them to a very considerable degree, and, to take more shame to ourselves, we cherish them because they are prejudices; and the longer they have lasted, and the more generally they have prevailed, the more we cherish them.[23]

In 1923 Stanley Baldwin claimed that he spoke 'not as a man in the street, but as a man in the field-path, a much simpler person steeped in tradition and impervious to new ideas'.[24] And in 1998 Jeremy Paxman, in his book on the English, asserts 'The English approach to ideas is not to kill them but to let them die of neglect'. Paxman also argues that the English approach to problems is 'empirical' and that 'the only ideology they believe in is Common Sense'.[25] Roger Scruton, too, argues that the English are much more interested in 'concrete realities' than speculation.

As English culture does not just value but venerates the tried and tested, personal experience and practicality, we can see that the mental process most promoted in English culture is what Jung defines as sensing. English culture is, as I argued in Chapter 3, more introverted than Scottish culture - more interested in the inner, rather than the outer world. That is why English culture does not have the oral, energetic and active quality which is so apparent in Scotland. The combination of introversion and sensing has certain undoubted strengths. An individual of these preferences is usually dutiful and hardworking, down to earth, and very good at attending to detail. Hence this type is good at creating and maintaining administrative systems. They are also fairly tolerant of others and good at creating an environment which allows individuals to get on with living their own lives. In

England's case this has helped to create an environment which is reasonably sympathetic to cultural endeavours of all kinds. However, in Jungian typology it is the people who combine introversion and sensing who are the most traditional and conservative types. Their inferior function, writes Jung, 'has an amazing flair for all the ambiguous, shadowy, sordid, dangerous possibilities lurking in the background.'[26] - a characteristic of English culture that, over the centuries, countless observers of English culture have identified. Of course, there are many individuals in England who do not share this fear of change and who like new ideas, but they are going against the grain of English culture. The innate conservatism of the English can be viewed as either negative or positive. Some take Burke's view that it is a source of great stability and strength. Others, like Paxman, are more critical. Much depends on the person's own preferences and attitudes to change and possibilities.

I certainly believe that England's love affair with the past is as big, if not a bigger problem than the Scots' obsession with logical thinking. England is a country with a great desire to preserve her traditions and institutions even though they are often at odds with her becoming a truly modern nation. And it is for this reason that Black Rod lives on within the Mother of Parliaments, as does much of the pomp and circumstance. It is this innate resistance to change which also leads to the type of deep structural problems which economic historians such as Martin Wiener and Corelli Barnett argue lie at the heart of the British economy. Of course, there have been occasions when significant sections of the English people yearned for change. One such occasion was the 1945 election and the Labour landslide. There have also been a significant number of great English radicals and visionaries such as Tom Paine, William Cobbett and William Morris. But such radical visions have rarely animated the spirit of the English nation as a whole. When Margaret Thatcher was Prime Minister she had a strong, if unattractive, vision of what she wanted to achieve. She was interested in possibilities. However, she understood the natural conservatism of the English people and that is why she based much of her appeal, not on a radical new vision of an enterprise culture, but on Victorian values, on the jingoism of the Falklands War and on a Little Englander mentality which devalues all things European.

As the world is now a fast-moving place, and we are in the midst of another great technological revolution, England's Achilles heel may become more and more of a liability. And not just for the English. Scotland has hitched her wagon to a rather old-fashioned, if once elegant and sophisticated, vehicle marked 'England' and her ability to find solutions to problems, even with devolution, will be constrained by what the English will accept.

Other characteristics which are often described as 'quintessentially English' also flow from this combination of introversion and sensing. Jung argues that this psychological type is the most likely to display 'rational self-control'. Another way to describe this quality in a person is to refer to their 'stiff upper lip'. The difficulty in seeing future possibilities in a positive light may also account for the inherent pessimism the English often display, not necessarily about their own individual lives, but about the future of England. Paxman gives many examples of this 'strong streak of natural gloominess'. He argues that not only are they likely to 'ignore the silver lining and grasp at the cloud' but also that they often believe the 'place is doomed', 'gone to the dogs' - that somehow England and the English are 'finished'.[27] And this may help us understand why Roger Scruton chose the title *England- an Elegy* for his book.

The picture which often emerges of England is of a fairly stable, inoffensive but rather dull place. In Jung's scheme there is a need for balance - the attitudes and functions which have been repressed will still find an outlet. That's why in Scotland we see the otherwise logical Scots declaring their love and values through their celebration of that great compensatory Scottish hero - Robert Burns. The English seem to find compensation for their heavy emphasis on privacy, conservatism and convention in that great English characteristic - 'eccentricity'. In a scholarly work entitled *The Character of England*, Richard Law describes the phenomenon in the following terms:

> ... the Englishman ... has a great respect and liking
> for the eccentric, for the 'queer one' ... Victorian
> Oxford swarmed with 'characters', from the top-
> hatted venerables and topers to 'the British
> Workman', last of the tribe. To this day the
> heretic, the grouser, or the crank is allowed full
> play in club or pub ... (As is) the Sabbatical
> Orator in Hyde Park ... But English eccentricity is
> always qualified. It is only permitted within the
> framework of the law or, at any rate, within the
> bounds which are laid down for it by social
> usage.[28]

At the end of the book, 'eccentricity' is listed as an essential
English characteristic and the editor observes that in England
there are even 'societies of cranks' and that English literature
is 'full of pictures of oddities'.[29] And as I write these lines I
cannot help thinking about all those things which seem to
emanate from English eccentricity and which make the toes of
your average Scot curl: Mr Blobby, The Monster Raving
Loonie Party, The Smurfs, Ken Dodd and his tickling stick,
Barbara Cartland, music hall, Stanley Unwin, Punch and Judy
shows, Boris Johnson, Kenny Everett, and the Temperance
Seven singing 'Winchester Cathedral.'[30] And, for me anyway,
the items on this list are every bit as embarrassing as the
Scottish Kailyard or the crocodile tears of the sentimental
Scot.

To conclude this section I want to return to Jung's own
comments on the theory of psychological types which I have
used in the past three chapters. Jung argues that his scheme
does not explain all differences between people and is not the
only way to understand type differences. But he argues it is a
useful 'compass' to help understand people and their different
journeys. In this section I have used Jung's compass to help us
understand various aspects of Scottish culture and national
character. And I believe it has been helpful in a number of
ways. Specifically it has allowed us to:

- challenge the notion of the 'divided', 'pathological' Scot
- see that perfection is unattainable and that development is inevitably one-sided, leading to strengths and weaknesses
- appreciate why the atmosphere which pervades Scotland is rather critical and judgmental
- understand some of the important ways in which Scotland and England differ.

Psychological type is, however, only a broad framework - a template to understand the pattern of growth and development an individual, or a nation, chooses. But it does not tell us everything we need to know to develop a full understanding. The types of preferences which Scotland has cultivated are similar to America's, for example. Many commentators have noted some similarities between the two countries, but there are also profound differences. To understand an individual fully we need to know not just about their type preferences, but also about their upbringing, religious beliefs and education. And, of course, all individuals are greatly affected by the various things which happen to them in life. In other words, we are to a large extent shaped, not just by our preferences, but also by our experiences. The same is bound to be true of a nation. So in the next section I shall examine how Scotland's history has shaped her citizens' beliefs and sense of national identity, before moving on to look at the relationship with England.

NOTES

[1] Quoted in Andrew Marr, *The Battle for Scotland* (Penguin Books: London, 1992), p. 97.

[2] Henry Thomas Buckle, *On Scotland and the Scotch Intellect* (The University of Chicago Press: Chicago, 1970), p. 243.

[3] Ibid., p. 243.

[4] Ibid., p. 21.

[5] Ibid., p. 264.

[6] Ibid., p. 255.

[7] Ibid., p. 256.

[8] Ibid., pp. 283-4.

[9] Ibid., p. 284.

[10] Ibid., p. 337.

[11] Neil McCallum, *A Small Country* (James Thin: Edinburgh, 1983), p. 100.

[12] C. G. Jung, *Man and His Symbols* (Arkana: London, 1990), p. 92.

[13] For further information see H. J. Hanham's introduction to Buckle in the 1970 Chicago edition of *On Scotland and the Scotch Intellect.*

[14] George Davie, *The Democratic Intellect* (Edinburgh University Press: Edinburgh, 1961), p. 321.

[15] Henry Thomas Buckle, *On Scotland and the Scotch Intellect,* p. 394.

[16] Ibid., p. 227.

[17] Ibid., p. 392.

[18] Ibid., p. 392.

[19] William McIlvanney, *Surviving the Shipwreck* (Mainstream Publishing: Edinburgh, 1991), p. 138.

[20] Charles Jennings, Faintheart: *An Englishman Ventures North of the Border* (Abacus: London, 2001).

[21] Irvine Welsh, *Trainspotting* (Mandarin Paperbacks: London, 1996), p. 165.

[22] Arthur Herman, *The Scottish Enlightenment: The Scots' Invention of the Modern World* (Fourth Estate: London, 2002), p. 76.

[23] Edmund Burke, *Reflections on the Revolution in France* (Penguin Books: London, 1968), pp. 181-183.

[24] Quoted in Jeremy Paxman, *The English: A Portrait of a People* (Penguin Books: London, 1999), p. 142.

[25] Jeremy Paxman, *The English,* pp. 192-93.

[26] C. G. Jung, *Psychological Types* (Routledge: London, 1991), p. 398.

[27] Jeremy Paxman, *The English,* p. 14.

NOTES

28 Richard Law, 'The Individual and the Community' in Ernest Barker (ed.),
    The Character of England (Oxford University Press: London, 1950),
    p. 41.

29 Ernest Barker 'An Attempt at Perspective' in Ernest Barker (ed.), *The
    Character of England,* (Oxford University Press: London, 1950), p. 568.

30 In 1936 Hugh MacDiarmid published *Scottish Eccentrics* (George
    Routledge: London). It is a series of essays on unusual Scots and ends with
    MacDiarmid's attempt to link such eccentricity to the 'Caledonian
    Antisyzygy'. It suits MacDiarmid to characterise the Scots as
    'idiosyncratic' as he wants to use this idea to help him portray Scotland as
    a land of extremes. But in all but the most repressive countries it is always
    possible to find oddballs, characters or social misfits of one kind or
    another. What is different about England is that eccentricity has a
    compensatory element and is institutionalised within the culture.

SECTION III

THE ROOTS OF
SCOTLAND'S
CONFIDENCE PROBLEM

6
My Brother's Keeper

'They will not leave me, the lives of other people.
I wear them near my eyes like spectacles.'

Douglas Dunn, *The Hunched*

Sometimes things happen in life which bring a vague glimmer or idea in to sharper focus. This is exactly what happened to me one day as I stood in a queue in a garden centre outside Glasgow. Service was slow and uncomplainingly we stood for what seemed like hours while assistants painstakingly checked the price of lobelia and petunias. A girl of eight took the opportunity to mount a campaign to get sweeties. Her mother was determined not to give in and tried reasoning with her: it was nearly teatime; she had sweets at home. But nothing would divert the girl's desire to get her teeth into the sweets she could see before her. The mother, increasingly embarrassed by the child's constant craik, then played her trump card. 'People are looking at you,' she said. And these five words worked a treat. Shirley Temple, the American child actress, would have taken this as her cue to entertain her audience with a chorus of 'the Good Ship Lollipop' but our Scots girl took it as her cue to be silent. The only words she then uttered were a few whispers in her mother's ear.

The Scots do not like to draw attention to themselves. It is a phenomenon I have observed at countless meetings and courses in Scotland where the Scots would often prefer to sit in embarrassed silence than speak and have people look at them. This is in stark contrast to Americans who do not have the same problem with being the centre of attention. I used to teach Scottish politics to American students at Edinburgh University summer schools and was continually amazed at how the students, both male and female, would gaily interrupt to ask questions or make points. As a critical Scot myself I was surprised at how inane these interventions could be. And this ease in talking in public was in sharp contrast to my own experience as a university student. I spent my first term at Strathclyde University in my Politics 1 tutorial not uttering a single word, and not because I had nothing to say. Later when I became a Politics tutor myself at Edinburgh University I saw the problem from the other side. Most of the Scottish students, except those classified as 'mature', were uncommunicative in tutorials. Most of the English students from middle-class backgrounds were prepared to talk. No doubt class played a part in all this, as the few English working-class students seemed rather inhibited as well, but there was a definite Scottish dimension to it all. Thirty years on it still has not changed that much. Scottish schools now try harder to encourage pupils to speak, and academics report some improvement, but it is slow because the problem does not lie exclusively with the schools. The roots of Scottish reticence and shyness run deep into Scottish culture.

As a trainer I talk for a living yet the fear of drawing attention to myself in public is still an issue for me even though I am now aged fifty. I love public speaking and have no fear in addressing hundreds of people - but only on one condition: I have to be the official speaker. In other words, I feel confident when I have been given the role and status as speaker and do not have to justify my right to speak. I feel entirely different if I am in a group where I am just one of the crowd. Then I feel inhibited, not by my lack of verbal fluency or by a deficit of opinions, but by my own doubts about whether I have anything important enough to say, or if my views will separate me from the majority. I may even doubt my right to take up other people's time or harbour a fear that they may think I am dominating or trying to take over. Some of these doubts and fears are heightened by the fact that I am female and come from a working-class background. But they are certainly due in large measure to my Scottish upbringing because rarely do the Scots seem to escape this fear. Of course, there are a few. I can think of half-a-dozen people myself who will not give up the opportunity to speak and be the centre of attention. But they are the distinct minority. It is much more common for the Scots not to draw attention to themselves even though privately they may have a lot to say. And it is this reticence which falsely gives rise to the image of the introverted, inarticulate Scots.

In Chapter 3 I argued that there is a deep-seated, cultural preference in Scotland for extraversion and I freely admit this looks like a paradox, a contradiction, for it is uncommon for extraverts to fear drawing attention to themselves to the extent the Scots do. Indeed, extraverts often crave the limelight. But there is an explanation and it lies at the heart of the way the Scots view the world.

Individuality v. Community

In Chapter 2 I pointed out, in response to arguments about the 'schizophrenic', divided Scot, that division is at the heart of human existence. One such dichotomy is between self and others; individual and community. Both poles represent essential facets of human life, for no person can exist as a lone individual and no two members of a community are the same. Each one of us has a unique, individual perspective on the world. And both individuals and communities can place greater emphasis on one side of the dichotomy or another. We can, for example, believe that the rights of the individual are sacrosanct and that the wider society's claim on a person should be limited. Alternatively, we can believe that it is the community, the rights and happiness of the many, which ultimately matter more than the individual and his or her rights or personal fulfilment.

At first glance it appears that introverts would be inclined to the individual pole of the self/others dichotomy and extraverts the community pole. But this is not the case. Almost all American extraverts, for example, are passionate believers in individual rights, for the US constitution is founded on such an ideology and Americans are brought up to uphold these beliefs. Japan, by contrast, has a strong belief in community - the primacy of the group over the individual - and these communitarian values can be seen in their working practices. This emphasis on the group in Japan co-exists with the Japanese preference for introversion. In Scotland's case the belief in the importance of community and the preference for the extravert world reinforce one another -

belief in social responsibility encourages and legitimises the preference for extraversion and vice versa. Indeed the belief in the importance of the outer world and the belief in the importance of community are like two threads woven into the fabric of Scottish society and they are difficult to disentangle. *Together they give great primacy in Scotland to the role other people play in our lives.*

A different dynamic is at work south of the Tweed. Some scholars argue that individualism is an important facet of English culture and can be traced back to medieval times. Jeremy Paxman in his book *The English* calls one of his chapters 'Home Alone' and argues that the English are a people with a 'curious reluctance to engage with one another'[1] and are greatly motivated by individuality and individual rights. Indeed Paxman states: 'If I had to list those qualities of the English which most impress me ... I think I would praise most this sense of "I know my rights"'.[2] Roger Scruton likewise argues that traditionally the English 'were individualists who prized the rights and privacy and freedom of the individual above all political gifts'.[3]

The difference in the Scots and the English orientation to other people is epitomised in the type of housing traditionally favoured by each country. This is a point made by the late nineteenth-century Scottish thinker who is hailed as the father of town planning - Patrick Geddes. In *Cities and Evolution,* published in 1915, Geddes argues that 'ordinary old-fashioned English readers' will find it difficult to understand the Scottish approach to housing because the English were brought up with the 'national idea ... of homes as separate houses, of each family with its own bit of ground, at least its yard, however small'.[4] In the Scotland of Geddes's day, by contrast, in both the cities and many burghs, over half the population were housed in tenements - an extremely communal form of living. In the majority of tenements it was common for members of a family to share one room (the 'single end') and for families to live side by side, sharing washing and sometimes cooking facilities. As shared toilets were commonplace many Scottish families did not even have the most rudimentary privacy and people often lived literally 'cheek to cheek' with neighbours. In such a set up, getting on with the folks over the landing, and what they thought of you, must have loomed large in everyone's lives. Our housing pattern may have changed over the years but much of the mindset has remained.

The Thatcher Legacy

In contemporary times the Scots belief in the importance of collectivity became more apparent and conscious thanks to the English - or, more specifically, to Margaret Thatcher. Ironically it was the detested Iron Lady who helped the Scots define their values and some basic differences with the English. It was the programme and ideology of her two Governments which gave a huge boost to Scottish nationalist sentiments. It is not difficult to see why. Thatcher was a convert to American individualistic ideology and her guru was the American right-wing ideologue Milton Friedman. So strong was her attachment to the value of the individual, Thatcher went so far as to claim that 'there is no such thing as society'. In 1988 she came to Scotland and addressed the General Assembly of the Church of Scotland. In her speech, now commonly known as the 'sermon on the Mound', she set out her belief in individualism and tried to link her ideology with Christian values. The ministers were not impressed. Indeed the Moderator promptly presented her with two Church reports on poverty and housing and urged her to study them carefully. It was her turn to be unimpressed. She had long harboured the view that the Scots had a dependency culture and had to be made to stand on their own two feet again. Erroneously, she thought this completely in line with the views of Adam Smith.

During her second term of office Margaret Thatcher's attempt to roll back the powers of the state and 'free' the individual were in full throttle. The Thatcher Government decided to abolish local rates, levied on property, and introduce instead a 'community charge', or 'poll tax'. Many Scots were outraged that a government, with no electoral mandate in Scotland, was muscling through a policy which ran against the grain of Scottish values. Here was a government who did not believe in society, putting a tax on democracy itself and taking little account of householders' ability to pay. Of course, the issue was not as clear-cut as that. The rating system itself was unfair, leading to a single-member household paying the same as the house next door occupied by five adults. But no matter, the Thatcher Government was seen to have attacked fundamental Scottish values. Anti-poll tax campaigns followed. Martyrs, like Tommy Sheridan, became heroes.

The Scottish writer and novelist William McIlvanney was one of Thatcherism's most eloquent opponents. In an address to the SNP in 1987 he claimed that the Thatcher Government was unlike any other:

> ... we have never, in my lifetime, until now had a government whose basic principles were so utterly against the most essential traditions and aspirations of Scottish life. We have never until now had a government so determined to unpick the very fabric of Scottish life and make it over into something quite different ... Under this government, it is not only the quality of our individual lives that it is threatened. It is our communal sense of our own identity.[5]

Aspects of the Tories' policies were publicly condemned in Scotland but embraced by individual Scots. Council house sales, for example, proved popular with tenants. In Scotland 54 per cent of the population lived in council houses in 1979, when the Tories came to power, and this had fallen to 38.8 per cent in 1991 - much of this drop was to due to the Government's sales policy. But despite the popularity of some of Margaret Thatcher's policies, the Tories' belief that individuals should cultivate their own life and not think about the community or their responsibility to others was ultimately the rock on which the Tory Party subsequently foundered in Scotland. Many civic, political and religious leaders in Scotland, such as Canon Kenyon Wright, led the charge against what they saw as 'an alien ideology' being imposed on Scotland by the New Right. They believed the only way Scotland could preserve her traditional ways of thought was by devolution. And so the Constitutional Convention and a successful campaign for devolution was born. Despite a solid tradition of Conservative support in Scotland (the Tories had 36 Scottish MPs in 1955), not one Tory MP was elected to the Westminster Parliament in 1997.

This prevailing sense of everybody's life being inextricably bound up with others is what I most like about the Scots view of the world. And it seems to shape the thinking of just about everyone who grew up in Scotland. Even Andrew Carnegie who acquired millions as an entrepreneur in America's highly individualist culture, believed that anyone who made money had a moral duty to spend it for the common good. By the time of his death in 1919 he had given away £325 million. In modern Scotland there is no shortage of people who have made something of their lives who feel a great need to do something for the commonweal. Undoubtedly this is what motivated Tom Hunter to fund a business school at Strathclyde University or Ann Gloag, who made millions running buses, to charter hospital ships to treat poor children from the third world. Sometimes the need to put something back and serve the community can take a political form, as is the case with Jim Mather who made his fortune in computers, who is now an active member of the SNP, and runs 'Business for Scotland'.

A Scottish Tradition

So why does this belief in community run so deep in Scottish society? One possible explanation is the inhospitable environment, resulting from a poor climate and a high proportion of mountainous terrain, for in circumstances such as these it is natural for people to feel they must rely on one another. Wallace Notestein points out in his historical survey of Scotland that the existence of clans, and the belief (often untrue) that members of a clan were blood relations of the chief, gave 'friendly personal quality to the feudal relationship'.[6] The Scots' relationship with England has also shaped their way of seeing the world. Undoubtedly it helped to create the Scots' love of freedom. The Declaration of Arbroath of 1320 reads:

> ... for, so long as there shall but one hundred of us remain alive, we will never submit ourselves to the dominion of the English. For it is not glory, it is not riches, neither is it honour, but it is liberty alone that we fight and contend for and for which no honest man will lose but with his life.

In some societies, including England, freedom has principally been about the rights of the individual vis á vis the king or state and has led to a focus on individual rights. In Scotland, freedom is the freedom of the Scottish people as a whole and the focus traditionally has been on the rights of the group, if not the country.

During the Scottish Enlightenment various Scots contributed greatly to understanding individual human beings better. Hume's pursuit of 'the science of man' led him to look closely at the way the human mind engaged with the world. Thomas Reid, the philosopher of 'Common Sense' also looked inwards to see how the mind constructed reality. And the type of individualism which was ultimately to triumph in the United States owed some of its thinking to Scottish Enlightenment figures. But one of the lasting legacies of these Scots is the creation of 'social' science. Indeed one of the key hallmarks of Scottish philosophy during this period is its emphasis on the social. This can be seen clearly in the Scots intellectuals' attitude to the evolution of the social and political order. English theorists such as Thomas Hobbes and John Locke believed that people had once lived as isolated, warring individuals in a 'state of nature'. This gave rise to Hobbes's famous claim that life for humankind was 'nasty, brutish and short'. The Scots were not impressed by such a line of argument, claiming it was ahistorical and simply did not correspond to the reality of human existence - at all times and in all parts of the world people had lived, not as individuals but as part of communities.[7]

As these thinkers were social theorists they were also interested in morality. Adam Smith has been claimed by the radical right in Britain and they have even set up a right-wing think tank in his name. Michael Forsyth was a founding member. But Smith is no American-style individualistic thinker. He too stresses the importance of people as social beings and maintains that sympathy with one's fellow creatures is at the very core of society and morality itself. 'How selfish so ever man may be supposed', writes Smith 'there are evidently some principles in his nature which interest him in the fortune of others, and render their happiness necessary to him, though he derives nothing from it except the pleasure of seeing it'.[8] Smith goes further and argues that the regulation of a person's behaviour is achieved because he/she has a sense of 'an impartial spectator' within. This spectator is 'the man within the breast, the great judge and arbiter' - a judge we consult on the right and wrongs of our actions. So, according to Smith, even our conscience is guided by others.

The Collectivist Mentality of the Scottish Church

If we examine the beliefs of John Knox and the Presbyterian Church we will find the origins of Scottish collectivist values. Presbyterianism is often thought to be a deeply individualistic and democratic religion. It places each man and woman in charge of his or her own spiritual destiny, for unlike Catholicism there is no intermediary between an individual and God, and no hierarchy. But this individualism is kept in check by much stronger group values. For example, *The Book of Discipline* clearly states:

> ... no one may be permitted to live as best pleaseth him within the Church of God; but every man must be constrained by fraternal admonition and correction to bestow his labours when of the Church they are required, to the edification of others.[9]

Knox and his followers made much of the importance of hard work, but this is to be channelled, at least some of the time, towards the social good and not just be used for the betterment of an individual or his or her family. Even the rich and powerful 'may not be permitted to suffer their children to spend their youth in vain idleness'. Instead they must be 'compelled to dedicate their sons ... to the profit of the Church and to the Commonwealth'.[10] As we have seen earlier, *The Book of Discipline* set out elaborate measures for the education of all, including the poorest members of society. It also exhorts everyone to 'have respect to the poor brethren, the labourers and manurers of the ground'[11] and states that the poor should be catered for out of parish funds. This did not happen, but from the intention we can see that Knox's religious ideology is essentially antagonistic to American-style Calvinism which does not see the poor as the responsibility of society at large. Even the nineteenth-century influential Scottish Church leader, Thomas Chalmers, who did not favour state handouts for the poor, argued strongly in favour of community support and urged the rich to honour their responsibilities to less fortunate members of society.

If we go on and look at other aspects of Church organisation in Scotland we shall see that its collectivist values have had both a positive and a negative legacy. Positive because they encourage us to acknowledge our social responsibility and negative because they have encouraged conformity and strict social control.

The Book of Discipline encouraged the elders and parishioners to watch the behaviour of the minister, his wife and family, to ensure they acted with propriety and set a good example. The minister and neighbouring ministers were likewise to observe the elders. And the parishioners were to keep a careful watch on one another. As Notestein observes, the Scottish Church reformers '... organised the censoring of behaviour so that even trivial faults were a matter for criticism. They put a premium on spying. They arranged for continuous moral judgements ... They raised the scrutiny of one's fellows to a public virtue'.[12]

So, paradoxically, while *The Book of Discipline* elevated the role of ordinary parishioners in the running of the Church, the Kirk session ultimately became complete master of the individual parishioner, for it took on the role of regulating the behaviour of all its congregation.

Knox's scheme for the denunciation of misconduct was indeed introduced in Scotland. How much people ate and drank, the kind of clothes they wore, the words they used, how they treated the poor, their sexual behaviour, and what they did on a Sunday - all came under legitimate public scrutiny. In *The Social Life of Scotland in the Eighteenth Century* a cleric writes of officers, beadles and deacons:

> There was not a place where one was free from their inquisitorial intrusion. They might enter any house and even pry into the rooms. In towns where the patrol of elders or deacons, beadle and officers, paced with solemnity the deserted causeway eagerly eyeing every door and window, craning their necks up every close and lane, the people slunk into the obscurity of shadows and kept hushed silence.[13]

In the Catholic Church, discipline is mainly achieved through private confessional, supported on occasion with public rebukes or excommunication. In Knox's reformed religion this was reversed. *The Book of Discipline* allows for transgressions, which were not widely known to be dealt with in private Kirk sessions, but, more commonly, alleged sinners were called before the minister, elders and congregation. The celebrated historian of Scottish social history, T. C. Smout, tells us that for sexual misdemeanours the sinner was:

> forced to stand dressed in sackcloth, bare-headed and bare-footed, first at the kirk door and then on the public stool of repentance in front of the congregation on every Sunday for six months or occasionally for several years, and sometimes by whipping and fining as well.[14]

Many of the sinners treated in this way were young women accused of fornication. Indeed as women were excluded from Church governance until the end of the nineteenth century, such discipline was always imposed by men, and women were often the recipients.

The system of discipline did, however, allow for repentance. If the sinner did repent (and most did) he or she could be admonished. Unrepentant sinners could be excommunicated and in that case no one, except their immediate family, was allowed to talk or have any dealings with the sinner. Fines and excommunications initiated by the Church were backed by the civil authorities. For example, people who had been excommunicated were not allowed to give witness in court or hold land. The Kirk's power over the population was so great in eighteenth-century Scotland that anyone wanting to move from one parish to another required a 'testificate' from the minister certifying the person's good behaviour.

The Church authorities also used prying to ensure the people of Scotland observed the Sabbath. People could even be censured for 'idly gazing out of windows'. A minute from the Edinburgh Kirk session of 1727 describes how each session was instructed 'to take its turn in watching the streets on Sabbath ... and to visit each suspected house .. and to pass through the streets and reprove such as transgress and inform on such as do not refrain.'[15] Again people could be referred to the Civil Magistrates for punishment.

The Kirk had other ways of enforcing conformity. For example, it was the session who appointed the parish school teacher and inspected their school and teaching methods. The Church also influenced the universities. As Smout shows, its reach and power was enormous:

> The emphasis in every home and school on repeating and understanding the catechism impressed on every child the importance of holding the right belief. Since justification was by faith and faith must be orthodox, orthodoxy was a prerequisite for salvation. On the other hand, by believing in the priesthood of all believers the Calvinist also stressed that every man must find his own way to God in his innermost thoughts and prayers. But this required the individual to become a reflective and intellectual

being, with all the dangers that he might reach an independent and unorthodox conclusion about God. To guard against this it was doubly necessary for the church courts to detect and call to heel a deviant before he imperilled his own soul and began to infect those of the rest of the flock.[16]

But for most modern Scots, the most significant reminder of the prying times comes via Robert Burns, himself a victim of such denunciation for his frequent sins of fornication. And, of course, Burns openly attacked the Church for such practices in his poems. In the 'Address to the Unco Guid' he writes:

> O ye wha are sae guid yoursel,
> Sae pious and sae holy,
> Ye've nought to do but mark and tell
> Your neebours' faut and folly.

The Questioning Scot

The penitence stool is a thing of the past and the days of Church elders peering in your windows to see if you were observing the Sabbath are long gone but some of this mentality remains. In Scotland there is still a strong sense that little is private and that we live under the gaze of others. Where we choose to live, how we make and spend money, how we dress, where we send our children to school, what we believe - are all part of the public realm in Scotland. Gossip is an important feature of Scottish life which has featured in many novels, and what is gossip if it is not an excessive interest in other people's business and a lack of respect for their privacy? The mentality which is still evident in Scottish life could be summed up in three words: 'our brother's keeper'. Yes, in Scotland we still act as if we are our brother's keeper and it means we are adept at doing two things: first keeping a watchful eye on others so that we know what they are up to and, second, being prepared to judge, criticise and censure their behaviour if we think it is warranted. Even before the Reformation this desire to know people's business was evident.

Notestein reports that even before Knox's time, the Scots were intensely curious about people and what they were doing. Indeed he thinks the Scottish curiosity about others is surely 'one of the most in-born Scottish traits'. He maintains that Scottish epics and ballads show the Scots always interested in other people's business and trying to find out more by asking questions. And Notestein, an American who has the benefit of perspective, adds:

> Here we may recognise the modern Scot who talks to one on railway trains and asks questions, often personal questions which the traveler not used to Scotland might resent. The Scot has long been interested in the stranger as well as in his neighbor, his place of living, his status in live, his occupation, and his success in it. He can hardly be turned aside from making inquiries.[17]

Countless other foreigners make similar points about the Scots. For example, Buckle maintains the Scots have 'a love of inquiring into the opinions of others, and of interfering with them, such as is hardly anywhere else to be found'.[18] Some share Buckle's view that the Scots' penchant for making inquiries is sinister; others put it down to friendliness. But, undoubtedly, the interest in others can amount to nosiness and can have a sinister aspect when it is twinned, as it often is, by that other Scottish trait - critical judgement. The Scots have a well-practised habit of finding out what others are up to and then criticising them or condemning them for it. Try eavesdropping, if you do not already indulge, on other people's conversations. Read Scottish novels and see how often authors present gossip as a central feature of community life. 'The speak o' Kinraddie' in *A Scots Quair* is a perfect example of this. Writing about nineteenth-century Scotland, Sydney and Olive Checkland point out 'that Scottish specialism, "pawky" humour.' And they add 'This was a dry, sly, cynical affair, never far from the frailties of neighbours and colleagues'.[19] Much of this criticism of others' behaviour is not said directly to the person's face and often happens behind the person's back.

If you are unconvinced of this sense of public intrusion into private lives, spend a few weeks reading the letters pages to Scottish newspapers and you will soon see what I mean. For example, in the midst of an acrimonious correspondence in *The Herald* about 'Nimbys' and wind farms, one man felt prompted to write: 'I have been married for 30 years and have two children, one grandchild, a dog, a cat, a mortgage on my ex-council house, and I consider myself to be happy'. Another included in his reply 'Oh, and by the way, we do have a small conservatory, but my wife's "burr" comes not from coffee clubs, but from Castle Douglas - dear me, another "monied area"'.[20]

The tendency to pry and criticise creates a culture which gives other people power over you and your actions. It is no coincidence that Adam Smith argued that our conscience is even dictated by other people - 'by the spectator within'. Nor is it any coincidence that one of Robert Burns's most quoted poems, 'To a Louse', deals with the issue of observing others and making judgements on them. Burns even says 'a wad some Power the giftie gie us/to see oursels as *ithers* see us!'. Judging from how often these lines are quoted in Scotland it is a sentiment which the Scots hold dear.

Little of this is as evident in English life. If anything the English are seen as lacking interest in other people. Paxman, however, argues that this does not suggest 'indifference', as some people claim, but illustrates what he sees as 'one of the country's informing principles' - the love of 'privacy'.[21] South of the Tweed 'an Englishman's home is his castle', for the English, by all accounts, believe passionately that they should be able to 'please themselves in their own lives'. There is also a great resentment at being 'overlooked and controlled'. At one point Paxman even argues that the English dream is 'privacy without loneliness'.[22] Scruton, too, stresses the importance of privacy and argues that in England, traditionally, there was no more valuable freedom 'than the freedom to close a door'.[23] 'The great English characteristic is the ability to leave you alone, to let you live your own life', is how one man summed it up in Harry Reid's book on England.[24]

The Tyranny of Public Opinion

The combination of the Scots' strong preference for extraversion, the importance of community and the experience of Presbyterianism, particularly its reliance on prying as a form of religious control and its system of public punishment, means that the Scots are overly concerned about what other people think of them. Over the years some discerning visitors to Scotland have observed this fact. In the early nineteenth century an English commercial traveller observed:

> A cautious reserve appears to pervade the breast of every Scotsman; he answers a question as if he were undergoing a cross-examination; the mysterious habit grows upon him, till he makes a secret of things which it would do him no manner of harm although all the world knew them.[25]

Notestein also writes that, given their history, it is no wonder that the Scots became 'sensitive to public opinion'. Ronald Mavor, son of the playwright James Bridie, also observes that 'a holy dread of what the neighbours may say' does little to encourage young artists in Scotland.[26]

It is more common, however, for commentators on the Scots not to notice this fear of what others may think and to claim instead that the Scot is a great 'individualist'. But it is not too difficult to understand why the Scots can, on the surface, appear individualistic. There are two basic reasons why people choose to toe the line, conform and let others' opinions of them rule what they say and do. The first is that a person can be genuinely concerned to maintain harmony in their personal relationships. They are keen to curry others' favour; they do not want others to think badly of them as people; and they do not want to upset others or offend them in any way. The second reason why people may conform to accepted forms of behaviour is that they are worried they may make a mistake; are seen to be 'wrong' and so make a fool of themselves. They may also be concerned that their conduct may lead others to denounce or damn them in some way.

And it is this second type of fear which tends to have the upper hand in Scotland. In other words, it is not fear of disharmony and giving offence to others but the fear of getting it wrong which is likely to keep people in check in Scotland. If we examine the occasions when Scots do take a stand and appear 'individualistic' we shall see that it is when they are operating on fairly 'safe' Scottish ground - they are being sceptical of something which appears illogical or unproven; they are arguing from first principles; or they are arguing on the basis of a fairly well-defined Scottish value such as equality or democracy. So, with a strong 'Scottish' wind at his or her back, a Scot will often appear bolshie or individualistic. Indeed the temptation to channel arguments into fairly safe, uncontentious territory helps us to understand why Scots often acquire the reputation for being pedants and nitpickers - people who argue about fine print and detail, rather than big issues. It is a courageous Scot indeed who battles against the prevailing wind of Scottish public opinion. Hence my claim that in Scotland it is collectivism, not individualism, which has the upper hand.

In a culture which elevates others' opinions in this way, and which has a tendency to sit in judgement on other people's behaviour, we are all tacitly encouraged from birth to be somewhat fearful of drawing attention to ourselves. Like Scots in the days described earlier by a cleric, we still have a tendency 'to slink into shadows and keep hushed silence'. Having the spotlight upon you is dangerous because it leaves you open to scrutiny and criticism. Australians call it 'the tall poppy syndrome'. Tall poppies stand out and are more likely to get their heads chopped off. So if we return to that wee girl in the garden centre who did not want to be the centre of attention, we now can understand why the phrase 'people are looking at you' may trouble her. But to understand fully why it should strike her dumb we need to examine a few more Scottish beliefs.

NOTES

1 Jeremy Paxman, *The English: A Portrait of a People* (Penguin Books: London, 1999), p. 116.

2 Ibid., p. 133.

3 Roger Scruton, *England: An Elegy* (Pimlico: London, 2001), p. 204.

4 Quoted in Douglas Dunn, Scotland: *An Anthology* (HarperCollins: London, 1991), p. 105.

5 William McIlvanney, *Surviving the Shipwreck* (Mainstream Publishing: Edinburgh, 1991), pp. 245-6.

6 Wallace Notestein, *The Scot in History: A Study of the Interplay of Character and History* (Yale University Press: United States, 1947), pp. 74-75.

7 See Christopher J. Berry, *Social Theory of the Scottish Enlightenment* (Edinburgh University Press: Edinburgh, 1997).

8 Adam Smith, *The Theory of Moral Sentiments,* D. D. Raphael and A. L. Macafie (ed.) (OUP: Oxford, 1976), p. 7.

9 'The Book of Discipline' in William Croft Dickinson (ed.), *John Knox's History of the Reformation in Scotland, Volume 2* (Thomas Nelson: Edinburgh, 1949), p. 316.

10 Ibid., p. 296.

11 Ibid., p. 303.

12 Wallace Notestein, *The Scot in History,* p. 128

13 Quoted in Lewis Grassic Gibbon & Hugh MacDiarmid, *Scottish Scene* (Hutchinson: London, 1934), pp. 315-6.

14 T. C. Smout, *A History of the Scottish People* 1560-1830 (Collins: London, 1969), p. 181.

15 Quoted in Lewis Grassic Gibbon & Hugh MacDiarmid *Scottish Scene,* pp. 316.

16 T. C. Smout, *A History of the Scottish People,* pp. 510-11.

17 Wallace Notestein, *The Scot in History,* p. 82.

18 Henry Thomas Buckle, *On Scotland and the Scotch Intellect* (The University of Chicago Press: Chicago, 1970), p. 394.

19 Sydney & Olive Checkland, *Industry and Ethos: Scotland* 1832-1914 (Edward Arnold: London, 1984), p. 134.

20 Correspondence published in *The Herald,* 3 -11 August 2001.

21 Jeremy Paxman, *The English,* p. 117.

22 Ibid., p. 118.

23 Roger Scruton, *England: An Elegy,* p. 51.

NOTES

24 Harry Reid, *Dear Country: A Quest for England* (Mainstream Publishing: Edinburgh, 1992), p. 208.

25 Quoted in W. Gordon Smith, *This is my Country:* A Personal Blend of the Purest Scotch (Souvenir Press: London, 1976), p. 45.

26 Ronald Mavor, 'Art the Hard Way' in Alastair M. Dunnett (ed.), *Alistair MacLean Introduces Scotland* (Andre Deutsch: London, 1972), p. 239.

7

Knowing Your Place

'What though on hamely fare we dine,
Wear hoddin grey, an' a that?
Gie fools their silks, and knaves their wine -
A man's a man for a' that.'
            Robert Burns 'A Man's a Man for a' that'

The centrepiece of the opening of the Scottish Parliament was undoubtedly Sheena Wellington's beautiful rendition of Robert Burns's famous lines. In the speech which followed, First Minister Donald Dewar reminded us that 'At the heart of the song is a very Scottish conviction: that honesty and simple dignity are priceless virtues not imparted by rank or birth but part of the very soul'. Like many Scots I felt proud of my country that day as I stood in July sunshine and listened to these words. But three years on as I write this book, I wonder if as Scots we pay a huge price for this passionate belief in simplicity and equality. Before looking at what's written on that price tag, I want to explain where this commitment to equality springs from. For the sake of clarity, I should also point out that this chapter only looks at the inequality arising from wealth and rank and I shall look at other aspects of inequality, such as gender, in the following chapter.

We're A' Jock Tamson's Bairns

One of the reasons why the Scots have a strong belief in equality is that Scottish Presbyterianism is a deeply democratic religion. It may have taken hundreds of years, and the spilling of blood during Covenanting days, but the Scots managed to separate their Kirk from the king and state and build it on thoroughly democratic foundations. The power of the Pope was abolished. Bishops were done away with. Church governance was put in the hands of ordinary parishioners who elected the ministers and elders. *The Book of Discipline* encouraged ministers not to pay too much attention to the rich or to important members of the parish. Their funerals, for example, were just to be carried out like any ordinary person's. As we have already seen, the reformed Church aimed to educate every child, irrespective of wealth or rank, and *The Book of Discipline* encouraged respect for the poor. Only 'stubborn and idle beggars' were singled out for criticism. The reason for such equal treatment of rich and poor was not superficial but sprang from the deep Calvinist belief that God is not influenced by a person's rank as it is by their deeds or their faith that people will be judged. In his own lifetime Knox was well known to be no respecter of rank. He denounced from the pulpit his critics and enemies, both rich and poor, high-bred and humble. He reduced Mary Queen of Scots to tears on more than one occasion and sent critical letters to Queen Elizabeth of England. Knox was not alone. Other Scottish religious figures also showed lack of respect for formal authority. Many have noted that Scottish Presbyterians even address their God in informal and almost irreverential terms; a style that was satirised to good effect by Burns in 'Holy Willie's Prayer': 'O Thou, that in the Heavens does dwell/Wha, as it pleases best Thysel...'. And over the years the Scots have acquired a reputation, even as servants, for not being obsequious. This was brilliantly demonstrated in the film *Mrs Brown,* which showed the Scots ghillie John Brown talking to Queen Victoria as if she was nobody special. In fact, an oft-quoted Scottish proverb proclaims 'Jock is as good as his maister'. Another is 'we're a' Jock Tamson's bairns'.

It is important to put the democratic instincts of the Scottish Kirk in perspective, however. Presbyterianism was a strongly patriarchal religion and for hundreds of years women were excluded from the Church's decision-making bodies. Within the Kirk itself most members were aware of distinct class divisions. Even in the 1950s and 60s Church congregations were often divided along strict class lines. The most well-off, respectable Church members occupied the best pews and did not mingle much with the lower orders who sat at the back.

Nonetheless it is still true to say that John Knox and his followers sowed the seeds of Scottish egalitarianism by establishing the new Kirk along fairly democratic lines. And once sown, these seeds were fed and watered by Robert Burns for it was he who ensured that egalitarian beliefs established deep roots within Scottish culture. Indeed Burns spoke not just for ordinary people in Scotland but for ordinary people round the world, for his poem 'A Man's a Man' is nothing less than an international anthem for the basic, irreducible equality of human beings. 'The rank is but the guinea's stamp/The man's the gowd for a' that.' But more importantly for our purpose, Burns became the carrier of the fundamental belief that *the Scots* are a people with deep democratic, egalitarian and humanitarian instincts: not only was Burns 'one of us', but by celebrating him in the way we do we annually pay homage to these democratic beliefs.

Just Plain Folk

It makes sense for people who believe in a common humanity and who dignify the poorest members of society in their thought, to uphold the values of ordinary everyday life. 'Common decency', 'honest poverty', 'plain talking' - in Scotland these are morally as good as more sophisticated, refined ways of living. 'High' culture usually emerges in societies which are wealthy enough to support a cultural elite, through patronage, for example, so Scotland, for centuries an exceedingly poor though well-educated country, was likely to be excluded from such sophisticated ways. John Grierson sums up this idea when he writes:

> The secret of it is that we're a peasant and a proletarian people and have never had courtly affairs to strait-jacket us. Our songs are the songs of the common people, our practicality is of a people with a living to make, and a daily job to do, and no fine airs to impose on anybody ... We never had anything but what we got out of our common doings as working people.[1]

If we examine Scotland's history we can find other reasons why the Scots were likely to be unimpressed by, if not actually hostile to, to the development of manners or cultural refinement. First,

Scotland lost her King and royal court to England in 1603 with the Union of the Crowns. In European countries the court was generally responsible for the development of art, culture and manners. So when Scotland lost her court in Holyrood to the south of England, she lost this refining influence. Secondly, simplicity is at the very core of Presbyterianism. This can be seen in its church service which is supremely simple and easy to understand. This is no small matter as the Covenanters fought and died for the right to simplicity in their service and against the imposition of English High Church ways, such as kneeling, candles, choir singing or even the prayer book. The interiors and exteriors of Scottish churches also display the desire for such simplicity. Historically Presbyterianism was opposed to cultural and artistic expression in theatre, for example - and so another refining influence was blocked in Scotland.

Pretentious? Moi?

For a variety of reasons, then, the Scots came to value the simplicity of ordinary people. Hugh MacDiarmid put the matter simply when he wrote of the Scots: 'we feel no necessity whatsoever to indulge in any airs and graces'.[2] Pomp and circumstance, frippery, finery, posh words, anything that can be dismissed as 'all meringue and nae mince' is easily suspect in Scotland as it suggests pretension - the desire to pretend you are something you are not. And it is in avoiding pretension that many Scots try to display their deep attachment to egalitarian and Presbyterian values. The nineteenth-century Scottish thinker and writer Thomas Carlyle is a perfect example of this. He was born in humble circumstances on a farm in Ecclefechan, Dumfriesshire. After a stint in Edinburgh and a farm outside Dumfries, he and his wife Jane moved to London where Thomas had more opportunity to make a living as a writer. In his day, Carlyle was seen as the cleverest man in the United Kingdom and dubbed the 'sage of Chelsea'. Carlyle is often decried by the Scottish literati for selling-out Scotland and going to live an affected life amidst English intellectuals and writers, but the old Presbyterian spirit triumphed in the end and he ultimately redeemed himself and proved his Scottish credentials. The Prime Minister, Benjamin Disraeli, offered Carlyle a state pension and an honorary title in recognition of his contribution to British cultural life. Carlyle refused both. On his deathbed he knew there were plans for an elaborate funeral and for an imposing grave among the great and good in Westminster Abbey. Again he refused and, according to his wishes, he was buried with no service in Ecclefechan, beside other members of his family.

One of the reasons Burns became such a Scottish folk hero is that he died penniless and unhonoured in a farm in Dumfries. And it is the same mindset which helps us to understand why Sir Walter Scott, a figure of huge importance in the making of modern Scotland and a man with a massive international reputation, should be thought so little of by ordinary Scots. As a friend of mine who grew up in a council house in the Borders once explained, Scott was 'a toff'. So Scott's baronetcy and his big house at Abbotsford effectively deprived him of an affectionate place in the hearts of ordinary Scottish people.

In contemporary Scotland we can still see this respect for ordinary, unpretentious ways. It is exactly these sentiments which underlie aspects of Gordon Brown's behaviour. A son of the manse, he refuses to wear the customary evening dress to deliver the annual speech the Chancellor of the Exchequer gives at the Lord Mayor's Banquet at the Mansion House. To avoid seeming ostentatious, he served £12 bottles of champagne from a supermarket at his wedding reception on the banks of the Forth. It is also the Scots' dislike of pretension which is so brilliantly satirised in BBC Scotland's comedy TV series *Chewing the Fat*. One regular sketch shows people shirraking anyone (with a cry of 'ooh' and affected hand gestures to the face) if they are seen to be getting above themselves. In one sketch, workmen compare what they have with them to eat during a break. One man says a cheese roll, another a ham sandwich; when the third says 'a baguette' he is taunted mercilessly. 'Real' Scots do not eat fancy things like baguettes. They eat plain bread. Even pan bread is suspect.

Of course, this is not as true as it used to be. The Scots are taking to foreign food in a big way even if it is often curry and chips. But what *Chewing the Fat* highlights so accurately is that the Scots are still on the look-out for pretentious behaviour in those round about them. If they spot it in people they know, they will mock them. If they see it in folk they do not know so well, they will talk about them behind their backs. 'What did you think of her saying ...?' 'What was he like with that cravat on?'

I had my own experience of this recently. I contacted some old friends from Strathclyde University to see if they wanted to come to my fiftieth birthday party. One man phoned me up to say he couldn't manage. Hardly had the pleasantries been exchanged when he said 'I saw that piece and the photie in the Sunday paper about you being a management consultant. Ye big pseud. I should have known that's what you'd end up doing. You always were a poser, even at uni'. And it all came flooding back. I had forgotten how this type of exchange was routine at university. It was how you got your laughs. Nor can I say I was an innocent victim, I was more than able to give as good as I got.

In an article on Glasgow, William McIlvanney argues that at the 'core' of Glasgow speech lie two key ingredients -'deflation of pomposity and humour'. Later he distils the essence of Glasgow to two words - 'human irreverence' - and adds:

> Those who are, for me, the truest Glasgwegians, the inheritors of the tradition, the keepers of the faith, are terrible insisters that you don't lose touch for a second with your common humanity, that you don't get above yourself. They refuse to be intimidated by professional status or reputation or attitude or name. But they can put you down with a style that almost constitutes a kindness.[3]

Openly 'taking the piss' out of people in this way is very Glaswegian, but I believe that the basic underlying belief, that getting above yourself is a bad thing, is essentially Scottish. In other parts of Scotland the criticism may remain unexpressed, but still be thought, or it may be said but with less humour or 'kindness'.

These basic values often lead to reverse snobbery. For example, it is common for Scots who have risen in the world to take pride in their proletarian roots. Indeed this is something which English commentators often deride. 'Nothing appeals so much to Scotch sentiment as having been born in the gutter', writes T. W. H. Crosland. At the end of his book on the unspeakably loathsome Scots, Crosland suggests ten rules to improve the Scots' conduct. Rule number 4 reads: 'There is nothing specially credible in having been born in a muck heap. Do not boast about it.'[4]

The Scots and the English share many attitudes in common but, historically, there are marked differences between their views on culture and manners. The editor of *The Character of England*, published in 1950, argues that 'position' is very important in England and that there is a great deal of 'snobbery'. He also argues that 'It is impossible to think about the character of England without also thinking about the character of the gentleman'.[5] The passage of time, particularly the ideology of the 1960s, has obviously eroded such a fascination with manners in English life and I cite this book to illustrate the historical difference between the two cultures. Most middle-class Scots have never been preoccupied with 'position' and manners to the same extent as their English counterparts.

With the impetus for cultural refinement and manners less strong in Scotland than in England, anyone who acted in such a way, or who was particularly attracted to high culture, was easily seen as 'Anglicised'. Even today, Scottish aristocrats come across as very English. And with good reason. The landed classes in Scotland are likely to be educated at English public schools, many attend English universities and have strong ties to the establishment in the south of England. Many do not even speak with a recognisably Scottish accent or act in ways which make them 'one of us'. So the Anglicisation of the Scots aristocracy has in this way reinforced the idea that anything 'upper crust', or even cultured, is essentially English and not authentically Scottish.

Toffs and Traitors
In contemporary Scotland there is still a quiet, and often unacknowledged, contempt for people who have been born into

wealth or rank. They are often viewed as people who just 'don't know the time of day'. At the first sign of a silver spoon in someone's mouth, many a Scot will be thinking, albeit privately, 'there's someone who has had it easy, so what does she or he know about life?' Such disrespect is evident in Burns's poem 'A Man's a Man':

> Ye see yon birkie ca'd "a lord"
>   What struts an' stares, an' a' that?
> Tho' hundreds worship at his word,
>   He's but a cuif* for a' that.
> For a' that an' a' that,
>   His ribband, star an' a' that,
> The man o' independent mind
>   He looks an' laughs at a' that.

*(ninny)

It is common for Scots to believe that wealth and position protect people from 'the real world of hard knocks' and undermine their credibility as people. Nonetheless such toffs are often tolerated and treated with polite disdain because they may have power over you as employers or landlords. And their existence can to some extent simply be shrugged off as proof, if any was needed, that 'the warld is ill-divided'.

In Scotland the real venom is saved for 'the poachers turned game-keepers' - for those of ordinary birth who seem to be enthralled by wealth, possessions, rank, or who have developed manners or affectations of any kind. People who are seen to have got on and turned their backs on their ordinary Scottish upbringing are particularly resented. 'Ah ken't his faither', 'who does she think she is?' or 'I knew him when he didn't have two pennies to rub together'. Whatever the formulation the meaning is the same: 'Here is someone from our own stable who is acting like he or she is better than the rest of us'. It is this sentiment exactly which underlies Billy Connolly's fall from grace with sections of the Scottish press and many of his fans. Once lionised for his original humour and complete lack of deference, this one-time shipyard worker had the temerity freely to admit that he not only consorted with English nobs and royalty but actually liked them! Sheena Easton, the wee girl from Bellshill who made it big in the pop world, went to America and loved it so much she was deemed to have turned her back on Scotland. She even started to speak with a mongrel American accent. During an appearance in Glasgow in the 1990s her 'disloyalty' was repaid in boos and hisses. And then there is Ann Gloag, one of the founders of the Stagecoach empire. A former nurse who grew up in a council house, she then spent some of her millions on a castle in Perthshire and was sometimes spat at when she made an appearance on the streets of Perth.

The Scots poet Alexander Scott brilliantly satirised the Scots attitude to equality in two lines:

> *Scotch Equality*
> Kaa the feet
> Frae thon big bastard.[6]

So we can see how the 'man's a man' sentiment can be something of a double-edged sword. On one side it is positive because it forces us to realise that people are human beings, and should be respected as such, irrespective of their economic circumstances or 'refinement'. In Scotland, we do not believe 'manners maketh the man'. And it is surely good for the rich, honoured or famous to realise that, despite all the trappings of their material success, deep down they are just like everybody else. But these sentiments have a negative side in that they can easily be used to try to keep people in their place. It is very ironical that a country which upholds egalitarian values should also communicate to ordinary people that they should be careful not to get 'above themselves'.

This sentiment is also prevalent in some English working-class communities. The tabloid press in Britain as a whole is often accused of having an 'anti-success' mentality. But such attitudes are more powerful in Scotland because we are not just open to the charge of being pretentious and putting ourselves above our community if we get on; our very right to call ourselves 'Scottish' is called into question. What's more, for reasons I set out in previous chapters, there is little sense of privacy in Scotland; it is very easy to feel that we live our lives under the glare of comment and with the threat of critical judgement and censure. By 'getting on' in life we can easily feel that we are setting ourselves up for criticism. In fact, the pressure just to be one of the crowd in Scotland can be so great that doing anything different can make people feel exposed. Hence the wee girl's fear in the garden centre when people were looking at her (see Chapter 6). Sometimes the fear is not simply about being criticised but that age-old fear of being 'cast out'. Of course, such a fear is quintessentially human, but in a society like Scotland, where other people play such an important part in our lives, it has much more power and resonance.

Getting On

It is not uncommon for societies to espouse communitarian values which keep people in their place. In Nordic countries, for example, the 'Janteloven' (Jante law) operates - dictating a moral and social standard which keeps individuals in check. This set of laws was first set out in 1933 by the Danish writer Aksel Sandemose in a novel about the imaginary community of Jante, but most Nordic countries recognise its relevance to them. The Jante law reads like the Ten Commandments and includes dictates such as 'You shall not think that you are special; You shall not think you are the same standing as us; You shall not think that you are smarter than us; You shall not think you know more than us; You shall not think that you can teach us anything'. And while there is obviously some overlap between the Jante law and what I have been describing so far in this and the previous chapter, it certainly does not describe the motivating force in Scottish culture. The Jante law is far too limiting and prescriptive. And it is not difficult to see why. In Scotland the pressure to be just like everybody else is just one side of the story. One of the great Scottish paradoxes is that existing alongside this notion that we shouldn't get above ourselves is the contradictory pressure to make something of ourselves and to show that we are at least as good as, if not actually better than other people. Confused? You certainly are on the issue of self-advancement if you were brought up in Scotland. Indeed one of the characteristics of Scottish culture is that it is extremely competitive, and there is a huge pressure in Scotland for us to prove ourselves in some way. Intellectually the Scots may disagree with 'status' but they will often strive to be in the one-up position. Indeed one-up-manship is something of a Scottish pastime. Consult a *Broons* annual, documenting the life of Scotland's most famous fictional family, and you will see that a regular storyline features family members competing with one another. Granpaw will even roll up his trouser legs and show he is better at water skiing than youngsters, like Joe and Hen. H. M. Paterson, in a book on Scottish education published in 1983, argues that schools uphold 'the ferocious stress on social conformity so characteristic of Scottish society' as well as the 'easy acceptance of a ruthless search for advancement to some position of reward, power and status within the undeniable social hierarchy - in the Kirk, in business, in politics, in sport, or in the professions'.[7] In Scotland we are reared to feel that we should be a nobody like everybody else, *and* that we must prove our worth by becoming a somebody.

A couple of years ago a young relative of ours called Janice came over from Nova Scotia to work in Scotland for a few months. She took a job as a waitress in a local hotel. When she was a student Janice had worked as a waitress in various places in the United States and Canada and she couldn't believe the difference in attitudes between Scotland and North America. 'Over there,' Janice told us, 'people just accept you as a person no matter what job you are doing. Even if it is a menial job they think you are trying to get your act together to do something with your life. Over here, people just look down on you if you are serving them. They treat you as if you are a nobody.' What else was there to say except 'Welcome to Auld Scotia, Janice, the land that celebrates Robert Burns and "simple dignity"'.

Traditionally, the most legitimate channel for competition and upward mobility has been the education system. Indeed, over the years when people have made the case for Scotland being an egalitarian country, they would often cite as evidence the fact that it is possible for people from lowly backgrounds to get on. The Scottish education system, they will argue, by being open to poor people has always been an important conduit for self-advancement. The theme of the clever but poor country lad (and they were all lads) rising through the education system is so well-worn in Scottish literature it is almost threadbare. What's more it is trotted out so often it is now simply referred to as 'the lad o'pairts'. In the mid 1970s, however, Scottish academics started to call this 'the Scottish Myth'. In the introduction to a book called *Social Class in Scotland: Past and Present,* Allan MacLaren maintains that there has always been social inequality in Scotland and that to allow the brightest from the lowest order to advance cannot be termed 'egalitarian' - it is in fact 'elitist'.[8] In previous centuries, a few may have risen through the education system but the rest, the vast majority, had little opportunity for advancement. Indeed MacLaren argues that the opportunities for poor, Scottish boys were extremely limited but since they were better than the opportunities in England it fed 'the myth' that Scotland was genuinely an egalitarian society.

Scottish Egalitarianism

Scottish sociologist, David McCrone, in a textbook on Scotland looks in depth at studies which could support or contradict the myth of 'Scottish egalitarianism'. McCrone is at pains to point out that myths are never based on facts and simply shape the way we see the world, so the Scottish myth cannot be proved or disproved. However, he concludes that the most striking factor to emerge from the data is that the pattern of class mobility in Scotland is very similar to other parts of the United Kingdom and that this is due in large part to a shared industrial heritage and to similar access to higher education north and south of the border. He also states that these surveys show that: 'Scotland has a slightly smaller middle class, a slightly larger manual working class, but the processes of social mobility which created these structures of opportunity are remarkably similar on both sides of the Tweed'.[9] McCrone does not think this means that egalitarianism in Scotland is based on nothing, as there is a reasonable amount of upward mobility, but he argues that in this respect Scotland is not substantially different from other parts of the United Kingdom. Earlier I argued that the English are more concerned with 'position' than the Scots, but that does not mean that they are opposed to the idea of social advancement for those born at the bottom of the social ladder if they have talent and ability. 'The ladder,' writes Ernest Barker, editor of *The Character of England* 'has always been a ladder of possible ascent'.[10] McCrone, however, argues elsewhere that in Scotland the belief that the Scots are more egalitarian than the English is a fundamental part of Scottish identity. It is, he claims, 'an ideological device for marking off the Scots from the English'. And, he adds, 'it becomes the essence of Scotland.'[11]

David McCrone also argues that 'the man's a man' sentiment can lead to two different political interpretations. The first is 'an activist one' which seeks 'the resolution' of the contradiction between aspiration and reality. It is, therefore, a call to political action or support of some kind. The other is, according to McCrone, a 'more conservative interpretation of the myth, that if man is primordially equal, then social structural inequalities do not matter, and nothing needs to be done. It is sufficient that "we're a' Jock Tamson's bairns"'.[12] Traditionally, Scottish politicians, at least of Labour or nationalist persuasions, have supported the activist interpretation and it is the more dominant interpretation in Scotland. In reality, however, we have done little to eradicate such inequalities and have had to fall back on the idea that somehow class and wealth do not matter too much in Scotland; it is respecting people's basic humanity which counts. Not much comfort for the one in three Scots children living in poverty.

The Class Divide

Gerry Rice grew up in the Gorbals and now works for the World Bank in Washington. In 2000 he returned to Scotland for a year to work at Scottish Enterprise. We used to meet regularly to talk about Scottish culture. Every time we met Gerry would reel off some of Scotland's appalling poverty and health statistics and express dismay that middle-class Scots just seemed to accept these facts and do nothing to bring about change. 'Why are people not talking about it much, or trying to do something about it?' Gerry would keep asking me. Every time he raised the subject of poverty I felt uncomfortable. I knew he was right and I felt guilty. But, eventually, I decided to mount a defence. 'You live in Washington. That city has some of the worst deprivation in the Western world. Some poor people do not even have basic health care and America is a much richer country than Scotland.' His answer was unforgettable: 'That's America for you. That's what they believe in. But the Scots are always proclaiming to the world what decent, egalitarian people they are'.

It may be painful for modern Scots to accept, but Scotland is a society deeply divided by social class. Educational attainment, life expectancy, physical health, mental health, crime - all are affected by wealth and post-code. This is a real, physical divide. Stand at the railway line which separates the affluent Glasgow suburb of Bearsden from Drumchapel, one of Scotland's poorest housing estates, or go to countless other points round Scotland and you will see this divide with your own eyes.

The great class divide in Scotland is often very apparent to outsiders. Here is how the New Zealand academic H. J. Hanham described it a few decades ago in his book *Scottish Nationalism*:

> To the outsider, Scotland, with its aristocracy still largely in being and the gracious living of its big town houses ... with the workers tucked away in their tenements out of sight, often seems much more of a traditional society than does that of England. It is the sense of social hierarchy that the outsider notices, not the native democracy ... Scottish democracy may be a powerful force as a myth, but it is a myth base on style, not on the absence of income or class differentiations.[13]

Poverty in Scotland

- A report on poverty in Scotland published in November 2002 estimates that one in four individuals in Scotland live in low-income households. It also estimates that one in three Scottish children live in poverty. [14]

- A report published by Save the Children in October 2002 claims that a staggering 96% of children living in Whitfield South in Dundee live in poverty and that 58% of children in Glasgow can be classed as poor. The Save the Children report also shows that stark inequalities exist within Scotland: their research indicates that the second lowest poverty rate for children in the UK was recorded in Kilmardinny, Bearsden, a wealthy Glasgow suburb.

- The gap in life expectancy between the affluent suburbs of Scottish cities and the poorer council estates can be as high as ten years. Those living in the most deprived areas are two and a half times more likely than more affluent Scots to die from coronary heart disease. The Scottish cancer rate is also 14% higher in poorer areas and cancer sufferers who live in these deprived areas are 40% more likely to die of cancer than more affluent Scots.

- Children living in Easterhouse are five times more likely to die before their first birthday than children living in Scotland's affluent suburbs.

- Educational sociologists, like Linda Croxford, believe that education in Scotland, as elsewhere, reinforces disadvantage rather than alleviating it. In a recent report she writes: 'It has long been believed that education is a means for reducing social inequality, but in fact pupils who start school with socio-economic and educational disadvantages make less progress than their more advantaged peers, and thus the gap between advantaged and disadvantaged widens in the course of school careers.' [15]

- Various experts estimate that the top 1% of Scottish society own more than 20% of the wealth while the bottom 50% has only 7%.

A Paradox

So how can we account for this paradox at the heart of Scotland - the fervent belief in social equality yet the reality of a real, palpable class divide? Poverty cheek by jowl with wealth; advantage and opportunity flourishing alongside deprivation? There are lots of possible explanations, including the fact that since 1707 Scotland has not been a sovereign nation able to pursue her own political agenda. But I think this is too easy an explanation and the answer seems to lie at a much earlier point in Scottish history. T. C. Smout tells us that the early Church reformers saw themselves as champions of 'the impotent poor and of the peasant and labourer'. One of the first acts of the reformers was to nail a 'Beggars Summonds' to the doors of the friaries 'calling on them to surrender their possessions to the poor "to whom it rightfully belongs".'[16] *The Book of Discipline* also outlined a scheme of funding poor relief from the patrimony of the Kirk and intended to make offences against the poor part of ecclesiastical discipline. None of this happened, prompting Smout to remark 'the complete failure of Knox's followers and successors to carry out any part of this programme makes the most depressing reading of anything in the history of the Godly Commonwealth.'[17] There were various reasons for lack of progress, including practical difficulties with appropriating the funds of the old Church. Ultimately, once the new religion was established and was supported by lairds, merchants and tradesmen, the Kirk 'became blind and silent before the prospect that the economic self-interest of landlords and the middle classes could be sinful'.[18] In short, the Kirk was not prepared to rock the boat, named 'economic self-interest'. Idealism was tripped up, and rendered impotent, by practicality - a sequence we can see on various occasions in Scottish history.

As an atheist I feel no need to justify the actions of Knox and his followers. Indeed I am well aware that they would have dismissed my thoughts since I am a mere woman. However, inequality is, regrettably, a fundamental aspect of human society. And even with the best of intentions it is almost impossible to eliminate. Those who have do not easily or willingly give up their advantage for the sake of the impoverished. The Scots Church failed to live up to its ideals, but so have countless socialist regimes right round the world. So we have in Scotland the rhetoric of equality, and the fervent belief in it, alongside the reality of a country deeply divided by class and wealth.

The Scots' myopia on equality issues - the fact that we tenaciously cling to a myth - is not due to some kind of 'schizophrenia' or fatal flaw in the Scottish character. It is not that uncommon for a people to uphold a myth of this type - that is exactly what millions of ordinary US citizens do when they cherish 'the American Dream'. Despite a wad of statistics to the contrary, Americans still believe that anyone, if they work hard, can become President or live in a lovely house in the suburbs with a swing seat on the porch. In reality, success is largely determined by family background, not simply by hard work. In America, being black is also a significant obstacle to realising the dream.

So it is for a variety of reasons, then, as I sit and think of the opening of the Scots Parliament, and play back in my memory Sheena Wellington's haunting voice singing 'A Man's a Man' and hear Donald Dewar's fine words about 'simple dignity' being 'part of the soul', that I see Scotland's commitment to egalitarian values as double-edged. Of course, we are right to affirm human dignity; right to be unimpressed by wealth and rank. But such sentiments all too often lead to an unwitting desire in Scotland to keep people in their place. And, no matter how much we may pay homage to such sentiments, they have done little to diminish inequality. In fact, they may even stand in the way of us being honest with ourselves about the extent of poverty and deprivation in contemporary Scotland.

NOTES

1 John Grierson, 'The Salt of the Earth' in Forsyth Hardy (ed.), *John Grierson's Scotland* (The Ramsay Head Press: Edinburgh, 1979), p. 33.

2 Hugh MacDiarmid 'The Dour Drinkers of Glasgow' in Hugh MacDiarmid, *The Uncanny Scot: A Selection of Prose* (MacGibbon & Kee: London, 1968), p. 99.

3 William McIlvanney, *Surviving the Shipwreck* (Mainstream Publishing: Edinburgh, 1991), p. 183.

4 T. W. H. Crosland, *The Unspeakable Scot* (Stanley Paul: London), p. 196.

5 Ernest Barker, 'An Attempt at Perspective' in Ernest Barker (ed.), *The Character of England* (Oxford University Press: London, 1950), p. 567.

6 *The Collected Poems of Alexander Scott,* David S. Robb (ed.) (Mercat Press: Edinburgh, 1994), p. 147.

7 H. M. Paterson, 'Incubus and Ideology: The Development of Secondary School in Scotland, 1900-1939' in Walter M. Humes and Hamish M. Paterson (eds), *Scottish Culture and Scottish Education,* 1800 - 1980 (John Donald: Edinburgh, 1983), p. 198.

8 A. Allan MacLaren, *Social Class in Scotland: Past and Present* (John Donald: Edinburgh).

9 David McCrone, 'We're A' Jock Tamson's Bairns' in T. M. Devine & R. J. Finlay, *Scotland in the 20th Century* (Edinburgh University Press: Edinburgh, 1996), p. 112.

10 Ernest Barker, 'An Attempt at Perspective' in Ernest Barker (ed.), *The Character of England* (Oxford University Press: London, 1950), p. 564.

11 David McCrone, *Understanding Scotland: The Sociology of a Stateless Nation* (Routledge: London, 1992), p. 120.

12 David McCrone, 'We're A' Jock Tamson's Bairns' in T. M. Devine & R. J. Finlay, *Scotland in the 20th Century,* p. 114.

13 H. J. Hanham, *Scottish Nationalism* (Faber and Faber: London, 1969), p. 27.

14 Usha Brown, Gill Scott, Gerry Mooney, Bryony Duncan (eds), *Poverty in Scotland 2002* (Child Poverty Action Group/Scottish Poverty Information Unit: 2002).

15 Linda Croxford in Usha Brown et al, *Poverty in Scotland 2002,* p. 148.

16 T. C. Smout, *A History of the Scottish People 1560-1830* (Collins: London, 1969), p. 91.

17 Ibid., p. 91.

18 Ibid., p. 92.

8

More Equal Than Others

*'I want to see ... (Scotland) as the most open, the most open-minded
and the most tolerant wee country in the world.'*
Jimmy Reid, *Power Without Principles*

I have little doubt that Jimmy Reid spoke for many people in
Scotland when he wrote these lines. But is Scotland as open and
tolerant of difference as many of her citizens would like?

Many English people have reason to believe the Scots are not
that tolerant and open-minded: if they venture north of the
Tweed they often feel the Scots are prejudiced against them, not
just as a nation but as individuals. As the journalist and critic
Joyce McMillan once remarked, anti-English passion in Scotland
'gives the nationalist movement a poisoned strength that can only
lead to racism and chauvinism'.[1] And the Englishman Charles
Jennings, after his recent tour round Scotland, argues that while
the Scots have historical reasons to hate the English he can't
understand why they haven't managed to let it go:

> After all, Denmark co-exists with Germany, Portugal
> with Spain, Canada with the USA - yes with frictions,
> misunderstandings, irritations. But they don't see it as
> an essential pre-condition of nationhood to
> characterise their larger neighbours always and forever
> as predatory, hypocritical, self-obsessed bastards.[2]

Rarely does this attitude degenerate into name calling and
outright discrimination but it does often mean that the English
get a frostier reception in shops and pubs, for example, than other
foreigners. It is also common for the Scots, partly as a response to
feelings of marginalisation, to portray the English as inferior,
almost sub-human. Even sophisticated, educated Scots often
stereotype the English as people who are morally inferior or less
compassionate than those living north of the border.

The Scottish writer Ian Rankin once remarked: 'the Scots aren't racially prejudiced - they're much too busy being bigoted.' And Rankin's line illustrates that the Scots like to see themselves as much less racist than the English. But in the mid 1980s a BBC Scotland Radio series *It Doesn't Happen Here* exploded this myth. Numerous Scots from ethnic minority backgrounds all over Scotland testified that they were often victims of harassment and prejudice: that the Scots were quite capable of being racist. In 1999 one black respondent in research undertaken by the Rowntree Trust maintained: 'As far as casual, unprovoked verbal racism is concerned, we just take it as part of living in Glasgow'.[3] That same year the Commission for Racial Equality produced figures showing that 'Scotland's black/minority ethnic groups were at least three times as likely to suffer racist incidents as black/minority ethnic people in England and Wales'. Such racism is not confined to verbal assaults. Just how racist the Scots can be was demonstrated tragically by the murder of Imran Kahn, a Glasgow schoolboy, and by the murder of a Kurdish refugee, Firsat Yildiz Dag, in Glasgow. In the wake of the latter murder the Scottish newspapers were full of quotes from refugees, some of whom had escaped persecution in their own lands, saying that they did not feel safe in Scotland. An opinion poll on attitudes to immigration in Scotland published in April 2002 showed that a staggering 46 per cent of those surveyed said they thought there should be 'a repatriation programme for immigrants'. And even though Scotland's population is falling, 34 per cent said there were 'too many immigrants in Scotland'. The only ray of sunshine in an otherwise bleak poll was that 46 per cent of Scots agreed that 'immigrants make a positive contribution to Scottish society'.[4]

In April 2002 Rowena Arshad, Director of the Centre for Racial Equality, and the Equal Opportunities Commissioner for Scotland, claimed that Scotland is inflicted by a 'polite and insidious racism' and is uncomfortable with the notion of diversity.[5] She also argued that one of the biggest barriers to tackling the problem is that the Scots liked to pride themselves on being a tolerant people who believe in equality. As with class inequality, denial is the name of the game. In August 2002 this denial became painfully evident with the publication of *Being Scottish* which gives 100 Scots the opportunity to elaborate what Scottishness means to them. Many of the positive comments made by white Scots contributors mention their pride in the 'man's a man' philosophy. Broadcaster Billy Kay even writes about his admiration for the Scots' 'rampant egalitarianism'.[6] Sheila McLean, a Professor of Law and Ethics at the University of Glasgow, claims that 'Everyone who lives here is accepted as Scottish irrespective of his or her original roots'.[7] But such views are in stark contrast to some of the contributions in the book by 'new Scots'. One of the most eloquent and funny pieces is by Mukami McCrum who was born in Kenya and has now lived in Scotland for almost thirty years. Mukami was taught in a Church of Scotland mission in Kenya before coming here so she already knew something of Scottish culture and aspirations. When she arrived she soon discovered a different ideology at work. She describes how over the years she has been spat at, had bricks through her car windscreen and been subjected to malicious phone calls, abusive language and hurtful remarks. No wonder she writes of her 'sense of alienation':

> I learnt too late that the Scottish people knew nothing or very little about my people, but I did expect to be treated like a human being. My Scottish teachers in Kenya never told us about the inherent fear and dislike some Scots have for people like me. Yet I was taught about their greatness, their sense of humour and about people like David Livingstone and Rabbie Burns who were noble, superior, brave, tolerant, hospitable, hard-working and kind.[8]

One of the contributions by Robina Qureshi, a young woman born in Scotland to Asian parents, oozes anger and indignation at how she has been treated by many Scots. She asserts that as a child she was 'loathed for being Asian' and goes on to denounce 'the veneer' of egalitarianism in Scotland. And again it is the duplicity of what she believes to be 'a deeply racist society' priding itself on its egalitarianism which sticks in her throat, and she demands of modern day Scots: 'At least admit your racism'.[9]

People from other minorities are also beginning to pluck up the courage to say that being different in Scotland is a problem for them - that they do not feel that they are accepted as Jock Tamson's bairns. In the midst of the Section 28 (Section 2a Scotland) debate, Tim Luckhurst, former editor of *The Scotsman,* described Scotland as 'a backward, repressed and socially conservative country'.[10] But he was wrong: Scottish attitudes towards homosexuality and other sexual morality issues are no longer that different from the rest of the UK. For example, the Scots are as likely as the English to believe that homosexuals should have the same legal rights as heterosexuals.[11] But it also true to say that homosexuals and lesbians have little presence in Scottish culture: there are no famous Scottish icons of homosexuality or gender bending - no Scottish Eddie Izzard, David Bowie or Boy George. Scots in the public eye also seem reluctant to 'come out' and openly acknowledge their sexuality. In 1993, Bob Cant, a Scottish gay social historian declared:

> Lesbians and gay men are, for the most part, invisible in modern Scotland. The few public references to us - by teachers, by preachers, by politicians, by pundits - imply that we are Other, that we are 'these people', that we do not belong.[12]

Almost ten years have elapsed yet Cant's words are still true. And I have little doubt that the fear of being cast out or ostracised for wanting to express your sexuality or sexual identity in different ways has, over the years, fuelled some of Scotland's startling migration figures. I know a number of young Scottish men who, after much soul searching and feelings of alienation, went down south in pursuit of a new identity. I also know two women, both nurses, who fell in love and wanted to set up home together. They felt they could not cope with the obtrusive interest in their private lives and the concomitant disapproval and so they emigrated to Australia where they felt they would have a chance to be themselves.

At the height of the storm over the repeal of Section 28 (2a) it appeared as if homosexuality is a divisive issue in Scottish life, but it is a small fissure in comparison with that yawning chasm - religion.

Being Catholic

As Scotland is a small country which likes to proclaim its egalitarian ideals to the world, when the composer James MacMillan got to his feet at the 1999 Edinburgh International Festival and gave a lecture about a 'prevalent, if not unspoken bigotry' against Catholics in Scottish national life he did not just spark off but ignited a blazing controversy. Even months after the speech various columnists and letter-writers were still debating the pros and cons of MacMillan's argument in the press and the fireworks continued to light up the Scottish firmament. The following year Tom Devine edited a book of essays about the controversy called *Scotland's Shame? - Bigotry and Sectarianism in Modern Scotland* and yet another debate ensued.

Few could dispute that religious tensions exist in some quarters of Scottish life. In 1995 Cara Henderson's boyfriend was killed for being a Celtic supporter and she went on to set up an anti-sectarian organisation called Nil By Mouth. She estimates that in 1999-2000 eight Scots lost their lives through sectarianism. Steve Bruce, Professor of Sociology at Aberdeen University, disputes this figure and claims that he knows of only 'four murders relating to Old Firm rivalry in 20 years' and adds that this is probably not much different from 'football-linked violence in Newcastle, London or Liverpool'. However, journalist Neil MacKay, in an investigation in *The Sunday Herald* in September 2002, asserts that there have been 12 sectarian killings in Scotland since 1995.

But leaving football aside, does the Catholic minority have reason to feel aggrieved at their treatment by the Protestant majority? It is undoubtedly the case that Scotland was once an anti-Catholic land. In 2002 the Church of Scotland even apologised for the sins committed in the early part of the twentieth century by some of their ministers who preached the virtues of forcible repatriation of Irish Catholics. Many Scottish intellectuals in the 1920s and 30s were likewise guilty of anti-Catholic prejudice as it was all too common for them to fret about Irish Catholic 'contamination' of Scottish Presbyterian culture. In employment too anti-Catholic discrimination was commonplace. But times have undoubtedly changed. Scotland is an increasingly secular society and only a minority care very much about religion these days. Making recruitment more professional, and the extensive use of 'person specs' and 'job specs' has also meant that while anti-Catholic prejudice may still exist in some quarters, it operates at the margins of Scottish life. The presence of Catholics in a large number of high-profile jobs testifies to the fact that being a Catholic in Scotland these days is no longer the barrier to professional, or political, advancement that it once was.

There's little doubt that MacMillan would have set off a less noisy pyrotechnic show if he had acknowledged this change in Scottish life. But it is also true to say that the media ignored much of the spirit of MacMillan's remarks and focused on whether discrimination against Catholics is still a significant feature of modern Scotland. As MacMillan points out in the conclusion to Tom Devine's book, in his original speech his concern was not with *'discrimination'* as such but with 'prejudice'. He maintains that his lecture was 'a plea for social inclusion' in the wake of the brave new Scottish Parliament being established. It was, he now claims, his attempt to 'call for pluralism and diversity'.[13]

James MacMillan would have furthered his cause of inclusion and harmony if he himself had refrained from using very negative language in his lecture and refused to act the part of the ultra-critical Scot. He would also have helped his cause if he had not simply trotted out the standard, but questionable, argument about Presybterianism restricting art of all kind. Jokes about similarities between 'Mao Tse Tung and John Knox, Pol Pot and Andrew Melville' were not that helpful either. It is also ironical that his call for acceptance and diversity were at points couched in terms which constitute much of the problem in Scottish public life. Here is one example of what I mean. MacMillan cites the case of a letter-writing campaign against all-faith prayers in the Scottish Parliament but rather than simply describing the intolerant behaviour he dislikes, he goes on to generalise and calls it 'an obsessive and paranoid flaw in the Scottish character'.[14] Sadly this makes some of his speech sound like confrontational name-calling. It also inspires pessimism for if such behaviour is 'a flaw in the Scottish character' then does that mean there is nothing much we can do about it?

James MacMillan would also have helped his case if he had acknowledged that in many incarnations Catholicism is not a very tolerant religion which encourages diversity or pluralism. This is a point Tom Gallagher makes in an essay in *Scotland's Shame?* Referring to the way Cardinal Thomas Winning eagerly headed the campaign against the repeal of Section 28 (2a) on giving information about homosexuality in schools, Gallagher writes: 'Cardinal Winning has attracted the scorn of many within his own Church appalled at his readiness to give free play to the kind of intolerance visited upon Scottish Catholics right up to our own time'.[15]

Despite these criticisms of MacMillan's original lecture, there is much in his argument with which I agree. Indeed many of the points he makes are similar to those I have advanced repeatedly in this book, for at the core of MacMillan's argument is the belief that in Scotland there is a strong tendency 'to restrict, to control and to enforce conformity and homogeneity'. An important strand in MacMillan's argument here is that Catholicism is not respected in Scotland; not seen as a conduit to Scotland's pre-Reformation history or part of the rich tapestry of Scottish life. Even liberals, he claims, at best tolerate Catholics only if they don't do anything too overtly Catholic like send their children to separate Catholic schools. In one of the most powerful passages in *Scotland's Shame?* Patrick Reilly, a retired professor of English at Glasgow University, writes:

> Scotland has ceased to be a Protestant country
> without ceasing to be an anti-Catholic one and it is a
> change that no Catholic will applaud. Catholics are
> still made to feel that their habit of kicking with the
> left foot is, at best, an inconvenience, at worst, a
> disaster. To do anything on or with the left, the
> sinister, side has long been a synonym for perverse,
> crooked, aberrant ... From 1872 onwards there was
> pressure upon Catholics to stop kicking with the left
> foot and to switch to the right. Today the pressure is
> for them to kick with no foot at all, to purge their
> schools of religious education other than as a purely
> academic discipline sanitised of faith commitment.
> Once the wish was to make them Protestant; now it
> will suffice if they stop being Catholic. They were
> formerly criticised for being Catholic; they are
> presently criticised for being religious by Protestant
> atheists (they do exist) and by those who have
> deserted Calvin for Marx. But whatever else changes,
> one thing abides: the animus against Catholics and
> their schools.[16]

For me, a self-confessed Protestant atheist, one of the most
challenging aspects of the MacMillan camp's argument concerns
this defence of separate Catholic schools. It is commonplace for
Scots to argue, including the EIS, the main teachers' union, that
Catholic schools should be abolished; that religion should play no
part in education. Mike Russell, the SNP's current education
spokesman, argues that there is increasing pressure on politicians
in Scotland to abolish separate Catholic schools. I am sure that
some of this pressure does come from religious prejudice but that
most of it is fairly well-meaning. Many would like to see the end
of separate Catholic and Protestant schools because they believe
this will help to heal the disfiguring scars of sectarianism in
Scotland. If everyone attends the same school, the argument goes,
then religion will cease to matter. Everyone will appear the same.
So essentially this argument is about the assimilation of the

Catholic minority into the 'mainstream'. Some academics in Scotland argue that this process of assimilation has already happened. For example, sociologists Michael Rosie and David McCrone argue in *Scotland's Shame?*:

> Whatever may have been the case in the past, the evidence from studies in the 1990s indicates an acculturation and assimilation into mainstream Scottish society. While others in this book are exploring directly the thesis that Catholics are systemically discriminated against in Scotland, our evidence here makes that a very difficult argument to sustain. Scottish Catholics at the start of the new millennium are not the people they were. Their past is indeed history.[17]

For me this is one of the most depressing articles I have read in a long time. With one high-handed swipe these two authors simply try to brush aside and render irrelevant the whole question of whether there is anti-Catholic prejudice in Scotland. Yet even on the subject of discrimination they are not standing on rock-solid ground. Fellow social scientists, Patricia Walls and Rory Williams, argue in the same volume that there simply is not enough evidence for academics to draw such categorical conclusions. More importantly, Rosie and McCrone are simply not prepared to engage with the argument MacMillan and others advance because, in this instance at least, they are only interested in what can be measured objectively. They just don't seem to understand that MacMillan's argument is largely about human feelings. MaMmillan and others *feel* that their Catholicism is an important part of who they are as people but they do not simultaneously feel that this aspect of themselves is valued by the wider Scottish society in which they live. And no one, not even number-crunching sociologists, can deny these feelings or the importance people attach to them.

One of the central issues here is about assimilation. Rosie and McCrone apparently see assimilation as the pinnacle of equality -

once this peak has been scaled and no differences can be identified there is no longer a problem to address. Next case. But assimilation usually means that a dominant group has absorbed a minority into its culture at the expense of that minority's own culture and differences. When I was involved in gender equality work in organisations dominated by men this type of issue kept coming up. What the majority of women repeatedly say, though often in private and out of earshot of management, is that they do not want to have to act like men. More than anything else they want to come to work and feel not only that they can be themselves, but also that they will be respected for it. Much of the equality issue here is about feelings of authenticity and about feeling valued.

Essentially James MacMillan and his supporters are saying they feel that Catholicism is not respected in Scotland. The idea that religion has no real place in school is largely a Protestant view, though undoubtedly a number of (assimilated?) Catholics now hold this view as well. So every time some well-meaning Scot argues that separate schools should be abolished, a significant number of Catholics, like James MacMillan, feel their point of view is being undervalued. And the sensitivity has become even more intense in recent years because Catholic schools are now performing very well.

Earlier in the book I argued that in Scotland the love of objective, logical thinking means there is a tendency to reduce issues to first principles. For many Protestant-minded Scots, including myself until I read some of the essays in Tom Devine's book, a first principle is that religion and education should be separate. But if we move into the realm of *realpolitik* it is easy to see that no political party which hopes to win power will put the abolition of Catholic schools on its election manifesto for the simple reason that they would stand to lose votes and engender huge splits within the party. Such a proposal would have repercussions not just for the Catholic community but for many Protestants as well. As Mike Russell has pointed out, it would inevitably entail the complete elimination of religion from schools, including any reference to God, as is the case in the USA.

So it is no exaggeration to say that if any political party put the abolition of state-funded Catholic schools on their manifesto in Scotland an unholy war would break out. The issue would dominate the political agenda for years and would make the controversy over Section 2a look like a row about which sandwiches to take on a Sunday-school picnic. It would plunge Scotland headlong into a religious dispute redolent of 1843 and the Great Disruption. And it wouldn't be the fiddle we would hear but the drone of bagpipes as Scotland's chance to make something of the devolution settlement went up in holy smoke.

As I shall show in Chapter 14, Scotland faces some huge educational challenges. To my mind, the issue of separate schools does not even register on the scale of problems to be tackled. Even if you still think on principle that religion and education should be separate - that the 1918 settlement should never have taken place - is it not about time to let the matter go? Undoubtedly sectarianism is an issue but should we not try to tackle the mindset that creates it rather than enforcing conformity, suppressing diversity and alienating those Catholic Scots who are passionate supporters of separate schools?

Not Out of the Ordinary
We may talk a lot about common humanity in Scotland but there is little doubt that Scots, like people in many other cultures, are prejudiced and are capable of marginalising and even dehumanising others who are different from them. Indeed it is no exaggeration to say that for many people in Scotland 'a man's a man' as long as he is not English, a homosexual, an asylum seeker, or kicks with the wrong foot. But this does not mean that we should go to the other extreme and berate ourselves for being hopeless, intolerant, prejudiced people. While writing this book I have been struck by how challenged human beings are, right round the world, by difference; just how many societies are trying to grapple with discrimination issues. In the past months alone the newspapers have been full of stories about intolerance and discrimination of one type or another: the war between Palestine and Israel; the problems facing asylum seekers, not just in Scotland

and England but in Australia where they have even refused to accept a boatload of refugees; Protestants in Belfast spitting at and abusing four year old Catholic girls on their way to school; Nato troops intervening in the guerrilla war in Macedonia between the Albanian minority and the predominantly Slav Government; terrorist bombs in New York and Washington provoking a confrontation between the West and Islam; and the Fascist leader, Jean-Marie Le Pen, attracting so many votes in France that he made it to the final ballot. I am not citing these examples so the Scots can just say 'it is so difficult to grapple with equality and diversity issues, let us not bother trying any more'. I am using them to show that for all our faults and prejudices we are not that bad; if we were to measure ourselves on a scale of prejudice and discrimination we are really rather ordinary. No better or worse than most other nations. We do ourselves no favours if we hold to the Scottish myth of equality so much that it blinds us to the reality of our circumstances. But neither is it beneficial for us constantly to indulge in thinking that ends up with the equation: Scotland = the worst, or with notions of Scottish pathology.

Women's Experience in Scotland

And finally, what about that other great 'minority' in Scottish life - women? Is *Mac*Hismo alive and well in Scotland? Before writing anything specifically about women I want to point out that right round the world men dominate and that many societies, even in the West, are not just patriarchal but downright misogynist. So in the pages which follow I am neither interested in trying to ascertain how women in Scotland fare in comparison with women in other lands nor am I interested in trying to quantify the extent to which women are marginalised in Scottish life. Instead I am merely going to look at a few of the ways in which women in Scotland are undervalued and traditionally kept in their place.

Calvinism postulates the spiritual equality of the sexes as it makes both men and women responsible for their own salvation. But Lesley A. Orr Macdonald, in a comprehensive review of women in the Scottish Kirk, argues that this 'potentially liberating' aspect of Calvinism for women was not realised for centuries. Indeed Macdonald argues that the Scottish Reformation ushered in a religion which was deeply masculine in both belief and practices. Catholicism had allowed for female religious communities, making it possible for some women to live almost independently of men. The cult of the Virgin Mary and the plethora of female saints also meant that Catholicism offered women role-models and emphasised the importance of female compassion. All this was swept aside by the Reformation. The Reformers' God was an authoritarian male figure and absolute masculine authority was considered appropriate not only for church governance but also for family life. The Kirk believed it was right and proper for women and children to be under the rule and supervision of a patriarch. Indeed they believed that it was unnatural and 'disorderly' for women to have any authority. As only men could become ministers or elders, the church discipline which I highlighted in previous chapters was the discipline of men, with women and girls often on the receiving end. So harsh was this discipline that the poet John Keats once remarked 'I would rather be a wild deer than a girl under the dominion of the Kirk'. As Macdonald shows, much of the Kirk's discipline attempted to keep women submissive and in a subordinate position:

> For a range of offences, from gossiping and slander, to adultery, harlotry and witchcraft, women in the 16th and 17th centuries were subjected to punishments which were intended to silence, to humiliate, to shame, to demonise and above all to control them for behaviour which was not in keeping with the submission required by the defenders of the faith. Those who committed sexual misdemeanours, or who chose to live on their own and not in a male-headed household, were liable to particular pursuit and censure. This atmosphere of repression, abuse and contempt reached its nadir in the periodic witch hunts of the period. In 1727, the last of thousands of Scottish women were tortured and burned.[18]

The complete domination of women in the Scottish Kirk continued until the first few decades of the nineteenth century. As the evangelical movement within the Kirk took off and encouraged a whole series of mission work to help build the Church, relieve the poor or convert natives and savages to Christianity, women were increasingly seen as particularly suited to carry out much of this activity. But while the Kirk changed its views on women's social role, it still saw women as subordinate to men. Even the women's organisations set up within the Church, such as the Women's Guild, were initially controlled by men. Not only were women still deprived of exercising any authority, they were also prevented from expressing their opinions. In 1847, Thomas Chalmers, the man who led the Great Disruption, said in response to the subject of women's rights: 'I have always looked upon this as a very paltry and distasteful question; I think that it is revolting to the collective mind of the Free Church.'[19]

But in encouraging women's mission, the Kirk had let the genie (or more precisely Jeanie) out of the bottle. As Macdonald shows so conclusively in her book, once women started to play a more public role their attitudes started to change. They soon began to acquire skills, knowledge, contacts and confidence which changed their lives irrevocably. It was these skills which they were later to utilise in proper, paid employment. It was their growing understanding of inequality and oppression, learned in their work with the poor and in anti-slavery campaigns, which helped women to see that they themselves had no rights and were victims of oppression. Before long, some women in Scotland, as elsewhere, were beginning to agitate for rights - not only in the Kirk but also in education and in politics.

Knox's vision of a literate and educated Scottish people included girls and women yet Scotland has never produced one female intellectual or scientific figure of national, let alone, international renown - no Mary Wollstonecraft, Madame de Stael, Rosa Luxemburg, Simone de Beauvoir, Madame Curie, Hannah Arendt or Iris Murdoch. The absence of women's presence in Scottish intellectual and cultural life until the mid twentieth century is not only striking in Scottish history books but unmissable by anyone visiting the Scottish Portrait Gallery in Edinburgh. Leaving aside the section dedicated to the twentieth century, the few women on display are mainly queens, and duchesses - women who have made their name through birth or marriage. The main exception is the celebrated Flora MacDonald whose only claim to fame is that she helped Bonnie Prince Charlie.

Of course, it is true that in any society dominated by men, many of women's achievements go unrecognised. This is the argument Joy Hendry advances in an article on Scottish women's writing. 'Scottish women writers, of all forms and genres, have had a pretty raw deal', writes Hendry. But she also says she doubts 'if any Scottish woman writer has felt that her environment was encouraging, sympathetic or favourable to her achieving the full extent of her potential'.[20] Indeed, Hendry adds 'those who succeed are those who thrive in an adverse climate'. Hendry is aware that Scotland's political status and Scottish culture as a whole have not been sympathetic to writers of either gender, but she maintains that Scottish women writers have been doubly disadvantaged - have had what Hendry calls 'the double knot in the peeny'. In a culture which undermines rather than builds individual self-confidence and which expects people to conform to rigid norms of behaviour, Scottish women have had good reason not to feel ambitious for themselves and to conform to the limited life which has, at least until recently, been on offer.

At various points so far in this book I have argued that what other people think of you is crucially important in Scotland and that, in an extremely critical culture, this combines with the fear of negative judgements to keep people in their place and limits individual initiative and action. These constraints affected, and continue to affect, both men and women but women are not just shackled and disadvantaged by them - they are more likely to be stopped dead in their tracks. It certainly stopped Susan Ferrier: the nineteenth-century Scottish novelist even abandoned novel writing because she felt the activity was 'socially unacceptable'. While writing this book I heard the story of a woman artist who moved to the Highlands with her family and was producing landscapes which her husband sold in the small gallery they ran.

Over time she became depressed. A friend visited to help raise her spirits and when the artist's husband and family were well out of sight, she opened a cupboard to reveal all sorts of canvases she had been working on but felt she had to keep secret. And amid this secret work were nude self-portraits and various paintings depicting her views of religion and feelings of repression.

Scotland's emphasis on respectability has weighed particularly heavily on women. Many social historians and sociologists have argued that 'respectability' has been a guiding principle in the lives of ordinary Scottish people. In 1936 the novelist Willa Muir, in her book *Mrs Grundy in Scotland* argued that 'respectability' had become a widespread Scottish disease. 'Behave yoursels before folk', writes Muir, 'has taken the place of the Ten Commandments'.[21] The social historian Richard Finlay argues that the Kirk's definition of respectability 'revolved round sobriety, temperance, thrift, hard work, religiosity, and self-improvement'. Finlay argues that there was 'widespread adoption' of such values in Scottish society and that they had a particular hold on the working class. He also points out that 'perhaps the greatest propagators of these values were members of the labour movement and trade unionists who sought working-class social and economic advancement'.[22] Finlay also argues, with much legitimacy, that the importance of these values in Scottish working-class life had less to do with aping 'bourgeois ideology' than with 'human dignity': life was tough for poor, working-class people in Scotland - if they practised restraint they could lead decent, if exhausting, lives. If they were not careful with money, if they did not work hard to maintain certain standards of cleanliness or worse still if they if gave into the temptations of drink, then there was nothing surer than that they would end up living in the most abject slum.

R. F. Mackenzie, the liberal educator, grew up in Aberdeenshire, and reports how the quest for respectability was acted out in his household:

> We were brought up to be 'respectable', doing the
> right things, not being uncouth in any way, throwing

under a cushion the socks that were drying at the
kitchen fire when somebody knocked at the door. I
wouldn't have admitted that we slept four to a room
and that we had a dry privy at a corner of the garden.
We maintained the façade that was considered
respectable. I felt vulnerable, dependent on the good
opinion of neighbours.[23]

These words chime with my own 1950s childhood. Having a
clean, tidy house was very important in the respectability stakes.
If we ever had visitors, a huge amount of time would be spent
cleaning and polishing. If the door-bell rang unexpectedly on a
Sunday the Craigs would rush about stuffing newspapers under
cushions just in case it was the minister or an uninvited visitor! In
England too, particularly in the poorer areas, respectability was
important but, for reasons I have advanced elsewhere in the book,
the nature of Scottish tenement housing and the elevation of
others in everyday life meant that being 'respectable' had even
more importance in the lives of ordinary people than south of the
Tweed.

Mackenzie argues that in Scotland the working- and middle-
class were obsessed by such respectability and that only the 'local
aristocrats' could afford 'the luxury ... of being themselves'.[24] He
then tells a wonderful story about a Scottish baroness who was
giving a talk to the Women's Rural Institute when she felt her bra
come loose. According to Mackenzie, 'without fuss or
concealment' the doughty baroness continued to give her talk
while making a manoeuvre which allowed her to deposit the
offending bra in her handbag. No doubt any Scotswoman of
more modest upbringing would have been 'black affronted', to
use Maw Broon's phrase, at the very idea of people knowing of
her embarrassing predicament.

In the past, everyone in Scotland, bar the real aristocracy, felt
the pressure to be respectable, but a family's respectability was
often seen as the responsibility of the mother - it was up to her to
ensure high standards of cleanliness and order in both the house
and its occupants. Poverty, poor living conditions and large

families meant that lives were particularly hard for many Scottish working-class women. As is the case in many male-dominated societies, any laxity in women's moral standards was judged much more harshly than men's. I am not arguing, however, that women's behaviour was, and is, only controlled and limited by men - that women are inevitably victims of *male* power. Often the pressure on women to conform, in the past as well as the present, comes as much from other women as it does from men.

Some readers may be wondering why in a book on understanding the Scots, their culture and confidence, I am devoting so much time to analysing the experience of particular groups within Scottish society. And the answer is quite simple: it is very difficult for people to feel confident if they do not feel valued. And it has been very hard in Scotland for women - more than half the population - to feel valued for being themselves. Indeed in many respects women have been ignored. As I have already pointed out, traditionally Presybterianism was an extremely patriarchal religion which, unlike Catholicism with its cult of the Virgin Mary and its galaxy of female saints, has tended to make little of women's maternal role. In cultures where there is a pronounced separation of heart and head women can still be given respect as they are seen as more in touch with feelings and the tender human side of life. This was the case to some extent in the Scottish Kirk in the early part of the nineteenth century. But, as I argued in Chapter 4, in Scotland the emotional aspect of life has been institutionalised in the work and cult following of Robert Burns. Indeed not only is Burns a man but the Burns cult itself is deeply male and, until recently, women were even routinely excluded from Burns suppers.

In the early 1970s the feminist Sheila Rowbotham argued that throughout the world women had been 'hidden from history'. Look at historical texts and you will see just how much they dwell on the activities of men and forget the lives of women altogether. Historians are now beginning to address this imbalance but Elizabeth Ewan and Maureen M. Meikle argue in the introduction to their edited volume *Women in Scotland* that 'Women's history has developed fairly late in Scotland in comparison with other Western countries'.[25] They acknowledge a complexity of reasons for this but maintain that in Scotland 'the focus' has been on identity and this means that 'political history' has tended to squeeze out social history - the branch of history which is more likely to examine women's role and contribution to society. And as Lynn Abrams points out in an article on the need to 'gender Scottish history', 'these preoccupations' with national identity and national politics 'have never led historians to examine how women have intersected with the discourses on nationalism and nation-state formation in Scotland'.[26]

Leaving aside politics and constitutional history, the type of Scottish issues and events historians and cultural analysts tend to focus on are exclusively male. Take the Scottish Enlightenment - there is a huge roll-call of names to mention, but they are all male and there are not even one or two minor female figures to consider. The 'lad o' pairts' and the issue of social mobility in Scotland has likewise been analysed repeatedly and, as David McCrone points out, there is no female equivalent - no 'lass o' pairts'.[27] The Labour Movement has also been responsible for marginalising the role of women in Scotland. Since the industrial revolution women have played an important part in the Scottish economy. Indeed whole industries - such as jute in Dundee and cotton in Ayrshire - were largely dominated by women. Nonetheless the most celebrated aspects of Scotland's industrial past are heavy industries - shipbuilding, engineering, mining and steel - where men dominated. Even though women did work in some of these industries their labour is often forgotten. Women also played a part in the Scottish Labour Movement, organising rent strikes for example, yet they are not accorded an important place in the story: unlike the heroes, the heroines are largely unsung. Given these last few points it is unsurprising that the images of Red Clydeside are resolutely male. Indeed the only statue in Scotland commemorating the activities of a female socialist figure is on the banks of the Clyde and it is to La Passionara - a Spanish leader.

As I have always been interested in gender issues it is tempting for me to write extensively about the specific masculine nature of

Scottish culture and the impact this has on both sexes. But since this is a book generally on Scotland, and not on gender, I shall confine myself to pointing out two straws which show that the wind blowing through much of Scottish culture is cold and hostile to women's lives and values. The first concerns the way women are routinely portrayed in an unflattering light in the highly influential Scottish working class novels penned by men like William McIlvanney or James Kelman. The women characters in these novels often have aspirations for a better house or more money, and these writers regularly depict them as the carriers of alien middle-class (and therefore English) values. In one of his novels McIlvanney mounts a vicious attack on 'genus surbanus'. 'After mating', McIlvanney writes, 'two offspring are produced at intervals mathematically calculated by the female, whereupon the female swallows the male whole and re-emits him in the form of a bank-balance.'[28] Neil McMillan, in an article about women in Kelman's fiction, asserts that the author is within a tradition of male Glasgow fiction which 'persistently identifies womanliness with negative bourgeois aspirations'.[29]

The second, and final, straw illustrating a decidedly anti-feminine wind blowing through Scottish culture, is the life and work of Hugh MacDiarmid - the man the Scottish historian Christopher Harvie claims 'stood guard over the Scottish intellect'[30] in the first half of the twentieth century. Alan Bold in his biography of MacDiarmid asserts that the author 'changed Scotland' and that in the course of his life gave 'the nation an ideal made in his own image'.[31] But what is the image of Hugh MacDiarmid? For me, it is of a churlish, critical patriarch who downplayed the importance of human relationships and exaggerated the importance of art - a viewpoint summed up in his memorable line that he 'would sacrifice a million people any day for one immortal lyric'.[32]

As a woman, and a mother, MacDiarmid's image is not one which I respect, let alone like. Of course, I feel dazzled by some of MacDiarmid's language and imagery and can appreciate how he managed to raise the level of Scottish culture, but I do not care for much of his philosophy of life. This philosophy is summed up

in the lines from 'A Drunk Man Looks at the Thistle' which are
reproduced on MacDiarmid's headstone:

> I'll ha'e nae hauf-way hoose, but aye be whaur
> Extremes meet - it's the only way I ken
> To dodge the curst conceit o' bein' richt
> That damns the vast majority o' men.[33]

Despite his claim that he does not have to be right, it is hard to
find a more certain or authoritative Scottish voice than
MacDiarmid's. It is true that he changes his opinion over time,
but when he makes his judgements he speaks with such certainty
and authority that his voice is not only intimidating it is
tyrannical. Indeed MacDiarimid does not just express opinions -
he writes in tablets of stone. It is he, the Great Man, who sits on
high deciding how to rank the work of his competitors or what
views are appropriately Scottish. In the article I referred to in
Chapter 2 where he complains about distractions, such as
women, in pubs, MacDiarmid writes:

> It is the old story of those who prefer hard-centre
> chocolates to soft, storm to sunshine, sour to sweet.
> True Scots always prefer the former of these
> opposites. That is one of our principal differences
> from the English. We do not like the confiding, the
> intimate, the ingratiating, the hail-fellow-well-met,
> but prefer the unapproachable, the hard-bitten, the
> recalcitrant, the sinister, the malignant, the sarcastic,
> the saturnine, the cross-grained and the cankered,
> and the howling wilderness to the amenities of
> civilization, the irascible to the affable, the prickly to
> the smooth.[34]

No doubt he was exaggerating for effect, but even so every time I
read these lines I want to shout - 'speak for yourself Hugh
MacDiarmid. You certainly don't speak for me or any Scottish
woman I know'. If women had managed to make their views and

presence felt over the last hundred years in Scottish culture, Alan Bold could not have blindly asserted that somehow MacDiarmid has given Scotland 'an ideal made in his own image'.

Women are still not making a big enough contribution to Scottish culture and society; too many women are still paralysed by fear of others' opinions and of being 'cast out'. Nonetheless there are more women's voices to be heard these days and reasons to believe that the tide has started to turn. For example, the Scottish Kirk's views on women have changed so much in the past few decades that they seem progressive in comparison with other churches. The political parties in Scotland, particularly Labour, have taken some positive steps to ensure that women have a strong, if not necessarily equal, say in the new Scottish Parliament. In the first in-take of MSPs 37 per cent were women - one of the highest percentages of female parliamentarians in the world. In a recent article, 'A Slow Revolution? Gender Relations in Contemporary Scotland', Fiona Mackay outlines some additional achievements:

> Girls have been outperforming boys in Scottish schools for decades. We can also see young women moving forward: they now consist of about half of new undergraduates in Scottish Universities, including medical students. Women have made significant inroads into many professions. For example, they account for 41 per cent of medical consultants aged under 35; one in three new police officers is female as is one in every two newly qualified solicitors.[35]

When I was young I was hard-pressed to come up with many names of famous Scotswomen. There was Mary Queen of Scots, Moira Anderson, Maw Broon and, of course, Maggie, Daphne and the Bairn, but once I had trotted out these names I was struggling. And presumably this is why my heroine was Doris Day in *Calamity Jane*. But nowadays there are a growing number of Scottish females who are making their mark one way or another. And this mark can be seen not just in literature and the arts but in the media, sport, politics and business. Now any Scots girl can become aware of the presence of women like Liz Lochhead, Kirsty Wark, Janice Galloway, Hazel Irvine, Margo MacDonald, Anne Gloag, Liz McColgan and countless more. Of course, there are still many hurdles for women to cross before we see anything like reasonable sex equality but nonetheless there are encouraging signs of what Fiona Mackay calls 'a slow revolution'. I have every confidence that if the Scots could stop being so judgmental and critical of others and start giving every individual more space to be themselves then this slow revolution would begin to speed up. And the beneficiaries would not just be women. For centuries women in Scotland have been silenced - Scotland would be all the richer if these voices could now be heard.

NOTES

1 Joyce McMillan, 'Tartan Special' in *Scotland on Sunday,* 15 July 1990.

2 Charles Jennings, *Faintheart: An Englishman Ventures North of the Border* (Abacus: London, 2001), p. 43.

3 Quoted in Rowena Arshad, 'Social Inclusion' in Gerry Hassan and Chris Warhurst (eds), *A Different Future: A Modernisers' Guide to Scotland* (The Centre for Scottish Public Policy/The Big Issue: Glasgow, 1999), pp. 221-2.

4 *Scotland on Sunday,* 28 April 2002.

5 *The Herald,* 26 April 2002.

6 Billy Kay in Tom Devine and Paddy Logue (eds), *Being Scottish* (Polygon: Edinburgh, 2002), p. 113

7 Sheila McLean in *Being Scottish,* p. 171.

8 Mukami McCrum in *Being Scottish,* p. 156.

9 Robina Qureshi in *Being Scottish,* pp. 218 -9.

10 Tim Luckhurst, *The Independent,* 7 July 2001.

11 For information on the Scots' attitudes to homosexuality see John Curtice, David McCrone, Alison Park & Lindsay Paterson, *New Scotland, New Society?* (Polygon: Edinburgh, 2001).

12 Bob Cant, *Footsteps and Witnesses: Lesbian and Gay Lifestories from Scotland* (Polygon: Edinburgh:1993), p. 1.

13 James MacMillan, 'I Hadn't Thought of It Like That' in T. M. Devine, *Scotland's Shame?* (Mainstream Publishing: Edinburgh, 2000).

14 James MacMillan, 'Scotland's Shame' in T. M. Devine, *Scotland's Shame?,* p. 16.

15 Tom Gallagher, 'Holding a Mirror to Scotia's Face' in T. M. Devine, *Scotland's Shame?,* p. 57.

16 Patrick Reilly, 'Kicking with the Left Foot: Being Catholic in Scotland' in T. M. Devine, *Scotland's Shame?,* p. 38.

17 Michael Rosie and David McCrone, 'The Past is History: Catholics in Modern Scotland' in T. M. Devine, *Scotland's Shame?,* p. 217.

18 Lesley A. Orr Macdonald, *A Unique And Glorious Mission: Women and Presbyterianism in Scotland* 1830-1930 (John Donald: Edinburgh, 2000), p. 25.

19 Quoted in Lesley A. Orr Macdonald, *A Unique And Glorious Mission,* p. 178.

20 Joy Hendry, 'Twentieth Century Women's Writing: The Nest of Singing Birds' in Cairns Craig (ed.), *The History of Scottish Literature: Volume 4* (Aberdeen University Press: Aberdeen, 1989), p. 291.

21 Willa Muir, *Mrs Grundy in Scotland* (George Routledge: London, 1936), p. 62.

22 Richard Finlay in Michael Lynch, *The Oxford Companion to Scottish History* (Oxford University Press: Oxford, 2001), pp. 522-3.

23 R. F. MacKenzie, *A Search for Scotland* (Fontana Paperbacks: London, 1991), p. 259.

24 Ibid., p. 259.

25 Elizabeth Ewan & Maureen M. Meikle, *Women in Scotland c.1100-c.1750* (Tuckwell Press: East Linton, 1999), p. xx.

26 Lynn Abrams, 'Gendering Scottish History: An Agenda for Change' in *Women's History Magazine,* Issue 40, February 2002, pp 11-12.

27 David McCrone, *Understanding Scotland: The Sociology of a Stateless Nation* (Routledge: London, 1992), p. 97.

28 William McIlvanney, *A Gift from Nessus* (Eyre & Spottiswoode: London, 1968).

29 Neil McMillan, 'Wilting, or the "Poor Wee Boy Syndrome":Kelman and Masculinity', in *Edinburgh Review* No. 108, p. 49.

30 Christopher Harvie, *Scotland and Nationalism: Scottish Society and Politics,* 1707-1977 (George Allen & Unwin: London, 1977), p. 193.

31 Alan Bold, *MacDiarmid: Christopher Murray Grieve - A Critical Biography* (John Murray: London, 1988), p. 438.

32 Lewis Grassic Gibbon & Hugh MacDiarmid, *Scottish Scene* (Hutchinson: London, 1934).

33 Hugh MacDiarmid, *A Drunk Man Looks at the Thistle* (Caledonian Press: Glasgow 1953) p. 6.

34 Hugh MacDiarmid 'The Dour Drinkers of Glasgow 'in Hugh MacDiarmid, *The Uncanny Scot: A Selection of Prose* (MacGibbon & Kee: London, 1968), p. 96.

35 Fiona Mackay, 'A Slow Revolution?: Gender Relations in Contemporary Scotland' in Gerry Hassan and Chris Warhurst (eds), *Anatomy of the New Scotland: Power and Influence* (Mainstream Publishing: Edinburgh, 2002), p. 279.

9
The Utopian Streak

'Och aye, it's the New Jerusalem! It's a land of milk and honey they're building up there in Scotland, laddie. They'll nae be doing it with your horrid Anglo-Saxon devil-take-the-hindmost approach. No, they're just more socialist than us sour-mouthed Sassenachs.'

This is how Boris Johnson, the English newspaper columnist and Tory MP, satirised the Scots' attitude to politics during the debate about the Scottish Parliament's support for free personal care. I am no fan of the maverick Johnson, but I think he is right - the Scots are a people with an inclination to Utopian dreams. These dreams may seem harmless, or even laudable, but they can be dangerous for they undermine our self-confidence. Indeed I believe one of the main reasons why we Scots are so self-critical is because we harbour dreams which are destined not to come true. And when they don't, the sense of failure catapults us to the other end of the scale and we end up knee-deep in feelings of shame, inadequacy and worthlessness. Of course, as rational, logical Scots we know that Utopia, or perfection, is unachievable, but lurking behind the logic is the belief that it should be achievable; that this is what we must strive for. It is simply no coincidence that it was a Scot, Andrew Young, who penned 'There is a happy land, far, far away'. And that happy land still haunts the Scottish consciousness. Given what happened in Scotland less than four hundred years ago it would be remarkable if such Utopian tendencies were not evident in Scottish life, for the most striking feature of our religious past is the sheer scale of what the nation tried to achieve.

Religious Revolutionaries
In Scotland, the Reformation was not a one-off event but a series of changes which occurred from 1560 to 1690. Knox and his contemporaries did not simply overthrow popery and Catholic ritual, they attempted to create the Kingdom of Heaven, to build

the New Jerusalem. In his acclaimed work, *The History of the Scottish People*, T.C. Smout argues that the Protestant reformers in Scotland were trying to create 'a perfect mirror of the Kingdom of God in Heaven'.[1] In this respect, as Campbell Maclean argues, the Scots were nothing less than religious revolutionaries:

> Most nations, however Christian, have retreated from this dangerously Utopian hope and have been content with more realistic and attainable ends. Where it has been tried, the communities have either been territorially smaller, as in Calvin's Geneva, or have opted out of general life in society, like Catholic monastics or like some of the Puritan primitives in the United States. But this is the single instance of a whole nation over centuries, being absorbed by the vision of communal attainment of such ambitious proportions. Only the great Communist states of the twentieth century have shared a like vision.[2]

One of the main obstacles to the creation of the Godly Commonwealth was the monarchy. King Charles I tried to re-establish royal supremacy by forbidding the General Assembly to meet and abolishing the presbyteries. But his attempt to impose a new common prayer book was the final straw. Rioting ensued. Churches were boycotted. In 1638 the Scots drew up a National Covenant requesting the King to respect the Presbyterian church. The Covenant was first signed in Greyfriars Kirk in Edinburgh but copies were made and dispatched round Scotland for the populace to sign. An astonishing three hundred thousand signatures were collected.

The National Covenant may read like a moderate and legalistic document but for many signatories it was much more than that. It was a vital step in Scotland's creation of the Godly Commonwealth. Archibald Johnston of Warriston, one of the document's creators, considered it to be 'the glorious marriage day of the kingdom with God'.[3] He also drew a parallel between Scotland and Israel - 'the only two sworn nations to the Lord' - a view which underpins the belief that the Scots are 'the chosen people'. In the decades which followed, Scotland embarked on Covenanting wars where people martyred themselves for their beliefs and for the great noble vision of 'Heaven on earth'. Anyone standing in the way of this vision was mercilessly killed in the name of God. But by 1690 it was clear to the Scots reformers that the Godly Commonwealth, the theocracy to which they aspired, had not been and could not be established. Religious toleration was forced on Scotland, following the Act of Union. Magistrates were forbidden from supporting the edicts of Kirk sessions and this meant that excommunication and other church discipline lost much of its power. Inevitably, the Church's control on the populace at large began to wane.

Over three hundred years have elapsed since then. Few Scots regularly attend church, yet that chapter in Scottish history lives on in Scottish life and it still shapes deep Scottish attitudes. It is for this reason that Wallace Notestein, in his historical survey of the Scottish character, argues that 'What differentiated the modern Scot in character from other peoples more than anything else was the Reformation. He may be an Episcopalian or a Glasgow Marxist, but he is in some degree a product of the Presbyterian movement'.[4]

The Scottish Dream

One of the enduring legacies of the Reformation is that many Scots, almost unconsciously, uphold the idea that we should still be striving for perfection. In a fascinating article on Scottish novels in the 1950s and 60s Glenda Norquay examines the work of four Scottish writers: James Kennaway, Alan Sharp, George Friel and Robin Jenkins. Ultimately she concludes that the central characters in these novels all feel dissatisfied with the judgmental, restrictive nature of Scottish culture and that 'the escape they envisage is not simply into an alternative world but into a world which offers perfection: flight must lead them into Eden'.[5] In their book, *Ten Modern Scottish Novels,* Isobel Murray and Bob Tait do not employ the same terminology as Glenda Norquay but nonetheless they still present us with the idea that Scottish writers long for Eden. 'It is possible to discern in many of them a yearning for a pre-industrial, pastoral Scotland', they argue, adding 'we are struck by a yearning for solidarity, for the very possibility of a sense of common purposes and values which would be life-giving rather than life destroying'.[6] A similar yearning can be found in the works of writers like Edwin Muir and Lewis Grassic Gibbon. In English literature there is a longing for Arcadia but this is the desire for a pre-industrial, green landscape where the English village reigns supreme. Jeremy Paxman argues that the 'English dream is privacy without loneliness' so it is a far cry from the longing for the communitarian paradise that dominates Scottish thought.

In Scotland, our Calvinist legacy has predisposed us to the need for redemption. It is a need which fuses the sense of a fallen, corrupted world, with the desire for salvation. As Scotland is no longer a culture dominated by God, nowadays redemption mainly takes a secular form. So the dream is of a world where flaws have been replaced by perfection. In America 'the American Dream' is the result of a fusion of strong Protestant impulses with migrants' ambitions to find a better life. It is primarily a dream of *individual* salvation via hard work and material success - a dream supposedly made possible by a land of opportunity and equality. By contrast, the Scottish dream rarely assumes a materialistic form. It sometimes takes an individual form, as is the case in some of the novels Glenda Norquay analyses. But the Scottish dream is mainly a dream of *collective* redemption and salvation; it is about us once again building the New Jerusalem.

According to Alan Sharp, one of the writers analysed by Norquay, the need for collective salvation is even apparent on the football terraces:

> Scotland lives in the grip of dream. The original dream was of a kingdom of heaven on earth, a serious attempt to produce a total theocracy. The failure of that attempt, it's my conviction, has left a psychic fault in the Scottish character. They're prone, at the drop of a whisky bottle, to commit themselves to

perfection, to Eden in a way, an Eden that they've never inhabited. At football they believe, as they stand there on the terracing, that they're going to see football played of the purest essence, that the game's suddenly going to be irreducibly perfect. They remain dissatisfied with anything less than this, and they remain hopelessly, endlessly optimistic that it will happen the next day.[7]

Stuart Cosgrove has also argued that for Scots fans, football is 'a dream that relates to the nation and its progress'. In recent years the performance of the Scottish football team has been so bad it has led to nightmares not dreams, but there is widespread agreement that Scots football fans for many decades lived in a world of fantasy and possibility - a world which bore little relation to what the Scottish team was likely to achieve on the park.

Scots often talk as if current social problems could suddenly be wiped out because people have a conversion as dramatic as Paul's on the road to Damascus - a conversion which turns good Scots folk from materialism towards wholesome pursuits and values. The Scottish-born journalist Ian Jack, in an article on his father, describes how he inherited this longing for a 'golden age' and day-dreamed about a time when people would see the light. 'The people ... would be filled with goodness. They would abandon Freemasonry and flee the public houses', writes Jack. '... and board tramcars for evenings organised by the Independent Labour Party. They would flood out of football grounds ... and cycle off with tents, to the Highlands'.[8] Of course, Ian Jack is being ironical and is all too aware of the naiveté of his daydreams but these are the types of dreams many Scots cherish. One of the most influential Scottish books of the 1980s was *A Search for Scotland* by the liberal educator R. F. Mackenzie. It is a beautifully written book about Scotland which is seductively idealistic and it is not difficult to see why it was hailed as a masterpiece by Scottish figures on both the left and right of the political spectrum. Near the end of the book Mackenzie writes: 'Self-interest and material comfort plays a larger part in the lives of most of us than we confess to',[9] yet his vision for Scotland is one where people have eschewed urban life and wealth. According to Mackenzie 'rural life' holds 'the prospect of happiness if we have enough food in our bellies and are free from back-breaking toil, so that we feel free to enjoy the sight of the dew-pearled hillside and the snail on the thorn.'[10] Describing the effect of an outward-bound trip to Rannoch on a group of teenagers in Fife, Mackenzie writes 'As they fitted comfortably into their natural habitat, we began to get glimpses of how a Scottish cultural revolution might be set in motion. It would begin in the country places'.[11] As the Scottish dream is for the nation as a whole, the dreamer must assume, as Mackenzie does, that it is capable of animating all Scottish people. So an essential feature of the Scottish dream is that it is blind to individual differences. In the Mackenzie example we will all come to love snails or countryside, once the scales of materialism have fallen from our eyes.

It is in politics, however, that we are most likely to see the Scottish dream in action, particularly the type of left-wing politics which have dominated the Scottish political landscape for decades. Jimmy Reid alluded to the dream in one of his newspaper columns when he wrote: 'My dad wept with joy when Labour won in 1945. He was dreaming of a New Jerusalem. John Smith would have understood, but not Blair and Mandelson. Their souls were never seared by the vision splendid'.[12]

'The Vision Splendid'

Almost all socialist creeds have idealistic or moral underpinnings but, paraphrasing George Orwell, some are more idealistic and moral than others. Marxist-Leninist thought is based on 'dialectical materialism' and sees itself as 'scientific'. As a result it has little time for socialist movements which are simply based on the idea that a socialist society would be morally better or more humane than capitalism. Within the Labour Movement which thrived in Britain in the early decades of the twentieth century, there was a huge range of opinion and again some of the parties and sects were more idealistic and moral in their views than others. What is clear is that socialists from Scotland, almost irrespective of grouping or party, had a strong ethical and idealistic base to their beliefs. Indeed many writers on socialism in Scotland point out how religion played a greater part in the movement's ideology than Marxism. For example, Keir Hardie, the man credited with founding the Labour Party, was from Lanarkshire and the influences on him were mainly religious. An ILP colleague said of Hardie: 'So far as he was influenced towards Socialism by the ideas of others it was ... by the Bible, the songs of Burns, the writings of Carlyle, Ruskin and Mill, and the democratic traditions in working class homes in Scotland in his early days'.[13]

Some of the great Scottish socialist politicians of this time - Hardie, Maclean and Maxton - passionately tried to improve the living conditions of ordinary people and their campaigns to raise men, women and children out of squalid poverty and inhumane working conditions cannot be seen as idealistic. But inevitably, as Scottish religious thought and history played such a large part in the creation of Scottish Labour ideology, these political reformers were not wanting to win mere palliative, economic measures; they were in their own way also attempting to create the Kingdom of Heaven on Earth. As one Scottish Labour Party pamphlet of the time argued, the change they were pursuing did not simply amount to capitalism being replaced by communism 'but also the greater transition from the semi-human to the wholly human ... Socialism is the only gospel on earth that makes for the spiritual emancipation of the human race'.[14]

For men like John Maxton, these socialist ideals became entwined with his aspirations for Scotland and the Scottish people. His was a huge vision not just of a Scottish Parliament but a 'Scottish Socialist Commonwealth'. At a rally in the St Andrew's Hall in Glasgow in 1924 Maxton declared:

> Give us our Parliament in Scotland. Set it up next year. We will start with no traditions. We will start with ideals. We will start with purpose and courage. We will start with the aim and object that there will

be 134 men and women, pledged to 134 Scottish
constituencies, to spend their whole energy, their
whole brain power, their whole courage, and their
whole soul, in making Scotland into a country in
which we can take people from all nations of the
earth and say: This is our land, this is our Scotland,
these are our people, these are our men, our works,
our women and children: can you beat it? [15]

Party Politics and Fallen Dreams

I am not suggesting that the creation of a socialist Utopia ever
gripped the whole Scottish nation, let alone the whole of
Clydeside, in the 1920s. Even in those elections where old-style
Labour did exceptionally well, they never won an outright
majority of votes in Scotland. And even when their vote was high,
many Scots voted Labour because they liked aspects of the
socialists' programme not because they shared the whole vision.
But the Scottish socialists' vision of Utopia owed so much to
Knox and the Covenanters that it became entwined with the
Scottish dream of collective redemption and still plays a huge part
in the psychology of the nation. This does not mean that a
majority of Scots consciously buy in to the notion of collective
redemption or live with a sense of Utopia. (Sadly many people in
contemporary Scotland live in such bleak circumstances that they
have little hope or optimism for their own lives, let alone an
aspiration for communal perfection.) But what it does mean is
that when people become involved in politics in Scotland they are
often animated by the Scottish dream. Lindsay Paterson argues
that it is Utopian attitudes and ultimately the Scots' 'fallen
dreams' which partly account for the disappointment many Scots
felt shortly after the Scottish Parliament was set up.[16]

Turning to party politics we can see Utopianism writ large in
Tommy Sheridan and his Scottish Socialist Party which openly
acknowledges itself to be a Utopian party, though it also
claims to put forward practical solutions to improve things for
people today. Nationalist politics has likewise been affected by
the Scottish dream. From the 1980s on, under the influence of

socialists like Jim Sillars and Margo MacDonald, the Scottish National Party, formerly a distinctly centrist party, has moved leftwards. A move which means the SNP now upholds many of old Labour's values and identifies with many of the radical socialist traditions of Scotland's central belt. As Gerry Hassan argues in his survey of the Scottish political landscape on the eve of devolution, the SNP 'try to cuddle up to institutional Scotland to capture intact the old Labour order, rather than critique and campaign against it'.[17]

Our Dream of Havana

Even outside conventional politics 'the vision splendid' still makes its presence felt in Scotland. For example, in the summer of 2001 a letter appeared in *The Herald* urging readers to ignore columnist Iain Macwhirter's claim that there is no alternative to 'liberal capitalism'.[18] Despite the collapse of socialist regimes right round the world, the writer urged *Herald* readers to see there is an alternative - Cuba. Scotland's salvation, indeed the world's salvation, depends on us seeing Cuba as a model for what we could achieve. Now I know that Cuba has many admirable qualities, but it is a fairly repressive country which teeters on the verge of bankruptcy. It has virtually no shops or basic consumer goods, such as soap. Despite these very simple facts a number of other Scots also wrote to *The Herald* to commend the idea that Cuba, with its excellent schools and hospitals, was a vision of what Scotland could attain.

The original letter was written by Mr Andrew Lockhart Walker from the affluent village of Dollar - not exactly the Red Clydeside of the new millennium. And this correspondence illustrates an essential point about the Scots' view of Utopia - it is a world where poverty and inequality have been abolished but where no one is rich. In fact a vital aspect of the Scots' version of Utopia is that money has become an irrelevance - it is a world where everyone has finally been saved from money's corrupting effects. So you can see why Cuba could become the New Jerusalem for many Scots. Indeed its poverty is partly what they find attractive. The people who wrote to *The Herald* urging us to consider Cuba as an alternative society, acknowledge quite openly how poor it is; that taking this route would inevitably mean a drop in the standard of living for the middle classes. Indeed a recurrent theme in many of the words written on Scotland is that to be authentic and true to herself she must consent to be a poor, but moral, country. The Scottish theologian and cultural figure, Anthony Ross, for example, passionately argued that Scotland must turn her back on materialistic values and 'that to win freedom we must agree to live simply and be poor, and learn to be open to people and ideas'.[19]

This argument, however appealing it might be to our values, is hopelessly naïve. It does not take account of political or human realities. Take the Cuba correspondence. The most appropriate response to the idea that Cuba is a role model for Scotland is - 'get real'. It doesn't matter how wonderful Cuba's education and health system is or how good her café culture, the Cuban way of life is so far removed from ours that we might as well urge the Scots to emulate the ancient Greeks. The Scottish electorate may vote to pay more tax as a way to help counter poverty, but as to becoming significantly poorer - I doubt it. I do not believe that human beings are wholly selfish or self-interested. Too much is made of competition in human and animal life when, in fact, there is strong evidence, even in animal behaviour, of the importance of co-operation and empathy. But immediate self-interest is a hugely important factor in private and public life. Regrettable, perhaps, but undeniable. So too is the natural conservatism of most people - a fear of the unknown, of change, which often stops them from positively choosing anything which is radically different from the present. Only an autocratic regime could force the Scots to embrace a Cuban-style, or genuinely socialist, political or economic system. In a democracy, where everyone has the right to vote, people's fears and self-interest are bound to limit political opportunities. The simple but brutal truth is that the realities of life in the twenty-first century make the Scottish dream of collective redemption impossible to achieve.

Panacea Politics

Even when Scots do not uphold notions of a full-blown Utopia - a perfect society where people all live happily together - a watered-down version of such thought processes persists. And the label we could give to this dilution is 'panacea politics'. Scottish politics is literally awash with examples of people claiming their schemes, notions and ideas could at a stroke cure many, if not all, of Scotland's ills. The early days of the National Party for Scotland, the forerunner of the SNP, were blighted by the political equivalent of such snake oil salesmen, all claiming that their idea, if adopted, would revitalise Scotland. A state of affairs which led SNP officials such as Lewis Spence to despair:

> I am all for the new nationalism, but at the moment it presents to me a maelstrom boiling and bubbling with the cross-currents of rival and frequently fantastic theories, schemes and notions ... Some hark back to the hope of a sixteenth-century Scotland regained, others suggest a national approchement (sic) with France, still others a Jacobite restoration. A certain group sees in the expulsion of all the English and Irish in Scotland the country's only chance of survival ... We are informed by one school of critics that only if Scotland returns to the Catholic fold shall she be able to rekindle the fires of her art, by another, equally absurd, that the Presbyterian faith alone is the true guiding star of Scottish artistic effort.[20]

In his book on Scottish nationalism, the New Zealand academic, Harry Hanham, maintains that even in the late 1960s SNP policy was essentially a weird mixture of notions from 'Douglas Social Credit' (a political scheme much loved by Scottish literary figures such as Hugh MacDiarmid and Lewis Grassic Gibbon), 'Christian Socialism, anarchism and political Radicalism'. 'Everything', Hanham caustically adds, 'except a frank acceptance of the modern state and of modern bureaucratized industrial, political, trade union, and commercial empires'.[21]

In more recent times, Isobel Lindsay, a politics lecturer and former member of the SNP, argued that the Party's belief that Scotland's salvation lies in independence in Europe was 'an escape into a Utopia' for, she maintained, the Party exaggerated the extent to which Scotland would be able to influence decision making in European institutions.[22] Indeed many Nationalists' commitment to independence appears to be so strong simply because they believe that breaking away from England will at a stroke solve many of Scotland's problems. And before the Scottish Parliament was in full swing, many pro-devolutionists argued that this simple transfer of power could remedy many of Scotland's ills. Months after the Parliament had been established, Gerry Hassan, now Director of Big Thinking, devoted a section of one of his articles to 'Caledonia Dreaming: The Vision Thing and Scottish Politics' and in it he writes:

> ... radicals of all political parties and none, must make sure that we shift the debate, challenging the Scottish political establishment, corporate Scotland and institutional elites in their old, cosy, closed ways, and demand a new, open, transparent order. This will require new visions for Scotland developing, as Churchill put it, 'a lighthouse not a shop window'; about how government works and best serves the people, new models of governance, and new ways of working in the public sector which tackle some of our worst inequalities in education and health. It is about an inclusive Scotland, with new models of partnership and mutualism, opportunity and choice expanded, and creativity and innovation championed in the 'old' establishment and 'new' sunrise industries.
>
> The dream of Scottish home rule was always about more than a Parliament on the Mound - our Camelot on the hill. The early labour movement pioneers and idealists who set up and maintained the nationalist movement through difficult times were inspired by

more than that. Their vision was of a Scotland which challenged the old vested interests of clubland and corporate Scotland and established a self-government beyond the political realm in the economic, social and cultural. That is a genuine clarion call for modernisers in any or no political party to unite behind today. We have achieved constitutional change our predecessors could only dream of; it is time to bring the political change and the new Scotland into being.[23]

Two years on from the establishment of the Parliament it is much too early to tell what benefits will ultimately accrue from devolution. But in the wake of Henry McLeish's ignominious retreat from high office, constant charges of cronyism at the heart of Scottish Labour politics and parliamentary debates redolent of 'yaboo' Westminster politics, it is hard not to see Hassan's words, and the countless others written in this vein, as little more than idle fantasy. It is a fantasy which I shared in earlier, halcyon days but which frankly looks rather daft in the cold light of devolution Scotland. I am not saying that none of this vision could ultimately be achieved, but like much in Scottish politics there is a strongly Utopian ('the lion will lie down with the lamb') quality about our aspirations and visions. After all, if we return to Hassan's vision, how realistic is it to expect people across the political spectrum to unite for anything (other than national security issues)? How realistic is it to expect the Scots, who have a long history of being disputatious, to pull together in the way that Hassan envisages? Has the Blair Government, with considerably more power than the Scottish Executive, managed to bring about either a new ethos in public sector working or genuine social inclusion?

And finally, the tendency to panacea politics has been evident in the way some Scottish Executive members have presented some of their policies. For example, when Henry McLeish was First Minister he passionately claimed that 'dignity' for elderly Scots would be achieved with the introduction of free personal care. In fact this initiative, although expensive to the public purse, does not mean any additional spending on the care of elderly people as it is a scheme designed mainly to reimburse the personal care costs of those elderly Scots who are already footing the bill out of their private income. It is, in effect, an expensive scheme which will contribute little to the lives of the vast majority of elderly people who struggle to cope because of inadequate pensions, the scarcity of residential care homes and sheltered housing, and a lack of home helps. But despite the limitations of the measure Henry McLeish presented it as a scheme which would, at a stroke, improve the day-to-day lives of older people living in Scotland. When Wendy Alexander was Enterprise Minister her pronouncements on broadband also suggested that this single initiative could transform the lives of people living in rural Scotland by getting them properly wired to the world. And a number of commentators dismissed her comments as overblown. Indeed a *Sunday Herald* editorial maintained that while it supported the initiative there is 'no virtue in fantasies regarding the transforming power of very modern miracles'.[24]

Idealists, Utopians and dreamers can be found in all cultures. There is nothing exclusively Scottish about such predilections. But in Scotland such dreams are not simply the dreams of individuals, or a few small-scale religious or political groups, they are woven into the fabric of Scottish life. And we can trace these Utopian threads right into the heart of Scottish culture and politics. Having a strong Utopian disposition myself I have no desire to knock this tendency in other Scots. I still believe it is noble for human beings to aspire to a world based on social justice, where poverty has been abolished. Indeed I would go further and say that this penchant to envision an idealised future where everyone is spiritually and culturally better off is a positive feature of many Scots and is much needed in a world where even the concept of continual social progress is struggling to stay alive. But like our commitment to egalitarianism, the tendency to Utopian ideas is double-edged. By encouraging us to dream of perfection it drains our energy and makes us cynical. Our Utopian longing also increases our frustration with ourselves and our culture and catapults us into feelings of worthlessness and self-criticism. And such feelings simply do not help us grapple with the very real problems which confront Scotland. Of course we need some inspiring visions but we also need pragmatic, realistic and achievable proposals which command widespread support and help us create a Scotland which may not be perfectly just and fair, but is significantly better than the one we currently inhabit.

NOTES

1 T. C. Smout, *A History of the Scottish People 1560-1830* (Collins: London, 1969), p. 72.

2 Campbell Mclean, 'Who is Their God?' in Alastair M. Dunnett (ed.), *Alistair MacLean Introduces Scotland* (Andre Deutsch: London, 1972), p. 201.

3 Quoted in Magnus Magnusson, *Scotland: The Story of a Nation* (HarperCollins: London, 2000) p. 424.

4 Wallace Notestein, *The Scot in History: A Study of the Interplay of Character and History* (Yale University Press: United States, 1947), p. 103.

5 Glenda Norquay, 'Four Novelists of the 1950s and 1960s' in Cairns Craig (ed.), *The History of Scottish Literature: Volume 4* (Aberdeen University Press: Aberdeen, 1989), p. 275.

6 Isobel Murray & Bob Tait, *Ten Modern Scottish Novels* (Aberdeen University Press: Aberdeen, 1984), p. 3.

7 Douglas Dunn, Scotland: *An Anthology* (HarperCollins: London, 1991), p. 34.

8 Ian Jack, *Before the Oil Ran Out* (Flamingo: London, 1988), p. 6.

9 R. F. MacKenzie, *A Search for Scotland* (Fontana Paperbacks: London, 1991), p. 261.

10 Ibid., p. 34.

11 Ibid., p. 172.

12 Jimmy Reid, *Power without Principles* (B. & W. Publishing: Edinburgh, 1999), p. 26.

13 Quoted in T. C. Smout, *A Century of the Scottish People* 1830-1950 (Collins: London, 1986), p. 256.

14 Ibid., p. 263.

15 Quoted in Gordon Brown, *Maxton* (Mainstream Publishing: Edinburgh, 1986), p. 160.

16 Lindsay Paterson, 'Scottish Democracy and Scottish Utopias: The First Year of the Scottish Parliament' in *Scottish Affairs,* Autumn 2000.

17 Gerry Hassan, 'Modernising Scotland: New Narratives, New Possibilities' in Gerry Hassan and Chris Warhurst (eds), *A Different Future: A Modernisers' Guide to Scotland* (The Centre for Scottish Public Policy/The Big Issue: Glasgow, 1999), p26.

18 *The Herald,* 27 July 2001.

19 Anthony Ross, 'Resurrection' in Duncan Glen, *Whither Scotland? A Prejudiced Look at the Future of a Nation* (Victor Gollancz: London, 1971), p. 126.

NOTES

20 Quoted in H. J. Hanham, *Scottish Nationalism* (Faber and Faber: London, 1969), p. 154.

21 H. J. Hanham, *Scottish Nationalism,* p. 175.

22 Quoted in Andrew Marr, *The Battle for Scotland* (Penguin Books: London, 1992), p. 192.

23 Gerry Hassan, 'Modernising Scotland: New Narratives, New Possibilities' pp. 26-27.

24 *The Sunday Herald* (Business Section), 9 September 2001.

10

Holier Than Thou

'Now what is man? There is one broad, sweeping answer which takes in the whole human race - man is a sinful being. All children of Adam born into the world, whatever be their name or nation, are corrupt, wicked, and defiled in the sight of God. Their thoughts, words, ways and actions are all more or less defective and imperfect ... We are like those animals in creation which are vile and loathsome ...'

These startling words on the hideous and corrupt nature of humankind are taken from a Free Church pamphlet circulating, not in a bygone age, but in November 2001. And it was handed out to unsuspecting shoppers in Glasgow's Byres Road, courtesy of Partick Free Church. The words were not penned by some fanatical Wee Free minister from the outer Hebrides but written in the nineteenth century by J. C. Ryle, the Bishop of Liverpool. This means there is nothing exclusively Scottish about such sentiments, but nonetheless it is true to say that such a harsh view of people as sinful and worthless beings has always been much more influential in Scotland than south of the border. So too has the 'thou shalt not' religion of the Old Testament, as opposed to the more tender and compassionate Christian teachings of the New Testament.

Writing this book at the dawn of the new millennium, centuries after the Reformation and Covenanting times, and with church attendance in rapid decline, it is tempting to conclude that leaving aside 'the Wee Free' these types of beliefs hardly feature in the day-to-day lives of ordinary Scots. But such conclusions would be wrong for we can still detect the hand of Calvin and Knox on modern-day Scotland. Contemporary Scots may not know very much about some of the great Scottish religious leaders. They may not understand why the Covenanters fought and died. They may be Catholics or Episcopalians or they may even be atheists, yet their country's religious history is imprinted on their psyche. In previous chapters I have shown some of the beneficial aspects of Scotland's Presbyterian past, most notably the focus on education and a history of staggering scientific and philosophical achievements. I have also shown how Presbyterianism underpins the Scots' love of equality and simplicity, the fear of scrutiny and being 'cast out' and the hankering after Utopia. In this chapter I look at some of the other characteristics that the Reformation has bequeathed to the Scots.

By all accounts, before the Reformation the Scots were a merry, pleasure-loving people who lived for the moment. But this new reformed religion was all about logic, reasoning and understanding. It was a cerebral religion which not only downplayed the importance of spiritual experience, aesthetic sense and beauty, but eventually demonised enjoyment of any kind. So the Kingdom of Heaven the Scots pursued was no paradise where people lazed about in beautiful palaces, thinking spiritual thoughts, being artistic, having fun, copulating or eating fruit; it was a world where everyone worked hard, led serious, frugal lives in accordance with the Bible and worshipped the Lord. For all that John Knox is seen as the kill-joy who turned the Scots into a guilt ridden people, he was not opposed to all forms of enjoyment. Nor was he particularly a promoter of Sabbatarianism. Such Puritanical edicts were a later development in Scotland's Reformation. And when they came they gripped the nation with a vengeance - doing anything on a Sunday, other than worshipping the Lord, was forbidden. So was celebrating Christmas or other traditional holidays. 'Gorgeous and vaine apparel' was criticised and people were exhorted to dress in sober colours. 'Hodden grey' was the Kirk's choice. Any form of enjoyment, such as card playing, gluttony, drinking, festive burials or weddings was also attacked. In 1649 the General Assembly of the Church of Scotland passed an act decreeing an end to 'promiscuous dancing'. Sex, the most natural of all human activities, was seen as vile by the Church authorities and any type of sexual activity outside the strict confines of the marriage bed deemed a serious breach of Church discipline. The elders even quizzed married couples on their sexual relationship.

At the height of its power, the Church was able to exert its authority over most people living in lowland Scotland and much of the Highlands. Only the nobility and vagrants managed to escape its discipline. Yet despite the obvious power of the Kirk, its ministers never managed fully to eradicate the Scots' liking for pleasure, and many Scots disregarded the Church's teachings in their personal lives. By the mid eighteenth century the power of the Kirk had waned so much that Robert Burns was not only able to reject its teachings but also to satirise its views. In his own life, Burns pursued pleasure, enjoyment, and romance and had the illegitimate children to prove it. He poked fun at 'the holy Willies' and celebrated love, sex and pleasure in his poems and songs. Burns was not a lone transgressor. Many historians comment that even at the height of Kirk authority in Scotland, fornication and drunkenness were commonplace and huge numbers of children were born out of wedlock.

Guilt-edged

But while the Kirk failed to regulate the behaviour of all Scots, and transgressions against its strict puritanical code were fairly common, it did manage to do one thing - inveigle its way into everyone's consciousness so that they believed they *should* behave in accordance with the Kirk's teachings. Inevitably this meant that when individuals transgressed they felt an overwhelming sense of guilt. And alongside football, guilt is still a national pastime. Those who are most sensitive to its powerful, but often invisible, presence are Scots exiles.

Alastair Reid is a poet and writer who, like many fellow Scots, has travelled the world. Born in Whithorn in 1926, he has lived in many places round the world including the United States, France, Greece, Spain and Central and Southern America. Reid is a gifted writer - a skill he used for many years as a columnist for *The New Yorker* - and this talent, coupled with his astute observations as both an insider and an outsider, mean he has written some of the most perceptive articles on contemporary Scotland. In his book *Whereabouts: Notes on Being a Foreigner,* he explains why he chose to leave his native Scotland behind:

The spirit of Calvin, far from dead, stalked the countryside, ever present in a pinched wariness, a wringing of the hands. We were taught to expect the worst - miserable sinners, we could not expect more. A rueful doom ruffles the Scottish spirit. It takes various spoken forms ... a man in Edinburgh said to me, 'See you tomorrow, if we're spared,' bringing me to a horrified standstill. 'Could be worse' is a regular verbal accolade; and that impassioned cry from the Scottish spirit 'It's no right!' declares drastically that nothing is right, *nothing* will ever be right - a cry of doom ... The wariness is deep-rooted. I prize the encounter I once had with a local woman on the edge of St Andrews on a heady spring day. I exclaimed my pleasure in the day, at which she darkened and muttered 'We'll pay for it, we'll pay for it' ...[1]

Columnist Anne Smith calls the complex blend of Scottish feelings of guilt 'the Knoxplex' and maintains that 'the victim ... is convinced that he is only truly alive if he is suffering, or working (one and the same thing usually)'.[2] Many Scots are also aware that they often feel guilty if they catch themselves having a good time or feeling happy. Andy Dougan, of *The Evening Times,* puts it down to 'that Calvinist thing that whatever good things happen to you they are all hideously undeserved'. Dougan adds that this means you 'are bound to ... be visited with some catastrophe in the near future in compensation'.[3] Many commentators on Scotland have observed how many Scots go through life seeing it as something to be endured rather than enjoyed.

Another prevailing belief is that enjoyment or even happiness is not only unimportant but potentially dangerous as such 'inessentials' divert your attention from life's true purpose. As a result of the Kirk's traditional teaching most Scots in earlier centuries saw 'real' life as being about hard work which should be undertaken, not so much for your own personal benefit, but for the benefit of God and others. This work ethic may have dimmed over time and with the advent of a more hedonistic society but it is still there. Indeed one of the reasons why Scotland is still a favoured site for inward investment is because the Scots are known to have very positive attitudes to work.

Many Scots, even today, uphold the essentially Calvinist idea that a person's life should be 'a pilgrimage towards an objective'. Just simply living your life unthinkingly is not good enough. To be meaningful, life has to be imbued with a sense of purpose. Andrew Carnegie, the Scottish self-made millionaire, would regularly remind young people, 'we've not been put in this world just to enjoy ourselves'.

Even when the power of the Kirk began to wane in Scotland, some individuals still continued to channel their sense of mission into religious activities and over the years many Scots became missionaries both at home and abroad. As Lesley A. Orr Macdonald shows in *A Unique and Glorious Mission*, many of those attracted to such work were women. As religion declined in significance, people redirected their need for a purposeful life into other activities. One obvious conduit for such a sense of purpose is the quest for knowledge and educational attainment. Many scholars in Scotland have pursued their studies with a quasi-religious zeal, often exhausting themselves in the process. Scots also commonly try to satisfy their need for meaning by entering occupations where they can be of service to others. This is surely why medicine and teaching have held such great attraction for the Scots. Indeed the idea of public service is particularly appealing to Scots, given the Calvinist legacy. And then there is politics. Politics, particularly radical politics, has also been an important avenue for the Scots to fulfil their sense of mission. According to one of his biographers, Keir Hardie, founding father of the Labour Party, was a man with a strong 'Covenanting temperament' and 'missionary style'.[4] In more recent times, John Smith, the Scottish MP and leader of the Labour Party until his untimely death in 1994, was one man for whom politics was a 'calling'. In a book about Smith's life and politics, Gordon Brown writes that the more Smith:

progressed in his political life the more he felt his actions closely bound up with his Christian beliefs - the desire to help others, to strive for a better and more just society, to seek to improve people's lives and opportunities through the power of the community.[5]

And the SNP too has had its share of purposeful Scots; men like Robert McIntyre, who was an important figure in the Party's reconstruction in the 1940s. McIntyre was the son of a United Free Minister and a specialist in tuberculosis working mainly with the poor before he dedicated his life to Scottish politics. He won a parliamentary by-election for the SNP in Motherwell in 1945 and was the first SNP MP at Westminster (though the seat was lost in the general election a few months later).

It is important to realise that the importance of mission and purpose may be a Calvinist legacy but it is so much part of Scottish culture that it has the capacity to affect all Scots, including those who are atheists or Catholics. Robert Crawford, the current Chief Executive of Scottish Enterprise, is a good example. Crawford was brought up a Catholic and attended a Catholic school but, as he himself admits, he is a 'driven' man, a 'secular Calvinist'.

Thinking in Black and White

As we have already seen in previous chapters, the Scots have a tendency to see everything as black or white. Things, people, events are either/or, good or bad. This tendency to polarise is characteristic of all Christian cultures and derives its power from the Christian belief that God is a single being who is all that is good and pure while the Devil incarnates all that is evil. The ancient Greeks did not worship one God but believed there were numerous gods, each with different personalities and manifesting different aspects of good and evil. Some Eastern religions do not split good and evil in this way. Instead they see the world as an interplay of two forces, such as yin and yang. Indeed God in some Eastern religions has many faces and characteristics and has both a good and bad side.

In Scotland, the influence of Calvinism may have increased the tendency to polarise even further. So too has the predominance in Scottish cultural life of the mental function Jung defines as thinking. Indeed as extraverted thinking itself can easily lead to fairly simplistic either/or categories, we can see why black and white thinking should be so prevalent in Scotland. For example, the Scots tend to see people in terms of good or bad; clever or stupid; generous or selfish; talented or hopeless. The old Scottish proverb 'Ye're either aa dirt or aa butter' sums up such a view of people.[6] Sydney and Olive Checkland, in their book on Victorian Scotland, argue that the Scots' tendency to Manichean thought polarised issues and 'left little room for the middle ground upon which real debate about human behaviour could take place, and where most of life resided'.[7]

A good example of how such a polarising mindset distorted political debate and comment occurred while I was writing this book. Donald Dewar's will was made public and almost overnight 'Saint Donald' became 'greedy, hypocritical Donald' in the minds of some Scottish commentators. But Donald Dewar's reputation was tarnished, not because of anything he did in his lifetime, but because the Scots find it difficult to stop seeing everything in 'perfect or worthless' terms. If the former First Minister was not the Saint the press had painted then he must be a sinner and a hypocrite. But neither summation is right, for like everyone else in life he had strengths and weaknesses - good points and bad points.

I knew Donald personally for over twenty years and both as a man and as a politician he was far from perfect. At a personal level he could be moody and bad-tempered. As a politician he was far from the visionary the press liked to portray at the end of his life. Yes he did have a vision - the creation of a Scottish parliament - but with that achieved he did not know what he wanted to do with the new-found power. In many ways he was a rather conservative character who did not want to rock the boat and who was at home with the political establishment. But he also had huge strengths which I hardly need repeat here. He was genuinely a man of principle. He was very considerate even to his opponents. He worked tirelessly for the things he believed in. He was not concerned about formality and could talk to anyone and I can well understand why he was so loved and respected by his Drumchapel constituents.

The controversy over the will was twofold: this supposed 'man of the people' left around two million pounds to his son and daughter and almost half that money came from a share portfolio which included shares in privatised utilities. But Donald never described himself as 'a man of the people'. He never pretended to be anything other than a former pupil of a lesser public school who came from a rather well-heeled Scottish family. He was middle class through and through. Everyone knew that. He never made a secret of his love of art and learning. For all that he had Peploes on his wall, he lived a fairly miserable existence (eating fish fingers with his books in cardboard boxes), but for no other reason than he was a divorcee with few homemaking skills. Nonetheless sections of the press charged Dewar with 'hypocrisy' and 'leading a double life'. Some called into question his right to call himself socialist. The freelance journalist Tim Luckhurst, who had once worked for Donald as a researcher and who never misses the opportunity to put the boot in to his former employer, came up with the hideous, and meaningless imagery that the Dewar will was 'a bolt of bile from beyond the grave'.[8] The lawyer Ross Harper, a lifelong friend of Donald Dewar, was so dismayed at some of the press reaction he tried to put the record straight. An article appeared in the press to explain how Donald Dewar had inherited the paintings from his family, and many of the shares, and why he had three houses.[9] He also explained that when Donald had become Secretary of State he had put his share portfolio in the hands of an independent stockbroker who then bought the shares 'outwith Donald's knowledge'. It was the stockbroker who had bought the shares in the privatised utilities. But that still did not deflect the criticism of hypocrisy. Two days later, Gerald Warner in *Scotland on Sunday* wrote:

> In future, every time that some sanctimonious media sycophant or Labour apparatchik puts the onion to

his eye and launches into maudlin Princess Donald mode, try reciting: 'Thames Water, Powergen, Railtrack ...'. If that does not put his privatised gas on a peep, ask him why the Fund Manger of the Nation had the Internationale played at his funeral, instead of *Money Makes the World Go Round?*[20]

A few, a very few, in our society opt to eschew money or comfort and live in the midst of some of the most deprived members of the community. And I am particularly thinking here about those ministers and priests who choose to live in some of Scotland's worst areas. The rest of us - Christians, humanists, socialists and social democrats alike - compromise in one way or another. We may do our bit here and there but we still make most of our decisions with reference to what would be best for ourselves and our families. And, unless they are martyrs, that no doubt includes Tim Luckhurst and Gerald Warner as well as Donald Dewar himself. Castigating each other is not the way forward. All it does is create yet more guilt - the least productive of all human emotions and one we already have in abundance. It certainly does not help Scotland solve the plethora of political and social problems. And it is exactly this kind of prurient, nasty comment on Donald Dewar's life which deters a lot of good people in Scotland from going into politics. Scottish politicians are acutely aware of this type of constant criticism. I remember one prominent MSP once saying to me: 'What I would like above all is for people in Scotland just to give you the benefit of the doubt from time to time. To accept that, while you may be wrong or misguided, you were genuinely doing what you thought was best'.

Good and Bad Faith

Another of the problems underlying Scottish thinking is that we make little distinction between good and bad faith. Acting in good faith includes those occasions when we make mistakes, not out of malevolence or from questionable values, but because we haven't thought things through properly or are forced to act in some ways because of external circumstances such as the pressure of time. Essentially we make mistakes or make questionable judgements in good faith because we are human. But when we act in bad faith we know that what we are doing is wrong and we still choose this course of action because it suits our own very narrow interests and we simply do not care about the wider repercussions. But in Scotland the prevailing mindset is that each individual is personally responsible, and culpable, for any mistake or questionable judgement that he or she makes. It is as if the Scots think that bad faith is the norm, not the exception. This means that in Scotland a common, if unconscious fear, is that at any moment you might be held to account for your actions by your peers and that no excuses, or mitigating circumstances, will be allowed.

A good example of this fear of being charged with bad faith occurred while I was writing this book. In 2001 the then Moderator of the Church of Scotland, Andrew McLellan, asked Harry Reid, the former editor of *The Herald,* to undertake a radical study of the Church and publish his findings. A year later Harry Reid published a book called *Outside Verdict.* This is widely recognised as a controversial book and Reid more than fulfilled the Moderator's request. But you just have to flick through the book to see the angst which must have gripped the author before its publication, for at the end of the book there are two pages entitled 'An apology'. What does Reid have to apologise for? What terrible writer's sin has he committed? Being too Edinburgh centric:

> ... I confess that Edinburgh probably dominates this book disproportionately. I am based in the capital, as also are the superb research facilities I have been using. In addition, the Kirk itself is very strongly rooted in Edinburgh ... . As I pursued my researches, I did travel round Scotland quite a lot (to do so was not a chore but a glorious privilege) - but I am conscious that I could and should have spent more of the six months outwith Edinburgh. For this, I apologise.[11]

His years spent having to understand and react to the Scottish mindset meant that Harry Reid was only too aware that in Scotland he could be hung out to dry for such an error. So to offset any charges of wilful neglect or bad faith it was best if he placed himself voluntarily on the penitent's stool, 'confessed' his sins and hoped that the Kirk session would be lenient with him.

Moray McLaren, in his edited collection called *The Wisdom of the Scots,* is so anxious about being denounced for the work that he prefaces the book with a six-page 'apologia'. Essentially it is an elaborate attempt to get his defence in first. It wasn't his fault, he tells us, he refused first time round, the publisher and his friends twisted his arm. McLaren even recounts the scene:

> Fighting a rearguard action, I then put it to my friend that I hadn't the temerity to place my name on an anthology impartially representing 'the wisdom of the Scots'. 'It would be all very well', I added, 'just putting forward my on own view. I can stand up to the knocks against them. But when it comes to what other people said and ... '[12]

I know exactly the type of thought processes which have led Reid and McLaren to get their defence in first, as every hour I have spent on this book I have also wrestled with these same Scottish demons. Apart from the fear of making mistakes and being denounced and reprimanded further down the line I have been plagued by a recurring question: 'Will so and so be offended and annoyed at me even questioning one of Scotland's holy cows let alone trying to slay it?' Indeed while on the subject perhaps I could squeeze in my own apology and say I know that I will have got some of my facts wrong but I am not an academic and I don't have ready access to a university library or colleagues to keep me right ... . And I'm sorry if I have offended anyone I didn't mean to and please believe me my intentions are good - I just want to normalise some of the debate about Scotland and make Scotland a better place to live for everybody ... Honestly!

You Tak the Low Ground, and I'll Tak the High Ground

The Scots' desire to see things in terms of black and white, right or wrong can easily lead to moral absolutism - the belief that your viewpoint is not only right but morally superior to others. Surveying Scottish history you can regularly see such a mindset in action. Of course, we can expect it in spades from religious figures, like John Knox or Andrew Melville, who believed with utter conviction that they were acting as God's emissaries and whose refusal to compromise was legendary. Leaving aside some of the Enlightenment geniuses such as Hume and Smith, who were open-minded, tolerant thinkers who wanted to learn from others, a strong sense of moral authority was evident in the attitudes and writings of many of Scotland's 'great men'. Thomas Carlyle is a brilliant example of this as is Hugh MacDiarmid. MacDiarmid may have been an atheist but in many of his journalistic writings he adopts the same tone to castigate others for their beliefs or shortcomings as many a minister denouncing sinners from the pulpit. In our own time, Jimmy Reid and other left-wing commentators, for all that they may be atheists, use religious imagery to attack opponents and argue that they are damned:

> Jesus went into the Temple and banjoed the money changers. Kicked over the tables. Told the greedy that they had only a snowball in hell's chance of ever getting through the portals of Heaven. His Heaven was obviously a Tory-free zone which effectively puts the bar up on the Blairites as well.[13]

One of the devices which is common in the writings of socialists like Jimmy Reid, William McIlvanney and Tommy Sheridan is to characterise an argument in totally black and white terms. 'Which side are you on?' they'll ask, and effectively this means, my side or the wrong side. Even when Scottish writers are not avowedly political there is still a tendency to characterise other people's motives and actions in simplistic terms. You are either out for number one or you are for the common good. No grey areas are recognised, let alone allowed. Any whiff of advantage or self-interest and that is you damned for ever.

Another device Scottish political or literary figures commonly use is to define Scottishness, not as something conferred by birth or residency, but by belief. In the past century these core Scottish beliefs have been delineated most clearly by those who are left of centre - by men like Hugh MacDiarmid with his notion of the 'true Scot', or by modern-day socialists like McIlvanney or Reid. The hegemony of left-wing views in Scotland undermines the political culture for it means that people cannot even question, let alone attack, key Scottish beliefs without feeling they are on the back foot - arguing from a defensive position.

Iain McLean, one of Keir Hardie's biographers, remarks: 'For Hardie the boundary was too vague between rightness and righteousness, and between righteousness and self-righteousness'.[14] Hardie, like many other Scots created in this mould, was only too ready to make personal attacks on political opponents who disagreed with him. The irony is that many of these thinkers stress the importance of co-operation and harmony yet, in reality, they are determined for their views to prevail. Edward Caird, in an article on Carlyle argues that he was 'quite incapable of the "give and take" of social life, or, indeed, of doing anything in regard to others, except simply to insist on his own will and his own opinions'.[15] And this assessment would fit a number of Scottish political thinkers. I must stress, however, that such thinkers' political ideology is rarely authoritarian in content and we can only use the term 'authoritarian' to describe their personal style and interactions with people.

My Way

Scotland's Calvinist past has bequeathed to contemporary Scots two potentially contradictory attitudes to authority and they lead inevitably to tension. The first flows from the central Calvinist tenet of God's magnificence and humankind's abject state. This means that in comparison with the majesty of God even our noblest achievements are worthless. Calvinism thus taught the Scots to feel humble and submissive and to obey unquestioningly their spiritual Lord and master. But alongside this essentially master/servant relationship, the Scots were also encouraged to see themselves as equal to others in the eyes of God. As we have already seen, the Scottish Kirk is built on democratic foundations - in place of religious aristocracy, the Scots have elected bodies. What's more, to ensure that the Scottish people would never again be 'hoodwinked' by priests or clerics, the reformers ensured that the Scottish people, even the poor, were taught to read and understand the Bible for themselves. The Scots were thus encouraged to be somewhat sceptical and independent-minded. And this spiritual independence of the individual parishioner is further encouraged by Presbyterianism's complete opposition to a priestly figure who acts as an intermediary between an individual and God. To this extent, every individual is equally in charge of his or her spiritual destiny.

So we can see how submissiveness to divine authority coupled with a belief in fundamental human equality means that the Scots are rather perplexed and confused by authority. The Victorian Scot Thomas Carlyle illustrated some of this Scottish ambivalence. Carlyle believed passionately in the importance of heroes and urged others to seek out and obey heroes. He wrote screeds on some of his own heroes - Napoleon and Oliver Cromwell, for example - but he was incapable of paying homage, let alone giving due respect, to any of his own contemporaries. With the rise of atheism in Scottish society it is easy to see why the historian Christopher Harvie has named one of his books on modern Scotland *No Gods and Precious Few Heroes* - lines borrowed from the Scottish poet Hamish Henderson. Or why some argue that a 'Scottish guru' is a contradiction in terms.

Individual Scots clearly vary in their attitude to authority. Some are prepared to accept authority and will eagerly toe the line. Others find it much more difficult to respect someone as a leader. But no matter what the outer behaviour is, I believe that most Scots deep down hanker after authority - that they are searching for an omnipotent God who knows all the answers and never makes mistakes. A perfect being. But, ironically, even God would find it difficult to convince many Scots of His perfection for, as Alexander Scott sardonically explains:

Scotch God
Kent His
Faither.[16]

NOTES

1 Alastair Reid, *Whereabouts: Notes on Being a Foreigner* (Canongate: Edinburgh, 1987), pp. 24-25.

2 Quoted in Iain Finlayson, *The Scots* (Oxford University Press: Oxford, 1988), pp. 44-45.

3 Andy Dougan, *The Evening Times,* 6 October 2000.

4 Iain MacLean, *Keir Hardie* (Penguin Books: London, 1975).

5 Gordon Brown, 'John Smith's Socialism: His Writings and Speeches' in Gordon Brown, James Naughtie & Elizabeth Smith, *John Smith: Life and Soul of the Party* (Mainstream Publishing: Edinburgh, 1994), p. 67.

6 David Murison, *Scots Saw* (James Thin: Edinburgh, 1981), p. 34.

7 Sydney & Olive Checkland, *Industry and Ethos: Scotland* 1832-1914 (Edward Arnold: London, 1984), p. 133.

8 Tim Luckhurst, *The Independent,* 3 July 2001.

9 *The Herald,* 6 July 2001.

10 Gerald Warner, *Scotland on Sunday,* 8 July 2001.

11 Harry Reid, *Outside Verdict: An Old Kirk in a New Scotland* (Saint Andrew Press: Edinburgh, 2002), pp. 232-3.

12 Moray McLaren, *The Wisdom of the Scots* (Michael Joseph: London, 1961), p. 15.

13 Jimmy Reid, *Power without Principles* (B. & W. Publishing: Edinburgh, 1999), pp. 247-8.

14 Iain MacLean, *Keir Hardie,* p. 162.

15 'Edward Caird on Carlyle' in A. M. D. Hughes, *Thomas Carlyle Selections* (Oxford University Press: London, 1957), p. XXV.

16 *The Collected Poems of Alexander Scott,* David S. Robb (ed.) (Mercat Press: Edinburgh, 1994) p. 144.

11

The Enterprise Problem

*'If we learn anything from the history of economic development, it is
that culture makes all the difference.'*
David Landes, *The Wealth and Poverty of Nations*

In his celebrated study of economic history, Professor David
Landes informs us that there is a joke in Russia that 'the peasant
Ivan is jealous of neighbour Boris, because Boris has a goat. A
fairy comes along and offers Ivan a single wish. What does he
wish for? That Boris's goat should drop dead.'[1]

It is fairly easy to understand why Russians, brought up in a
collectivist state, should be rather envious of others' success and
lack motivation and ambition for themselves. But research
undertaken by Jonathon Levie and Laura Steele at the Hunter
Centre for Entrepreneurship shows that at least one in four Scots
share Ivan's views and that the Scots are more jealous of other
people's success than the citizens of any other small nation. This
study also shows that three quarters of Scots believe that everyone
should have the same standard of living regardless of effort, skill
or risk.[2] And it is these types of attitudes which experts believe
underlie Scotland's low business birth rate.

Levie and Steele collect data for the Global Entrepreneurship
Monitor (GEM) which allows researchers to make international
comparisons in entrepreneurial activity. And GEM shows that
while the prevailing business climate in Scotland should be
'reasonably good' for starting a business, Scotland's
entrepreneurial performance is poor. Tom Hunter, in his
introduction to the 2001 report, states that Scotland remains 'a
Division Three player and our rates of opportunity
entrepreneurship are at half the levels of other small nations'.[3]

Nowadays those who are keen to promote entrepreneurship in
Scotland, like Tom Hunter, are fond of saying that the major
obstacle to entrepreneurship in Scotland is 'culture'. But they
are unable to give an adequate account of what this culture is let

alone explain how it may have arisen. I have already described a number of aspects of Scottish culture which are likely to keep entrepreneurship in check in Scotland, such as the fear of drawing attention to yourself and the constant desire to keep people in their place. The GEM study in 2000 highlighted the fact that more Scots than the inhabitants of any equivalent nation report 'fear of failure' as one of the biggest obstacles to starting a business. There is little doubt that the Scots' fear of failure is a legacy of the country's Calvinist past, and the type of thinking I have outlined in previous chapters. I shall return to this topic and examine it in more depth when I look at the importance of confidence issues in everyday life in Section V. This means that in this chapter I can look more generally at Scotland's past to discern the possible origins for Scotland's 'dependency culture'.

A Capitalist Cradle

Before beginning my brief survey of history, it is worth pointing up that what is surprising about Scotland's low level of entrepreneurship is that eighteenth-century Scotland furnished many of the ideas necessary for the Industrial Age to take off and for capitalism to become the dominant economic system. Lord Kames argued that private property was central to industrial development and without it societies do not develop beyond savagery. David Hume argued that it is the need to preserve property rights that gives rise to government and laws. Adam Smith produced the bible of capitalist economics - *The Wealth of Nations*. Smith not only coined the phrase 'the division of labour' but also showed how important it was in the creation of wealth. The Scottish contribution to the revolution in economic production in the eighteenth century was not confined to intellectual ideas. It was James Watt from Greenock who perfected the steam engine which literally powered the industrial revolution. One of the consequences of Watt's invention is that factories could be footloose - they no longer had to be sited near swift running rivers or close to sources of coal.

Arthur Herman argues that much of Smith's theory in *The Wealth of Nations* came from his observations of Glasgow merchants, particularly tobacco lords, when he was Professor of Moral Philosophy at Glasgow University in the mid-eighteenth century. Glasgow was one of the first cities to capitalise on trade with the American colonies. The money from such activities, the natural resources and geography of the Clyde, the enduring Scottish interest in science and engineering as well as the determination and seriousness of purpose encouraged by Presbyterianism, all contributed to the explosion in industrial activity in the west of Scotland. Men who had made a comfortable living running small businesses now invested time and money developing the new industries. By the nineteenth century Scotland was a world producer of ships, coal, steel, iron, cotton and other textiles.

Nowadays Scotland is not only a country with a poor business birth rate but also has low economic growth and low productivity. Scottish productivity is 40 per cent below the United States and 20 per cent lower than in France and Ireland. Scotland's population is also declining, making it more difficult for the economy to expand. Scotland has also acquired the reputation as a country with a dependency culture. The Scots are seen by outsiders as a people who expect the state to house them and give them dole money when the economy is in the doldrums. So, what has occurred in the past century or so to put a spoke in the wheel of this once great engine of enterprise?

The Loss of Entrepreneurial Attitudes

One plausible explanation for Scotland's loss of entrepreneurial spirit is that successful Scots became enthralled by English values. The American history professor, Arthur Herman, takes this view and argues that at the end of the nineteenth century:

> ... Scotland's upper and middle classes were losing that hard-driving entrepreneurial edge which had been a part of their cultural heritage. They increasingly settled into the ideal of the English gentleman. The values of Eton, Cambridge and Oxford, of the Reform and Athenaeum clubs, and of

Lord's Cricket Ground steadily replaced those of a grittier homegrown variety.[4]

The Tennant family personifies such Anglicising tendencies. Originally a poor family from Ayrshire, the Tennants lifted themselves out of poverty through basic enterprise and education. Charles Tennant, a gifted scientist, refined the process of chemical bleaching in the eighteenth century and founded the St Rollox work in Glasgow which ultimately became a huge industrial empire. A vastly wealthy family, they later established a family seat in Peebleshire. By the 1880s the Tennant boys were educated at Eton and the girls came out in London society. A baronetcy followed as did intermarriage with some of the English aristocracy. In our own time, most people know of the family only as a result of the socialite Colin Tennant's association with Princess Margaret and his life on the island of Mustique. He was just one in a long line of family members who had no interest in making money but only in spending it.[5]

Undoubtedly there is some truth in Herman's explanation of the loss of Scottish entrepreneurial spirit, but there is nothing uniquely Scottish in this phenomenon. Countless commercial dynasties in England, America and elsewhere have likewise become enfeebled following the death of the self-made man who founded the enterprise, and his replacement by sons who do not share their father's drive or values. Herman also argues that the middle-class Scot became obsessed with respectability and that this further undermined and 'distorted' the Scottish entrepreneurial spirit. He specifically claims that it 'blocked innovation and creativity in ways that could be stifling, even dangerous'.[6]

It is certainly true that successful entrepreneurs need to follow their hunches and be creative and that usually means careering along oblivious to the dictates of conventional life. A society with very prescriptive rules of how people *should* behave will probably find it difficult to sustain high levels of entrepreneurship. It is not uncommon for nationalist commentators to argue that the Scots' obsession with respectability is simply further proof of the imposition of bourgeois English values. But it is easy to find indigenous Scottish reasons for the importance of respectability in Scotland. Herman links the 'need to conform to social norms' and 'the emphasis on conformity' to Enlightenment ideals. Ideals which confirm the importance of others in both social and moral terms. But Herman does not probe far enough to find that the taproots nourishing the importance of respectability in Scotland run deep into the nation's cultural life: the combination of the cultural preference for the outer, extravert world, the supremacy of collectivist values and the rigid social control once exerted by Kirk sessions mean that in Scotland other people's opinions assume enormous importance in an individual's life. So conforming to established notions of 'respectable' behaviour is very important to the Scots. But this poses an important question: why did business activity in Scotland become separated from what people deemed to be respectable? Are we simply to blame this on the English as well or is there another answer?

The Scottish Experience of Industrialisation

After reading various historians' accounts of Scotland's social and economic past I am convinced of one thing: the vast majority of working-class Scots from the early nineteenth century on did not feel positive about capitalist wealth creation for the simple reason that they were either direct casualties of it or their families had suffered acutely from its effects in the past. In the nineteenth century Scotland was the second most urbanised country in the world. And perhaps it was the speed of this urbanisation and the predominance of heavy industry which explain why industrialisation wore such a particularly harsh and brutal face in Scotland. In industrial areas the vast majority of inhabitants lived in tenements. In late nineteenth-century Glasgow this was as high as 85 per cent of city dwellers. The tenements were often warm and dry, and so in some ways preferable to the black houses or damp cottages many had left in rural Scotland or Ireland, but the conditions were often appalling. In 1890 more than half of families lived in one room - called 'single-ends'. Sanitation was inadequate and often shared. Many buildings were infested with vermin and suffered from an acute lack of ventilation and light. No wonder visitors to Edinburgh, Glasgow and Dundee were appalled at some of the living conditions they witnessed. A nineteenth-century reporter for the West of Scotland Handloom Weavers Commission asserted that he had 'seen human degradation in some of its worst phases, both in England and abroad' but it was not until he visited Glasgow's wynds that he believed 'that so large an amount of filth, crime, misery and disease existed in one spot in any civilised country'.[7]

There were many reasons for Scotland's atrocious housing conditions but one is worth highlighting here. The Scots like to think of themselves as more compassionate to the poor than their southern neighbours when in fact throughout the nineteenth century the English were much more generous to those in need. Professor Tom Devine reports that even in the early twentieth century 'the annual cost of relieving paupers per head of population in Scotland was a full 50 per cent lower than in England.'[8] The Scottish Kirk was responsible for poor relief and firmly believed that people would not work if they were given money for nothing. They also believed the poor were generally responsible for their own predicament. This is why the Checklands write: 'In a sense it is fair to regard Scottish welfare provision in the nineteenth century as being, even more than that of the English, mean, grudging and censorious'.[9] This lack of entitlement to adequate poor relief in Scotland, during periods of unemployment or sickness, meant that workers felt very vulnerable. Many Scottish jobs were heavily dependent on world markets and so were precarious. So the prudent Scottish worker, forced to accept an annual lease on a tenement house, would play safe and commit himself and his family only to the most basic accommodation just in case he fell on bad times. As tenements were the principal type of housing in the urban areas, workers who did manage to accumulate some savings were less likely to become owner occupiers than their counterparts in England because tenements, involving a system of factors and common repairs, were not such attractive propositions for home ownership.

In 1917 the Government appointed a Royal Commission on Housing in Scotland which reported an 'almost unbelievable density'. The Commission pulled no punches: the free market and private landlords - many of them employers and churchmen - had completely failed to provide adequate housing for Scotland's working class. The Royal Commission believed a radical solution was necessary and proposed that 'the State must at once take steps to make good the housing shortage and to improve housing conditions, and that this can only be done by or through the machinery of the public authorities'.[10]

Over the following decades massive programmes of municipal housing took place in Scotland. Given the scale of the problem the provision of decent housing for everyone in Scotland was a huge task. Even in 1951, decades after the launch of countless slum clearance projects, 15.5 per cent of Scots lived in overcrowded accommodation compared with 2.1 per cent of English people. Nowadays, it is easy to look at some of the huge council schemes (or 'deserts wae windaes' to use Billy Connolly's phrase) that were created in places like Pilton, Craigmillar, Easterhouse or Drumchapel and ask why on earth they were ever built. But when you read about the scale of Scotland's housing problems over centuries it becomes clear that desperate solutions were needed. The tragedy is that within decades of these brave new council housing programmes, thousands of new Scottish slums had been created.

But to return to our quest to unearth the reasons why a strong Scottish spirit of enterprise did not survive the nineteenth century. From even a cursory inspection of Scottish housing and poor relief we can see that the Scottish working classes' experience in previous times bred two attitudes which do not help the creation of an enterprise culture. Trapped in atrocious living conditions where there was little prospect of improvement, the Scots often developed a strong dislike, hatred even, of an economic system whereby more fortunate individuals make money out of the less fortunate. The second attitude, which the experience of bad housing and meagre poor relief has bred, is an overwhelming desire for financial security and an unwillingness to take risks. A wrong decision could mean the difference between a life which, although poor and miserable, had some semblance of dignity and respectability, and the most wretched existence in an infamous slum.

In 2001 Thomas Stanley and William Danko published a booked called *The Millionaire Next Door* which examines the background of American millionaires and shows how, generations later, Scots still display this intense fear of falling on hard times. The authors' research shows that while people of Scots ancestry make up about 1.7 per cent of all US households, they account for 9.3 per cent of the millionaires. (Scots were three times more likely to be millionaires than those of English descent.)[11] However, Stanley and Danko also show that the Scots are the least entrepreneurial of all the successful ethnic groups and have usually accumulated money through saving and prudent investment. In other words, even centuries after the actual experience of life in poverty-stricken Scotland, Scots are often unprepared to take financial risks.

The Autocrats

The Scottish working classes' experience of private enterprise was not confined to housing; most worked in Scotland's industrial enterprises. Apart from the scandalous conditions which endured throughout the industrial world at that time - the employment of children, long working hours and the lack of basic health and safety measures, for example - Scottish workers had other reasons to feel aggrieved. In the late nineteenth century wages in Scotland were significantly lower than in England. Although they improved considerably in the early twentieth century, even as late as 1924 Scottish incomes were 8 per cent lower than in the rest of Britain. More important for our understanding of why the Scots were no great admirers of private enterprise, is the fact that many of Scotland's workers were employed in capital-intensive industries dominated largely by autocrats. Sydney and Olive Checkland argue that in the nineteenth century at least, these autocrats were very much moulded in the Presbyterian image:

They included such names as Colville, Baird, Yarrow, Tennant, Lorimer, Elder, Pearce, Neilson and Beardmore ... They were autocrats, their decisions were made, conveyed, and not discussed. They had a strong desire to keep everything in their own hands. A man like Beardmore, perhaps the greatest of them, took his own authority over the concern to be absolute and rightful: he and his peers were not given to self-doubt and self-questioning ... though the business might be slipping away or heading into a crisis, it would be a courageous junior who would raise his voice ... The magnates of the Scottish basic industries at the end of century may perhaps be taken as a distillation of the Victorian ethic. It centred upon the dominant male of middle age or over, brooking no interference, speaking only with his equals so far as there was any conferring at all, keeping under authority not only his labour force but also his wives and daughters. Even his sons could be kept under tutelage until old age or death broke the grip.[12]

Unsurprisingly, the Checklands argue that these men believed that workers were there just to obey orders - 'to be tell't'. In the mid nineteenth century there had been some consultation with the workers in Scottish enterprises but, according to the Checklands, this had disappeared by 1900 and they were given little information about the company. 'Labour had become in large measure merely a hired input', they write, 'with an underlying fear of dismissal'.[13] No wonder labour relations were terrible in many Scottish industries and that many became heavily unionised. So the owners of Scotland's great industries may have been grudgingly respected by fellow Scots but they were feared, intimidating demigods rather than attractive, enterprising role models.

An Alien Culture
In the Highlands too people continued to view capitalist business as alien. After the failure of the 1745 Jacobite rebellion the

Government in Westminster attempted to eradicate the threat posed by the Highlands by brutally eliminating its distinctive culture. Highland dress and music were proscribed. The speaking of Gaelic was forbidden. The authorities confiscated estates which had been held by Jacobite rebels and various schemes were introduced to stimulate the economy and introduce industry. The people were to be encouraged to be entrepreneurial and industrious. The Highland threat was reduced by such means but economic development did not happen in the way London envisaged. There were various reasons for this including lack of capital, the lack of a middle class and the sheer number of people, arguably the most entrepreneurial, who emigrated. But, according to Graham Watson, the bigger obstacle to business development was that Highland culture was based on kinship and communal values and stressed the importance of helping one another. It also frowned on risk-taking and encouraged conformity to group norms and so inhibited the development of entrepreneurship.[14]

For a variety of reasons then, many ordinary people in Scotland had very little reason to feel positive about capitalism. As realists, however, once they won the right to vote, many supported the Liberal or Conservative Parties, both of which espoused the virtues of capitalism. But, as Highlanders or members of the Scottish working class they often had very little reason to embrace the capitalist business ethic as their own. Of course, similar attitudes could be found in industrial areas of England, but the difference is that such anti-capitalist attitudes fitted more neatly with the Scots' view of the world. Throughout Scotland people held strong collectivist values and inevitably found it more difficult to embrace an economic system which resulted in a few becoming exceedingly rich while the vast majority lived in poverty. The Utopian nature of Scottish religious beliefs also predisposed the Scots to the idea that everyone should be working towards some kind of collective redemption.

So in Scotland, ordinary people who wanted their sons to get on encouraged them to acquire jobs as draughtsmen or clerks, for example. Indeed any 'collar and tie' job in a safe, secure establishment was respectable. Better still was going to university and then entering a profession such as teaching, medicine, law, accountancy or the ministry. For girls, an office job was respectable as was entry into an acknowledged female profession such as primary school teaching or nursing. And, judging from Scotland's low business birth rate, these attitudes are still very much in force.

The Influence of Thomas Chalmers

So much for the working classes. Let us move on to look at the attitude of the middle class and the Church to wealth creation. If you read about the early days of Scotland's industrial revolution it is easy to picture these entrepreneurs as men with a bible in one hand and a ledger in the other: men who saw no tension between the two sets of philosophies - God and Mammon. But by the nineteenth century the huge social costs of industrialisation in Scotland were so appalling they were impossible to ignore and the Kirk in Scotland became dominated by attempts to find solutions. One of the leading figures in this movement was Thomas Chalmers. He was an influential figure in nineteenth century Scotland and the fact that an estimated 100,000 people attended his funeral in Edinburgh in 1847 testifies to his importance and popularity. Chalmers was an evangelical within the Scottish Kirk and was particularly concerned about the spiritual and physical condition of Scotland's poor city-dwellers. He was a constitutional radical (and led the Great Disruption in the Church of Scotland) but his views were politically conservative:

> He stressed the correctness of the laws of political economy, the futility of trade unionism and democracy, the divine origins of a hierarchy where rich and poor had their obligations and their place, and the prime responsibility of the individual for his own material and spiritual health.[15]

Chalmers believed that the solution lay in creating a 'Godly commonwealth' made up of parish communities. Chalmers's views were complex. Although he believed that the poor were often responsible for their own suffering, and rejected the notion of compulsory poor relief and state intervention, he also believed passionately in community and that the rich had social obligations:

> The other part of his message, that the possession of wealth and power was ignoble without equivalent philanthropy and a sense of personal responsibility, was the inspiration to generations of soul-searching men to give generously of their money and time to the community. That Victorian Scotland was as world-famous for serious philanthropists - like William Collins of the temperance movement and William Quarrier of the children's homes - as it was for drunkenness and bad housing was due in no small degree to Thomas Chalmers.[16]

As a result of Chalmers's evangelical zeal, the nineteenth and early twentieth century in Scotland was a time of 'aggressive Christianity'. Sunday schools were set up and temperance societies and missions of all kinds appeared throughout Scotland. Chalmers himself attempted to show in a couple of experimental projects how the ethos of a rural parish could be transplanted to the city. One such experiment was in the Tron parish in Glasgow. Poor relief was suspended in the area and money was gathered from voluntary donations. Only the poor who passed a character test were awarded any monetary benefits. This and other similar projects initiated by Chalmers were finally judged to be failures. Quite simply the scale of Scotland's social problems was too huge for such palliative measures to have any real effect.

Professor Tom Devine argues that Chalmers's belief that poverty was the fault of the poor and their immoral ways held sway in the Scottish Kirk until the 1870s and only began to crumble in the last quarter of the nineteenth century as a result of the 'impact of intellectual and social forces in the secular world'.[17] Research and reports from social pioneers like Charles

Booth and Seebohm Rowntree showed how poverty was more the result of social factors than individual moral character. At the same time a more liberal theology was gaining ground within both the Church of Scotland and the Free Church. By the end of the nineteenth century the notion of 'the elect' had disappeared altogether from the beliefs they espoused. A number of ministers even began to adopt radical political views. Although members of the established Scottish Kirk varied enormously in their attitudes to trade unionism or Christian socialism, for example, it is fair to say that it was no longer intent on blaming the poor themselves for their misfortunes. By the same token, it also stopped portraying the rich as spiritually favoured. The rich were not often condemned as such - after all their money was needed by the Church itself - but those who had money were in a sense stripped of the Kirk's explicit blessing.

So it is not difficult to see why Scotland's middle classes increasingly preferred, and still prefer, their offspring to go into respectable and secure professional careers rather than get their hands morally dirty in real capitalist enterprise. Indeed, as it became abundantly clear in nineteenth-century Scotland that the country's growing wealth and economic success would not automatically, as many religious and Enlightenment figures once believed, raise the masses' living standards to tolerable levels, the enthusiasm of the Scottish middle and upper classes for the prevailing economic system appears to have weakened.

Throughout this book I have argued that Presbyterianism has had a huge impact on Scottish culture and character. I have also argued that Presbyterianism has both an individualistic strand - the individual's personal relationship with God - and a collectivist strand expressed in the idea that we are responsible to and for one another. But by the late nineteenth century, due to the ultimate failure of men like Thomas Chalmers to make a dent on Scotland's endemic social problems, the collectivist strand gained the upper hand in Scottish culture. The significance of this is best seen if we compare Scotland with the United States - a country which places a great emphasis on the individual.

America, America

In his book *American Exceptionalism,* Seymour Martin Lipset maintains that Americans see the world in substantially different ways from Europeans and that to understand this you have to understand the American creed. At the heart of this creed is a belief that the powers of the state should be curtailed and that state intervention should be kept to a minimum. In America, Protestant sects have had a huge impact on shaping the nation's mentality but their core beliefs are somewhat different from the original ideology which influenced Knox and his supporters. As the economic historian David Landes points out, it was later versions of the 'Protestant ethic which degenerated into a set of maxims for material success and smug, smarmy sermons on the virtues of wealth.'[18] Under the influence of such ideology, Americans believe that the moral person *should* work hard and strive to make money. Indeed survey evidence shows that 88 per cent of Americans say they admire people who have become rich through hard work.[19] For Americans, therefore, there is nothing contradictory in a religious person being rich.

America is the wealthiest country in the world but is also the country with some of the largest disparities in income. The very rich and the very poor do not quite live side by side (the rich ensure this is not the case as they often live in developments surrounded by security fences) but they inhabit the same cities, albeit on different sides of the track. To the European mind these huge inequalities are outrageous, particularly in a society which claims to be religious, but the American mind sees no contradictions. In fact many Americans would attribute the poverty that exists to government welfare programmes. A staggering 85 per cent of the American population believe that even in the land of minimal welfare provision and health care, 'Poor people have become too dependent on government assistance programs'.[20]

Lipset subtitles his book on American exceptionalism, 'a double edged sword', as he argues the country's ideology has both positive and negative aspects:

> ... it fosters a high sense of personal responsibility, independent initiative, and voluntarism even as it also encourages self-serving behaviour, atomism, and a disregard for the communal good. More specifically, its emphasis on individualism threatens traditional forms of community morality, and thus has historically promoted a particularly virulent strain of greedy behaviour.[21]

So Lipset associates with the American creed various unfortunate developments within that society - the high divorce rate, crime rate, drug taking and litigiousness. He does not mention, though it is obviously linked to the protection of individual rights, the gun culture and the deaths caused by firearms. America's reluctance to sign up to international protocols to limit global warming can also be seen as part of this individualistic philosophy.

We can also find an explanation for the high crime rate in the USA - a rate Lipset shows is three times higher than most other developed countries - in the emphasis American society places on personal success. Individuals are not simply encouraged to stand on their own two feet, they should also be 'winners'. 'The moral mandate to achieve success', argues the famous American sociologist Robert Merton, 'thus exerts pressure to succeed by fair means, if possible and by foul means if necessary'.[22] No doubt this is one of the reasons why there has also been such a prevalence in America of lawlessness, risky business ventures, 'rackets', bootlegging and so on, as people will take large risks or resort to illegal means if necessary to make money. In fact some American analysts believe this is the inevitable outcome of a society which places a high value on material success.

Scotland's Economic Salvation

I have devoted time to summarising some of the key aspects of American beliefs not because I think these are the attitudes we should import, but simply to show how different they are from the contemporary Scottish view of the world. Andrew Carnegie once famously proclaimed that 'the United States was Scotland realised beyond the seas'.[23] But he was mistaken. Even if Chalmers and the evangelicals had won the battle for Scotland's heart and mind in the nineteenth century the country was unlikely to have developed along American lines because the notion of community and the sense of being responsible for other people are deeply held Scottish values. Ultimately Scotland found the solution to her pressing social and economic problems in collectivism, not individualism and thus Scotland followed a decidedly un-American path.

By the mid to late nineteenth century, many of those who had wealth and power in Scottish society were increasingly won round to the importance of municipal or state action to solve mounting social problems. Even many of Scotland's great entrepreneurs became advocates of state planning and intervention. As many of the industries these men, or their families, had created were dependent on world markets and vulnerable to foreign competition, by the end of the nineteenth century much of Scotland's industry was built on an increasingly shaky foundation. A major problem was that Scotland was too dependent on heavy industry and had too few growth industries. Compared with England it also had too little indigenous demand for service jobs and consumer durables since wages had traditionally been lower in Scotland than England. This problem was exacerbated further by the fact that Scotland had a smaller professional or middle class as a result of centralisation of such jobs in the south of England. So by the early twentieth century it was clear that more economic diversity was needed in Scotland. In 1931 a group of leading industrialists, led by the influential Clyde shipbuilder Sir James Lithgow, set up a Development Council which aimed to attract new industries north of the border and counter Scotland's reputation for shop-floor militancy. But, partly as a result of the activities of Tom Johnston, the Labour MP who was Secretary of State in Churchill's coalition Government from 1941 to 1945, they soon became passionate corporatists. The Development Council quickly became a strong advocate of the kind of powerful central government planning of the economy that was to become such a feature of post-war Labour government strategy. Johnston then went on to create various organisations which finally became what is still known as the Scottish Council for Development and Industry (SCDI). Following its creation, post-war Scotland benefited from a number of significant inward investment projects from the rest of the UK and from the United States. By 1951, Ferranti, NCR, Honeywell and IBM had all set up in Scottish locations. Scotland also took state-led corporate planning to its heart with the Toothill Report on the Scottish Economy, the creation of the first new towns and the establishment of the Highlands and Islands Development Board. When the HIDB was launched in 1964 it was estimated that the SCDI had been instrumental in bringing more than 250,000 new jobs to Scotland.[24]

Private enterprise and the free market had, historically, failed the Scottish people. As is clear from looking at the west end of many of Scotland's towns and cities, some Scots became incredibly rich as a result of industrialisation but the vast majority lived mean, deprived lives in the midst of industrial squalor, yet often alongside wealth and grandeur. This is why Professor Smout says at the end of his book on Scotland from 1830 to 1950 that 'what was shocking to contemporaries, and is shocking to us, is how little one of the top two or three richest countries in the world did for its citizens until well into the twentieth century'.[25]

It was the machinery of state which did much to improve the lives of most ordinary Scots. It was the government or local councils which cleared the slums, built decent houses, introduced sickness benefits and old age pensions and provided free health care. It was the government which forced employers to operate within a regulatory framework which guaranteed fair treatment for workers. And it was also central government, through its regional policies, which managed to attract some foreign investment, and hence jobs, into Scotland from the 1950s on. The benefits of such policies were not just felt in the urbanised Lowlands but the Highlands and Islands as well. This is exactly the point James Hunter makes in his book *The Last of the Free* when he writes: ' ... to grow up in the Highlands and Islands in the 1950s and 1960s was to have access to opportunities of a sort never before on offer to the area's population.'[26]

The Makings of the Dependency Culture

The state certainly did much to improve life for thousands of ordinary Scots, but inevitably this approach also created many of the problems of contemporary Scotland. Just as Lipset refers to America's creed being a 'double edged sword', with positive and negative outcomes, the creed that Scotland adopted similarly has had good and bad effects. Government solutions did improve living conditions for many Scots but it ushered in a culture where decisions are made by committees of experts far removed from the lives of the people affected by them. In other words, it is a system completely at odds with the philosophy of self-help and self-determination advanced by socialist radicals of the past. For me one of the finest moments in Scottish history was when socialist radicals, like Jimmy Maxton, inspired poor working-class people to love learning and to hanker after a society which would create the circumstances which would allow them to maximise their potential. Nowadays people may be better housed, clothed and fed, but poverty still remains in whole tracts of Scotland. And the poverty I'm referring to is not just material deprivation but the lack of desire and ambition to make something of yourself and your life. As I demonstrated in Chapter 6, in Scotland the combination of strong collectivist values and the belief in egalitarianism (even though everyone does not start out in life equal) encourages people to know their place. It encourages us all to toe the line and conform. When we add to these attitudes the dependency which welfare policies and corporatism can encourage, it is easy to see why we have some significant economic problems in Scotland - low productivity, low business birth rate, and many impoverished communities where people seem to be devoid of motivation and ambition for themselves or their families. Often it is outsiders who are most able to pick up on attitudes which we take for granted so it is interesting to read what the New Zealand academic H. J. Hanham writes about this aspect of Scottish life in his book *Scottish Nationalism:*

The ordinary Scot since the 1930s has simply sat back and waited until the good things from the south have at least reached Scotland - new shops, new social security benefits, new industries, new towns. There has been a clamour when they have not come soon enough to please him. But there has been little disposition to do anything positive to help, or appreciation of the invaluable work done in Scotland by ... bodies devoted to the fostering of Scottish industry. The ordinary Scot has been prepared to accept that his more enterprising fellows will emigrate as a matter of course and that Scotland will become a pensioner dependent on England.[27]

The Safety Valve

Hanham is right to raise emigration in this context. One of the pressing questions which arises from the analysis which I have set out in this chapter is this: why did the Scots who once had the reputation for being a lively, active, intelligent and inventive people become subdued and somewhat dependant? And the answer lies partly in emigration, for it acted as a safety value, allowing those who were not prepared to accept the limited life on offer to escape. In *The Scottish Nation 1700-2000*, Professor Tom Devine explains that the period from 1821 to 1915 saw a huge amount of emigration from Europe, particularly to North America and Australasia. Throughout this period three countries topped the list for emigration - Norway, Scotland and Ireland. For most decades it was the Irish who came top but for four of the great surges of emigration (in the 1850s, 1870s, the early 1900s and the inter-war years) Scotland was the country producing most emigrants. Between 1841 and 1911 over 600,000 Scots emigrated to England, and Devine argues that if this migration is included in Scotland's figures 'Scotland then emerges clearly as the emigration capital of Europe for most of the period'.[28]

The Museum of Scotland houses a famous Scottish painting called *The Last of the Clans,* by Tom Faed. Painted in 1865 it depicts the tragic plight of Highlanders forced to pack up and leave their native land. But throughout the nineteenth century and into the twentieth many more Highlanders chose to leave than were actually forced to go. In the words of Marjorie Harper, a Scottish emigration specialist, 'the Highland diaspora ... owed as much to persuasion as persecution'.[29] In their introduction to *The New Penguin History of Scotland,* the editors argue that the enforced clearances of the Highlands have dominated the debate about emigration from the area. Effectively they argue that Highlanders were traumatised by the experience and that 'such bitter memories' have become 'embedded in its oral culture'. And they explain that a possible answer for such deeply held feelings may lie in the traditional Highland attitude to land:

> One answer may be the existence of a widely held belief that land was a communal entity within a moral economy ... Those doing the evicting were held to have a moral responsibility towards those under them, including obligations based on real or notional kinship. Associated with this is the fact that the Gaels were subject to a cultural displacement that was more severe than for Lowlanders, who were more used to cities and commercialism ... The dissolving forces of political and cultural change which ... turned landowners from chiefs into landlords during the eighteenth century had a profound impact on Gaelic society, also turning kinsmen into crofters.[30]

There are many reasons why emigrants choose to leave their homeland. Experts refer to them as the 'push/pull' factors. The Scots were, as we know from the clearances, often pushed by landlords who wanted to do something else with their estates. They were also pushed to leave Scotland by unemployment, poverty and atrocious living conditions. But often it was not those suffering the poorest conditions who left. Many emigrated because they were pulled by the opportunities and the possibilities of life in a new country. And this was true in the

Highlands and the Lowlands. In 1906 the Board of Agriculture, concerned about the declining rural population, reviewed the reasons and reported that particularly in Scotland 'many of the best men have been attracted to the colonies, where their energies may find wider scope and where the road to independence and a competency is broader and more easy to access'.[31]

Emigration siphoned off the Scots who wanted to make something different of their lives. It helped to remove those who were the most curious, the most opportunist, the most restless and the most ambitious. And the constant removal of people with such characteristics must have had a profound effect on Scottish culture and attitudes. This process is still at work in contemporary Scotland.

Some regard emigrants as Scotland's major export, but exports bring benefits to a country. In Scotland's case emigration was, and still is, a brain drain. It is a route out of Scotland for those who are not content with the limited world on offer to them or who simply want to leave Scotland's constricting attitudes so that they can spread their wings.

Scotland's Economic Choices

For centuries Scotland, unlike Soviet Russia, has always had a capitalist economic system yet I think it is fair to say that whole sections of the Scottish population have never made their peace with it. And given Scotland's history it is not difficult to see why. But this presents a huge challenge for all of us living in contemporary Scotland. From the days of Karl Marx right through to the fall of the Berlin Wall it was commonplace for socialists to believe that capitalism was only an economic phase which would finally come to an end as a result of internal conflicts and contradictions. But capitalism has been remarkably resilient and, if anything, seems stronger as it enters its global phase. What's more it is socialist regimes right round the world which have collapsed or had to reshape themselves. So no matter how much we may dislike the ethics of capitalism, its materialism or its environmental effects it is impossible to believe that it will not see us all out. We may dream of a society which is fairer and more equitable but we simply have no reason to believe, as Burns did, that 'it's coming yet for all that'.

As we enter the new millennium, Scots should realise that there are only three economic and cultural choices facing us as individuals. The first is to give full rein to our Utopian streak and say, uncompromisingly, that we do not want to play the capitalist game. If a person chooses this stance then he or she will salute Tommy Sheridan as a hero and may well cast their vote for the Scottish Socialist Party. If enough of us choose this route it will colour the Scottish debate about politics. But, since democracies rarely deliver enough power to a full-blooded socialist party for it to wrest the control necessary for effective socialist action, much of our energy will be diverted into talk about how things *might* be. In other words, taking this stance might increase the aspirations in Scotland for a fairer society but it will not deliver the fairness it seeks. The second choice is simply to continue with the type of policy which has dominated Scotland as a whole for decades. Effectively it means saying that for whatever reason - English domination, dislike of capitalism, lack of drive or imagination - the Scots are not able to deliver economically for themselves and so need to attract foreign companies into Scotland. In other words, taking this stance means seeing inward investment as our economic salvation. As we know to our cost, this strategy has many weaknesses. It means that the ownership and control of Scottish industry increasingly lie outwith Scotland. It means that Scottish jobs are still prey to the vicissitudes of international markets. It means many Scots working in foreign multinationals - the sector least likely to feel loyalty to a place or its workforce. And it also means that the jobs created are rarely high level research and development jobs but more basic production jobs which can disappear overnight with changes in technology. These are precisely the problems we have seen in the Scottish economy in the past decade as companies like Motorola, NEC, Compaq, Mitsubishi and Lite-on have either laid off workers or closed down their Scottish plants altogether.

The third stance an individual Scot can take is to accept that, like it or not, we all have to work within the current economic system and make the best of it. It means becoming genuinely enthusiastic about creating *Scottish* businesses. This way means trying to ensure more long-term commitment to Scottish jobs. And if Scots really are the compassionate, egalitarian people we like to think ourselves to be, then perhaps we can create businesses which manifest more integrity, principles and concern for all stakeholders and the environment than many multinationals do at present. Traditionally, Scotland's geography meant it was at a disadvantage economically because it was remote from many of her potential markets. The world of e-commerce, however, means that much of this disadvantage could be (and is already being) neutralised.

Indigenous business development has been part of the UK government's economic agenda since the 1970s, and the three main parties in Scotland support the idea in principle. Scottish Enterprise, through its Business Birth Rate Strategy, launched in 1994, has thrown millions of pounds of public money at the problem yet the figures have hardly budged. Not only has Scottish Enterprise achieved less than 10 per cent of the target for new business creation that it set itself, but between 1993 and 1999 the figure actually fell. Much of the difficulty the Scots have with setting up in business emanates from the type of personal issues I highlight in this book - a general lack of confidence, a fear of failure, a fear of success, an ambivalence about money, an over concern with others' views. But just as important is the fact that Scottish culture as a whole is ambivalent about wealth creation. This attitude has been there for over a century but sharpened in the 1980s as a result of Margaret Thatcher's occupation of Number 10 Downing Street. Many Scots have simply taken the view that being Scottish means playing down the importance of money-making and a pro-business agenda.

If we want to change Scottish culture to make it more positive about wealth creation we must separate it from an excessively Thatcherite ideology which encourages greed and argues that there is no such thing as society. We must also refuse to accept that being more positive about wealth creation means embracing and importing American ideology and values. We have to find our own way - a way that removes the specific Scottish blockages to entrepreneurship and business development; a way that respects, not negates or denies, Scottish history and culture. If we want to study cultures where a spirit of entrepreneurship has developed we should look to Australia and New Zealand, both of which have highly entrepreneurial cultures - and significant numbers of Scots.

One of the best actions that Scottish agencies could take to stimulate more interest in business development is to promote business not just as something which you can do to improve your own life but as something which has positive social benefits for the community. Building a business creates jobs. Spending money also creates jobs and puts money in other people's pockets. Making money also gives people the opportunity to spend some of it for the collective good. Indeed there are many cases of Scottish entrepreneurs who have made substantial sums of money and then spent much of it on a variety of charitable or educational programmes. These initiatives need to be more widely known. The more difficult part will be emphasising the importance of entrepreneurship and the collective good while at the same time trying to free up individuals so that they feel enabled to be more creative and independent; less worried about what other people think of them and whether they are going to fail.

Given Scotland's history I believe we can only become more entrepreneurial if we do not become too ideological about it. We must not demonise the public sector or continually portray private enterprise as consistently better when this is not the case. But neither should we automatically assume that public is always better than private. We must also show that it is possible to have more positive views of entrepreneurship and still be in favour of public spending and a fairer distribution of wealth. I also think it is a mistake to argue that Scotland will only become more entrepreneurial if the country embarks on substantial deregulation or becomes a giant freeport. As Tom Hunter points out, entrepreneurs do not decide to set up in business because the tax rate is favourable, they do so because they feel inspired and motivated. And such feelings are largely encouraged by an individual's prevailing environment. It is this that we have to change if we want Scotland to have a more enterprising culture - a culture where we cherish our own dreams rather than wish the demise of our neighbour's goat.

NOTES

1 David Landes, *The Wealth and Poverty of Nations* (Abacus: London, 1999), p. 518.

2 Dr Jonathon Levie and Dr Laura Steele, *Global Economic Monitor, Scotland 2000,* University of Strathclyde.

3 Tom Hunter in Dr Jonathon Levie and Dr Laura Steele, *Global Economic Monitor, Scotland 2001,* University of Strathclyde, p. 3. For further information on Scotland's low business birth rate see 'Promoting Business Start-ups: A New Strategic Formula', Fraser of Allander Institute, University of Strathclyde, June 2001.

4 Arthur Herman, *The Scottish Enlightenment: The Scots' Invention of the Modern World* (Fourth Estate: London, 2002), p. 349.

5 For a history of the Tennant family see Simon Blow, *Broken Blood* (Faber and Faber: London, 1987).

6 Arthur Herman, *The Scottish Enlightenment,* p. 353.

7 Quoted in T. M. Devine, *The Scottish Nation 1700-2000* (Penguin Books: London, 1999), p. 334.

8 T. M. Devine, *The Scottish Nation,* p. 343.

9 Sydney & Olive Checkland, *Industry and Ethos: Scotland 1832-1914* (Edward Arnold: London, 1984), p. 99.

10 Quoted in T. M. Devine, *The Scottish Nation,* p. 346.

11 Thomas Stanley and William Sanko, *The Millionaire Next Door* (Simon and Schuster: USA, 2000).

12 Sydney & Olive Checkland, *Industry and Ethos: Scotland 1832-1914* (Edward Arnold: London, 1984), p. 178..

13 Ibid., p. 178.

14 Graham Watson '"Nothing New Under the Sun": Are there Lessons to be Learned Today from Government Support for Businesses in the Highlands after the Uprising of 1745?', M.Sc. Thesis in Entrepreneurial Studies, University of Stirling, 1993.

15 T. C. Smout, *A History of the Scottish People* 1560-1830 (Collins: London, 1969), p. 186.

16 Ibid., p. 186.

17 T. M. Devine, *The Scottish Nation,* p. 380.

18 David Landes, *The Wealth and Poverty of Nations,* p. 176.

19 Seymour Martin Lipset, *American Exceptionalism: A Double-edged Sword* (W. W. Norton & Company: London, 1997).

20 Ibid., p. 287.

21 Ibid., p. 268.

22 Quoted in Seymour Martin Lipset, *American Exceptionalism,* p. 47.

23 Quoted in Arthur Herman, *The Scottish Enlightenment*, p. 328.

24 For further information see Alf Young, 'The Scottish Establishment: Old and New Elites' in Gerry Hassan and Chris Warhurst (eds.), *Tomorrow's Scotland* (Lawrence and Wishart: London 2002), pp. 157-9.

25 T. C. Smout, *A Century of the Scottish People* 1830-1950 (Collins: London, 1986), p. 275.

26 James Hunter, Last of the Free: *A Millennial History of the Highlands and Islands of Scotland* (Mainstream Publishing: Edinburgh, 1999), p. 347.

27 H. J. Hanham, *Scottish Nationalism* (Faber and Faber: London, 1969), p. 47.

28 T. M. Devine, *The Scottish Nation*, p. 468.

29 Marjorie Harper in Michael Lynch, *The Oxford Companion to Scottish History* (Oxford University Press: Oxford, 2001), p. 232.

30 R. A. Houston & W. W. J. Knox, *The New Penguin History of Scotland: From the Earliest Times to the Present Day* (Penguin Books Ltd: London, 2001), p. xxxiii.

31 Quoted in T. M. Devine, *The Scottish Nation*, p. 484.

SECTION IV

SCOTTISH IDENTITY

12

Complex Inferiority

'What is Scotland? A nation, a province, a lost kingdom; a culture, a history, a body of tradition; a bundle of sentiments, a state of mind; North Britain or Caledonia? Such are the questions which Scots have been asking themselves, implicitly or openly, ever since 1707 ...'

Janet Adam Smith is right to point out how since the Union of the Parliaments the Scots have been obsessed by issues of Scottishness and Scottish identity.[1] Over the years, countless Scottish writers have prodded the subject with their pens to check that it is still breathing; many have pronounced that Scotland and her people are not in good health. G. M. Thomson in his 1920s book, *Caledonia,* asserted that 'the Scots are a dying people'.[2] George Scott Moncrieff described Edinburgh as 'dead' and the whole of Scotland as 'an abortive carcass rotting somewhere to the North of England.'[3] Edwin Muir's journey round Scotland in the mid 1930s convinced him that although 'Scotland has not been a nation for some time, it has possessed a distinctly marked style of life; and that is now falling to pieces, for there is no visible and effective power to hold it together.' [4] And a decade or so before devolution, the nationalist writer P.H. Scott warned that various developments 'threaten the survival of the national identity'.[5] In recent times Cairns Craig has argued that 'Scottish culture has ... always lived under the shadow of its possible annihilation.'[6]

In Chapter 2 I showed how cultural analysts in Scotland often portray Scottish identity and consciousness itself as problematic. The Scottish literary expert, Douglas Gifford, even writes about 'the schizophrenic Act of Union in 1707' and claims it 'contained the seeds of Scotland's nineteenth-century crises of identity'.[7] But while literary specialists and political theorists such as Tom Nairn may claim that in the past there was something double and divided about the Scots' sense of themselves, historians are much more circumspect. In *The New*

Penguin History of Scotland, for example, Graeme Morton and R. J. Morris argue that in the nineteenth century 'Scotland had a remarkably confident national identity'[8] - that just as Scots today can have complex political identities, combining a sense of Britishness with Scottishness, so too did our forebears. In short, these historians believe there was nothing strange or pathological about the Scots' sense of themselves in the nineteenth century.

Over the years the Scots have fretted about the health of Scotland and Scottish identity yet, paradoxically, a sense of Scottishness has been robust and fairly impervious to Anglicisation. Even when the Empire and feelings of Britishness were at their height Scottish identity was strong enough to see off the nineteenth-century attempt for Scotland to become simply 'North Britain'. And in the twentieth century it was in such good health it became an effective springboard for varying degrees of political nationalism. The rise of the SNP and the popularity of various devolution campaigns would not have been possible without a strong Scottish identity. Now a Scottish Parliament once again sits in Edinburgh, after almost three hundred years of suspension, and survey evidence shows that a growing number of Scots say they feel much more Scottish than British. Brown, McCrone and Paterson in *Politics and Society in Scotland* show how, since survey data became available in 1986, 'it is clear that people living in Scotland give priority to being Scottish' rather than British. Indeed they add 'between six and nine times more people stress their Scottishness than their Britishness. This is a remarkable and consistent finding.'[9] It is impossible to read the recent volume *Being Scottish* and not be struck by how strongly Scottish most of the contributors feel. Indeed a few remark that it is so much part of them it is difficult to analyse. 'For the most part being Scottish', writes Ruth Wishart, 'is a garment you never shed to examine the fabric, design or texture. You wear it like the second skin it is'.[10]

So why has Scottish identity been so resilient? I believe there are four simple explanations.

A Negatively Defined Identity

First, Scottish identity is so strong because it can be reduced to a few simple words - *The Scots are not English*. Few countries can distil their identity into a soundbite and, like it or not, in the modern world soundbites are often more powerful than complex, sophisticated arguments. So the simple fact of not being English has afforded the Scots a strong, albeit negatively defined, identity. Many Scots analysts and commentators remark on this feature of Scots identity but they usually label it as wholly negative - a sign of rampant insecurity which gives rise to petty anti-English feeling. There is little doubt that the Scots' negatively defined identity displays itself in all sorts of unwanted ways and is a manifestation of a previous power battle which Scotland lost. But despite its weaknesses it has considerable strengths; it has been a constant star in the Scottish firmament. No matter what happens it is still there. And the very fact that it is always there has helped the Scots resist some of the pressures of continual Anglicisation and assimilation, and ensured the continuation of a strong Scottish sense of self. So if we are trying to chart why *Scottish* identity since 1707 has been robust and resilient, the sense of 'not being English' is our first port of call.

Distinctive Scottish Institutions

The second reason why Scottish identity has remained so strong following the Union is the terms of the Act of Union itself. There was no popular will in favour of the Union and rioting broke out in the streets in the days leading up to it. As there was no stomach in Scotland for an incorporating Union with England, the Scottish Parliament, thanks to the tenacity of men like Andrew Fletcher of Saltoun, did its best to ensure that Scottish identity and institutions would survive the union of the parliaments. So Scotland lost political sovereignty in 1707 but retained her separate Church, legal system and schools. Religion had played an important part in the formation of Scottishness as we know it and the Church's continuing influence was not threatened by the Union. What's more the Act allowed the Scots to administer and determine policy in education and poor relief - services which had most impact on the lives of ordinary people in the days and centuries which followed.

So the Scots may have been bribed and browbeaten into the Union but they still managed to secure terms that permitted a distinctive sense of Scottishness to remain following the joining of the parliaments.

A Storehouse of National Symbols

A third explanation for the resilience of Scottish identity is the wealth of Scottish 'iconography'. National identity is inevitably abstract and difficult to define. So a country's identity must not only be able to persist over time it must also be capable of transmission from one generation to the next. This means it needs to attach itself to easily understood symbols or icons. As various commentators, such as David McCrone, have pointed out, Scotland is knee-deep in national symbolism:

> ... if anything, it is overwhelming. It appears in films, novels, poems, paintings, photographs, as well as on shortbread tins.
> ...tartan; kilts; heather; haggis; misty landscapes; couthy (and slightly weird) natives; Jekyll and Hyde; Scottish soldiers; Take the High Road; MQS (Mary Queen of Scots); BPS (Bonnie Prince Charlie); Balmorality; Harry Lauder ...[11]

Not only are these symbols strong and enduring they are quite different from the symbols associated with England. For example, among the English symbols Paxman lists in his book on England are 'village cricket and Elgar, Do-It-Yourself, punk, street fashion, irony, vigorous politics, brass bands, Shakespeare, Cumberland sausages, double-decker buses, Vaughan Williams, Donne and Dickens, twitching net curtains ...'[12] And so the list goes on. A lot of the items on Paxman's list, like 'fish and chips, curry and bad hotels' apply to the whole United Kingdom not just England. And many of them are not that distinct. None of these symbols has the immediately recognisable quality of tartan or pipe bands, for example. This is why Charles Jennings writes: 'Englishness, unlike Scottishness, is baffling, diffuse.' And a few sentences on he asks: 'What common culture do we, the English, hold dear?'[13]

A striking feature of any list of Scottish icons is that it is dominated by Highland symbolism. There's little doubt that Scotland's fascination with tartan is attributable to Sir Walter Scott. He was made a Baronet in 1820 and two years later was responsible for stage managing George IV's state visit to Scotland in which the king wore a kilt (and pink tights) and the entourage were similarly decked out in tartan. The Westminster Government banned the wearing of Highland dress in 1747 and it is Scott who was responsible for its reappearance as elite costume. And this was just the beginning of royalty's love affair with the Highlands. Queen Victoria bought the Balmoral estate in 1848, opening yet another Scottish tourist trail. So for all these reasons Scott is credited with, or more accurately blamed for, giving Scotland an anachronistic and bogus national identity. Thanks to him, and James Macpherson of Ossian fame, Lowland Scotland literally stole the clothes off Highlanders they had previously despised. As we have already seen in Chapter 2 the Scottish literati's condemnation of tartanry and use of Highland symbolism has fuelled a great deal of negative comment on Scotland and the Scots yet as the celebrated historian William Ferguson points out:

> In the ethnic or cultural sense the words Highland and Lowland now have little relevance. Most Scots of the old ethnic stock nowadays are of mixed Lowland and Highland forebears - and the word 'most' here is used advisedly. This can be proved by a glance at the telephone directory of any major urban community in Scotland. There will be found a plethora of Highland names, in Glasgow or Edinburgh, Aberdeen or Dundee. Where have all those Gaelic names come from ...?[14]

Whatever view you take on the appropriateness of Scottish iconography one thing is clear - it has made a huge contribution to the continuation and strength of Scottish identity.

Scottish Beliefs and Preferences

Our fourth port of call in this quest for the strength of Scottish identity is that many Scots feel that the mindset they are encouraged to adopt is distinctly different from their neighbours'. This comes over clearly in *Being Scottish*. Sheila Brock, for example, writes that being Scottish is not about a 'genetic imprint' it is 'more a way of thinking, an acquired culture ... a vocabulary, an attitude ... '[15] Ruth Wishart even argues that 'the notion of thinking as if I were English would seem to require a head transplant, or, at best, some form of precision lobotomy'.[16]

However, as I argued earlier, most Scots are not aware of the forces in Scottish culture which shape their mindset. Sheila Brock simply attributes Scottish thinking to 'cold winds and midges'. Ruth Wishart does not even venture an explanation for differences in Scottish and English thinking styles. In Sections I and III of this book, I have tried to explain the forces in Scottish life which shape a distinctively Scottish mindset and for brevity I have summarised the main points in Table 1 below. For comparison, the table includes a similar list for England. In reading this table it is important to bear in mind that this summary is trying to capture the essence or spirit of Scotland and England. Of course, it does not describe every individual in each country. So it should read as the characteristics and values which the culture of each country encourages.

Over the years some of these Scottish characteristics have been watered down as a result of pressure from England. This is most true of Scotland's desire for generalism in education and the love of speculation and reasoning from first principles. These were features of Scotland's traditional approach to education but in the nineteenth and early twentieth centuries Scottish universities were forced to model themselves along English lines. But it is also true that English culture has been moderated as a result of Scottish preferences. It is impossible to read the history of Britain in the nineteenth and twentieth centuries and not be struck by how often it was the Scots who provided progressive thinking within the United Kingdom. In the nineteenth century much of the progressive thought behind the Liberal Party and the ruling class's openness to demands for the extension of the suffrage came from Scots such as Lord Brougham and Lord Macaulay within the Westminster Parliament.[17] The Labour movement too was heavily influenced by Scots like Keir Hardie or John Maxton who were animated by their Presbyterian background. Even the contemporary Labour Government has a number of Scots in key Cabinet positions and Tony Blair himself has been strongly moulded by Scottish preferences and beliefs. Blair's father was Scottish and Tony Blair was educated at Fettes, a public school in Edinburgh.

Table 1 Comparison of Scottish and English cultures

Scotland	England
Active, energetic	Reflective
Outward looking	Insular
Emphasis on speech (even in literature)	Love of the written word
Sociable	Private - emphasis on 'home'
Collectivist	Individualistic
Group rights (e.g. focus on Scottish freedom)	Individual rights (e.g. against the state)
Belief that what a person does affects others	Emphasis on the importance of privacy ('an Englishman's home is his castle')
Preference for generalism in education; breadth	Emphasis on specialism in education; depth
Principles	Pragmatism
Opinionated, passionate, committed	Open-minded
Judgemental (pronounced sense of right and wrong)	Tolerant; live and let live
Drawn to abstract thought and ideas	Prefers concrete information and facts
Speculative	Cautious, guided by experience

Table 1 Comparison of Scottish and English cultures contd.

Scotland	England
Forward looking	Backward looking
Drawn to vision and possibilities	Traditional
Initiate change or are at least open to the idea of change if it seems logical	Conservative; hark back to the past
Motivated by Utopian dream of collective redemption for all Scots - a perfect community	Dream of 'privacy without loneliness'; drawn to a green, isolated landscape
Emphasis on individual mission to improve the world for others	It is up to the individual to choose his or her own life
Emphasis on plainness and simplicity	'Manners maketh the man'; like refinement
Equality important	Fair play important
No disgrace to be born poor	Snobbery
Prone to sentimentality	Prone to cultivate cranks and eccentrics
Sense of under confidence and seesawing from feelings of inferiority to superiority	Sense of superiority

So even though Scotland lost her sovereign parliament, her distinctive language and many traditional ways of life, her strong preferences and unifying belief system means that the Scots have retained to this day a distinctive set of attitudes and beliefs. In other words, despite all the fears of Scottish soothe-sayers, who have predicted the demise of Scotland as a separate cultural entity over the years, Scottish identity, consciousness and preferences have more than just survived. They have remained remarkably strong and resilient. And I think it speaks volumes for Scottish tenacity and strength of character that it has endured in the way it has. As the historian J. M. Reid once remarked: 'For centuries the Scots had to fight bitterly and almost continuously for the mere chance to remain Scottish'. Reid is also right to say that as the Scots 'were poor, few and remote from the great centres of European life' they have every right to feel proud that 'in spite of everything, they had contrived to remain themselves.'[18]

Complex Inferiority

My argument that Scottish identity has always been robust despite the fear that it would fade away is not the same as arguing that Scotland's relationship with England has not been psychologically damaging for the Scots. The relationship has undermined Scottish confidence and self-esteem and the problem may well have predated the Union. The American historian Wallace Notestein, in his book *The Scot in History - a Study of the Interplay of Character and History*, argues that early records show the Scots were well known to be 'proud' and 'boastful' and that these traits seemed due in part to their insecurity. Notestein writes:

> The sensitiveness of the Scots to what was said about them was not unrelated to their habit of boasting about themselves. The chronicles furnish abundant proof that the Scots were peculiarly sensitive to what the English thought about them and any criticism of their courage or military prowess met with instant notice and reply.[19]

In other words, the Scots may well have had a hang up about the English long before the Union. So what is this 'sensitivity' or lack of confidence all about? There are various ways to characterise and analyse the relationship between Scotland and England. We could liken the two countries to siblings and look at the rivalry between them and its psychological effects on the junior partner. We could follow the example of Beveridge and Turnbull and show how the Scots were repeatedly told they had been civilised by the Union and so developed an 'inferiorist' mentality similar to that of colonial peoples. But the conceptual tool which I think best helps us to understand the psychological relationship between Scotland and England can be found in the famous work of the great French intellectual, Simone de Beauvoir - *The Second Sex.*

De Beauvoir's Concept of 'The Other'

De Beauvoir argues that in the natural relationship between two human beings both see themselves as sovereign beings - the One

- and they define the other as just that - 'the Other'. This 'fundamental hostility' between individuals and groups is not usually a problem as the Other 'sets up a reciprocal claim'.[20] Foreigners abroad, for example, view the inhabitants as 'Others' but they must come to see that they too are defined as abnormal and alien. For de Beauvoir the tragedy of woman's experience is that historically she has given up her own claims to sovereignty and accepted man's definition of her as the 'inessential Other'. Man is the neutral sex - the norm - whereas woman is defined with reference to him. This notion helps us to understand that while there are countless books on women's condition, men do not need to write specific books on their experience or interests as they constitute the 'mainstream'. It is the so-called 'ordinary' books on history, philosophy, religion, literature and so on which represent men's perspective on the world. Unconvinced? Then how about the fact that in the English language the word 'man' is used interchangeably to mean homo sapiens and to describe an individual male. Many men fail to understand why modern women can make an issue of nomenclature, and seem blissfully unaware that language is symbolically important as it underscores women's marginality from 'mainstream' culture - from the norm.

Table 2 Comparison of women's and the Scots' view of themselves and reactions to their inferior position

WOMEN	SCOTS
Women perceive themselves as different from men.	The Scots perceive themselves as different from 'the English'.
Women know they are judged by men as 'inferior' both because they are the 'Other' - a marginal afterthought - and because men have power over them (money, status, legal rights).	The Scots fear they are seen as inferior because the English - as the larger, stronger, richer partner - use their experience and views to define, for example, a good education, good manners, proper pronunciation. Also the English have more political and economic power.

Table 2 Comparison of women's and the Scots' view of themselves and reactions to their inferior position contd.

WOMEN	SCOTS
Women feel themselves to be inferior (because they are socialised in a society which accepts male dominance) and therefore they lack self-confidence.	Scots believe that Scotland was a barbaric, uncivilised place before the Union. They feel they couldn't do without the English to keep them civilised and well-governed. They may talk confidently (Wha's like us?) but secretly fret about being inferior.
Women may begin to resent the way their marginalisation is symbolised in language so they become hypersensitive to terms such as 'chairman'.	The Scots become very touchy about the use of language. They write letters to the BBC's *Points of View* programme about sports commentators' use of British and English.
As women's consciousness of subordination grows, men are often portrayed as inferior or inadequate in some way. Gross generalisations abound (e.g. 'all men are bastards').	The Scots often stereotype the English as arrogant people who talk loudly in restaurants. They tend to blame the English and their own lack of political power for anything which goes wrong.
As women's collective confidence grows and they become more financially independent of men, what would be denounced as 'sexism' in the past sometimes gets ignored or is deemed irrelevant.	As the Scots' confidence grows and they have their own parliament, and so more ability to control their own affairs, there is less reason to pay attention to the English let alone blame them for all their ills.
The increasing empowerment of women leads men to question the meaning of masculinity. Males begin to suffer an identity crisis. They start to write books on the topic.	As the Scots, and others, grow in confidence and in power, the English start to worry about their identity. Jeremy Paxman and others write books on the subject.

For brevity, I have charted the parallels between women's growing consciousness and Scots consciousness in the accompanying table. As you will see, women's experience of marginalisation is similar to the daily experience of many Scots.

This helps to explain the Scots' great sensitivity about terminology on the BBC or other English-dominated media. When 'England' is used instead of 'Britain' many Scots intuitively know it symbolises Scotland's marginal status; her role as 'inessential Other'. Their sensitivity on such apparently trivial issues can then make Scots look like paranoid, nit pickers - even to fellow Scots. Giles Gordon, for example, wearily asks:

> Why should the Scots ego be so vulnerable that whenever some British (sorry, English) journalist writes 'English' when he means 'British' we all know that a subsequent issue of the paper will contain a snide, facetious little letter pointing out that the problem with England is that it thinks Scotland a part of it.[21]

Isobel Lindsay illustrates the way Scots culture is marginalised in other ways. She writes that 'the Scots as a nation', both middle and working class, 'have experienced something akin to what the lower classes experience as a sub-group in the larger society. Our language or dialect was rejected as inferior and the centres of power and influence increasingly moved outwith the country.'[22] Following the Union, the definition of good manners, pronunciation and correct usage of the English language emanating from the English ruling class led the Scots to question their speech and manners. No doubt the lure of English patronage ensured that many an ambitious Scot paid attention to what the English defined as 'proper speech'. This comes across clearly in accounts of the Scottish Enlightenment when even these intellectual giants, in the wake of criticism from the South, were embarrassed by their Scottishness and became obsessed by expunging 'Scotticisms' from their speech and writing. Many even participated in elocution lessons run by the poet James Beattie. David Hume's lack of confidence in his native language led one wag to remark that the atheist Hume 'died confessing, not his sins, but his Scotticisms'. Hume himself wrote:

> Is it not strange that, at a time when we have lost our
> Princes, our Parliaments, our independent
> Government, even the Presence of our chief Nobility,
> are unhappy, in our Accent & Pronunciation, speak
> a very corrupt Dialect of the Tongue which we make
> use of; is it not strange, I say, that, in these
> Circumstances we shou'd really be the People most
> distinguish'd for Literature in Europe? [23]

As the stronger and more dominant partner in the Union, the English were able to arrogate to themselves the notion that they were right - the defining point, the barometer - and were able to judge anything different from them as inferior. Even Sir Walter Scott, a committed Unionist, believed this to be the case. 'The English act on the principle that everything English is right', he wrote, 'and that anything in Scotland which is not English must therefore be wrong'.[24] A sentiment echoed centuries later when the former Historiographer Royal in Scotland, Gordon Donaldson, claimed that 'in English eyes anything that is not English is peculiar; worse than that, it is backward if not actually barbarous'.[25]

De Beauvoir's theory, like that of the great German philosopher Hegel, on which it is based, is founded on the notion that rightness and selfhood are at the heart of any notion of sovereignty and that this plays its part in the relationship between two individuals (the master and slave, for example) and in the relationship between groups or nations. According to this theory, there is nothing unusual in the English defining themselves as the One, the norm, for that is the nature of sovereignty. The tragedy for Scotland is that, for both physical and economic reasons the English were able to impose their sense of superiority on 'the Other'.

The Relationship with England

So the sense of being if not exactly 'wrong', then 'not right' - a marginal Other - is, I believe, a key aspect of Scottish consciousness and it has been around for a long time. I am not arguing that the Scots over the generations have simply accepted the superiority of the English or their status as inferior, wrong 'Other'. If you read Scotland's history after 1707 it is clear that sometimes it suited the Scots to play second fiddle to England's 'superior' performance. And if that meant accepting the 'rightness' of the English approach, or emulating what Scots have sometimes described as their 'more mature' neighbour, then so be it. On other occasions the Scots have balked at the very idea of playing second fiddle and have been fiercely opposed to their own distinctly Scottish tunes being drowned out by English ways. Indeed there have been times when the Scots believed that if they took up the inferior fiddle and played England's tune, Scottish identity itself may disappear.

The historian N. T. Phillipson has shown how throughout the eighteenth and nineteenth centuries the Scots vacillated in their attitude to assimilation and subordination. In the nineteenth century the Scots demonstrated most opposition to assimilation when the English attempted to abolish small Scottish banknotes in 1826. And it was during the time of this perceived threat to Scottish identity that Sir Walter Scott, a great believer in the benefits of the Union, took up his pen and lambasted the English for always thinking they were right. Phillipson argues that this is an important incident in Scottish history as it highlighted an on-going dilemma for Scots: how to maintain a Union which did 'boast advantages', while asserting their independent identity as Scots. Phillipson argues that they needed 'a passive ideology' and the formula was provided by Sir Walter Scott himself. He claims that Scott:

> ... showed Scotsmen how to express their nationalism by focusing their confused national emotions upon inessentials, like the few sinecures and offices of state ... like the use of the word 'Scotch', the phrase 'north Britain', or the present queen's monogram on letterboxes; like the campaign to prevent the disbanding of the Argylls. By validating the making of a fuss about nothing, Scott gave to middle class Scotsmen and to Scottish nationalism an ideology - an ideology of noisy inaction.[26]

But this is much too rational and mechanistic an argument for the Scots' sensitivity to so-called 'inessentials'. Life is not as simple as Nick Phillipson makes out. A few letters, a persuasive argument and the viewpoint and activities of a nation are cast for centuries to come? - I think not. Phillipson's notion takes little account of how people's identity is formed or maintained, whereas the idea of the Scot as marginal Other leads to a much fuller, more human, understanding of the importance of these types of symbolic issues and the protests which ensued. The Scots did not need to be taught the importance of symbolism by Sir Walter Scott; they would have felt sensitive to marginalisation anyway because they were able to decode the significance of this symbolism and to see how it posed a *real* long-term threat to Scottish identity and self-esteem. Indeed some of the things which Phillipson cites as 'inessentials' are very pertinent. As any psychologist will tell you, what we call ourselves, and what names others use to refer to us, are major elements in our identity and sense of self. Using the term 'North Britain' instead of Scotland is a denial of the Scots' history and sense of distinctive culture. No wonder most objected and the term gradually disappeared from view - living on for many years only on hotel fronts.

Phillipson may dismiss such protests as 'noisy inaction' but, as Lindsay Paterson points out, they were often successful. England did withdraw her proposal to abolish Scottish banknotes and the same formula worked on other occasions for the Scots. Paterson writes:

> ... the English had no particular interest in imposing on Scotland ... The worst that could be said was usually that the English acted in ignorance of Scotland and were willing to rescind a policy only when the Scots complained loudly enough and with enough of a consensus.[27]

In truth, England has always featured heavily in Scottish identity. Pre-Union the dominance of England, and the threat she posed to Scotland, affected how Scotland behaved. William

Ferguson asserts, for example, that even in medieval times Scottish historians attempted to give weight to the distinctiveness of the Scottish Church to create a 'bulwark' against York and Canterbury's 'jurisdictional claims' over the Church in Scotland.[28] Post-Union, Scotland's relationship with England, and the Scots' views of the English, have been complex and have varied enormously. Sometimes the Scottish elite and the Scottish people as a whole have believed they were working in partnership with the English - a feeling which guaranteed the Scots were energetic partners in the building of the British Empire or in fighting alongside the English in battle. In the nineteenth century there were even those, such as the great literary figure, Thomas Carlyle, who strongly supported the idea of Scotland simply becoming North Britain. But they were in the minority and by the mid twentieth century it was evident that British identity had weakened with the loss of Empire and the decades of peace.[29]

Even when the Scots feel most in step with England, and in partnership with them, they still succumb from time to time to paranoia, imagining all kinds of slights and plots where all that may really exist is English insensitivity or even indifference. In this mode the Scots can become bitterly anti-English. But on occasions these negative views are justified as England is indeed seeking to encroach on Scotland's jealously guarded territory. Margaret Thatcher's poll tax was just such an encroachment. But it is also possible to move to the opposite end of the spectrum and see that there are occasions when the Scots believe that the English are in some ways superior. However, this is not a position which any self-respecting Scot can hold for long and so there is a tendency to seesaw back and forth between dislike and admiration for England and her ways.

So the Scots' views of England and the English are complex and vary enormously. The range of views testifies to one important fact about the Scots - England matters very much to them. Yet Scotland barely registers on the English horizon. A fact that prompted Alastair Reid to observe that 'of all the grievances nursed by the Scots, none is greater than the fact that the English apparently do not bother to hate back.'[30]

Many commentators on Scotland simply blame the English for the Scots' lack of self-confidence. 'It was towards the middle of the eighteenth century that the intrepid Englishman discovered Scotland', writes George Scott Moncrieff. 'He found a great deal for horror, ridicule, and pious defamation, and succeeded in leaving Scotland with an inferiority complex to this day.'[31] It is not uncommon for Scots to attribute any Scottish problem you can name to 'the auld enemy'. If anything, the 'blame the English' mentality in Scotland has grown in recent years and is becoming irritating even to committed Scottish nationalists. They see the Scots' attempt to attribute everything they do not like about Scotland to the Union with England as part of the problem which must be solved. In other words, such nationalists know that blaming the English is a manifestation of Scotland's political and cultural immaturity and must stop if the Scots are to build their confidence and start solving the myriad of problems they face. That's why Andrew Wilson, the SNP Economy Spokesman, bravely urged Scots to stop hating and blaming the English and even urged Scots football fans to support England in the World Cup. This plea was treated with derision by many Scots and one of the leaders of the Tartan Army went so far as to claim that 'the Scots' hatred' of the English was 'genetic'.

I have argued in this chapter that there are various reasons why the Scots' relationship with England undermined, and continues to undermine, Scottish self-esteem and confidence. However, it is mistaken to believe that the Union and the relationship with England is the sole cause of Scotland's feelings of inferiority. Indeed rather than seeing Scotland as a country with an inferiority complex it is better to see Scotland as suffering from *complex inferiority*. In other words, the reasons for the Scots' lack of confidence are many and varied. Politics is one important strand in this confidence crisis but it is interwoven with many other threads. Throughout this book I have tried to unravel the reasons for the Scots' lack of confidence. For example, I have shown how much of the Scottish belief system is designed to encourage individuals to know their place and so is more likely to undermine than to build confidence.

So if Scotland were able to take more charge of her own affairs and feel less insecure about her neighbour, Scotland's confidence problems may be ameliorated but I do not believe they would disappear. In short, Scottish independence *on its own* would not be enough to build confidence in Scotland.

NOTES

1 Janet Adam Smith, 'Some Eighteenth-Century Ideas on Scotland and the Scots' in N. T. Phillipson & Rosalind Mitchison (eds), *Scotland in the Age of Improvement* (Edinburgh University Press: Edinburgh, 1970), p. 107

2 G. M. Thomson, *Caledonia: Or The Future of the Scots* (Kegan Paul, Trench, Trubner: London), p. 10.

3 George Scott Moncrieff, 'Balmorality' in David Cleghorn Thomson, *Scotland in Quest of her Youth* (Oliver & Boyd: Edinburgh, 1932), p. 83.

4 Edwin Muir, *Scottish Journey* (Victor Gollancz Ltd: London, 1935), p. 25.

5 P. H. Scott, 1707: *The Union of Scotland and England* (Chambers: Edinburgh, 1979).

6 Cairns Craig, 'The Fatricidial Twins' in Edward J. Cowan & Douglas Gifford, *The Polar Twins* (John Donald: Edinburgh, 1999), p. 27.

7 Douglas Gifford, 'Introduction' in D. Gifford (ed.), *The History of Scottish Literature: Volume 3* (Aberdeen University Press: Aberdeen, 1989), pp 5-6.

8 Graeme Morton and R. J. Morris 'Civil Society, Governance and Nation' in R. A. Houston & W. W. J. Knox, *The New Penguin History of Scotland: From the Earliest Times to the Present Day* (Penguin Books: London, 2001), p. 410.

9 Alice Brown, David McCrone & Lindsay Paterson, *Politics and Society in Scotland* (MacMillan Press: Hampshire, 1998), p. 208.

10 Ruth Wishart in Tom Devine and Paddy Logue (eds), *Being Scottish* (Polygon: Edinburgh 2002), p. 287.

11 David McCrone, Angela Morris & Richard Kiely, *Scotland - the Brand: The Making of Scottish Heritage* (Polygon: Edinburgh, 1999), pp. 49-50.

12 Jeremy Paxman, *The English: A Portrait of a People* (Penguin Books: London, 1999), pp. 22-23.

13 Charles Jennings, *Faintheart: An Englishman Ventures North of the Border* (Abacus: London, 2001), p. 88.

14 William Ferguson, *The Identity of the Scottish Nation - An Historic Quest* (Edinburgh University Press: Edinburgh 1998), p. 315.

15 Sheila Brock in Tom Devine and Paddy Logue, *Being Scottish* (Polygon: Edinburgh, 2002), p. 35.

16 Ruth Wishart in *Being Scottish,* p. 288.

17 See Arthur Herman, *The Scottish Enlightenment: The Scots' Invention of the Modern World* (Fourth Estate: London, 2002), Chapter 10.

18 J. M. Reid, *Scotland's Progress: The Survival of a Nation* (Eyre & Spottiswoode: London, 1971), p. 9.

NOTES

19 Wallace Notestein, *The Scot in History: A Study of the Interplay of Character and History* (Yale University Press: Yale, US, 1947), p. 95.

20 Simone de Beauvoir, *The Second Sex* (Penguin: Harmondsworth, 1972), p. 17. For a full exposition of de Beauvoir's concept of 'the Other' see Carol Craig, 'Simone de Beauvoir's "The Second Sex" in the light of the Hegelian Master-Slave Dialectic and Sartrian Existentialism', PhD Thesis, University of Edinburgh, 1979.

21 Giles Gordon 'The Three Estatis: Scotch, Scots, Scottish' in Trevor Royle (ed.), *Jock Tamson's Bairns* (Hamish Hamilton: London, 1977), pp. 146-7.

22 Isobel Lindsay, 'Nationalism, Community and Democracy' in Gavin Kennedy (ed.), *The Radical Approach: Papers on an Independent Scotland* (Palingenesis Press: Edinburgh, 1976), p. 23.

23 *Letters of David Hume,* edited by J.Y.T. Grieg (Oxford, 1932), 1, p255.

24 Quoted in Paul Henderson Scott, *The Boasted Advantages - The Consequences of the Union* of 1707 (The Saltire Society: Edinburgh, 1999), p. 5.

25 Quoted in Paul Henderson Scott, *The Boasted Advantages,* p. 1.

26 N. T. Phillipson, 'Nationalism and Ideology' in J. N. Wolfe (ed.), *Government and Nationalism in Scotland* (Edinburgh University Press: Edinburgh, 1969), p. 186. My emphasis.

27 Lindsay Paterson, *The Autonomy of Modern Scotland* (Edinburgh University Press: Edinburgh, 1994), p. 63.

28 William Ferguson, *The Identity of the Scottish Nation - An Historic Quest* (Edinburgh University Press: Edinburgh, 1998).

29 For an interesting account of the creation of British identity see Linda Colley, *Britons: Forging the Nation 1707 - 1837* (Vintage: London, 1996).

30 Quoted in Douglas Dunn, Scotland: *An Anthology* (HarperCollins: London, 1991), p. 25.

31 George Scott Moncrieff, 'Balmorality', p. 73.

13
The Scottish Self

'Mirror, mirror on the wall, Who the hell am I at all?'
William McIlvanney, *The Kiln*

When I was almost finished writing this book I came across Colin Manlove's *Scottish Fantasy Literature*. Over the years Scottish fantasy literature has helped to sustain the notion that duality and division lie at the heart of Scottish consciousness and that there is something essentially divided about Scottishness itself. Two books in particular have encouraged such a view - James Hogg's *The Confessions of a Justified Sinner* and Robert Louis Stevenson's *Dr Jekyll and Mr Hyde*. Manlove's work is a scholarly survey which includes these two books as well as a number of other Scottish fantasy books such as Neil Gunn's *The Green Isle of the Great Deep*, J. M. Barrie's *Peter Pan* and Alasdair Gray's *Lanark*. In the introduction Manlove compares what he sees as the key aspects of these books with England's, albeit thinner, fantasy literature. The English books to which Manlove refers include J. R. R. Tolkein's *The Lord of the Rings*, C. S. Lewis's Narnia books and Charles Kingsley's *The Water-Babies*. As I read Manlove my heart sank as his conclusions about Scottish and English fantasy literature were in every respect the opposite of my own conclusions about the culture of the two countries. But Manlove's observations were so much the opposite of mine it was uncanny. And then I realised that this mirror image was to be expected and was completely consistent with Jung's theory. Jung argues that in human life there is a 'principle of compensation':

> The psyche is a self-regulating system that maintains its equilibrium just as the body does. Every process that goes too far immediately and inevitably calls forth compensations, and without these there would be neither a normal metabolism nor a normal psyche. In this sense we can take the theory of compensation

> as a basic law of psychic behaviour. Too little on one side results in too much on the other. Similarly, the relation between conscious and unconscious is compensatory. This is one of the best-proven rules of dream interpretation. When we set out to interpret a dream, it is always helpful to ask: what conscious attitude does it compensate?[1]

When Jung writes 'conscious' he does not mean that people are necessarily consciously aware of such attitudes but that the attitudes are in the realm of the conscious rather than the unconscious. A person who reflects very little on him or herself may still be unaware of such attitudes.

Clearly, dreams are the main way in which this compensation principle makes itself felt in an individual's life. But such a principle can also be evident within cultures and what Jung calls the 'collective unconscious'. *In Modern Man in Search of a Soul,* Jung writes: 'What is of particular importance for the study of literature in these manifestations of the collective unconscious is that they are compensatory to the conscious attitude'.[2] And then he adds that such literary manifestations 'can bring a one-sided, abnormal, or dangerous state of consciousness into equilibrium in an apparently purposive way.'[3] In other words, what we see in literature may often be the opposite of what pertains in real life. And if *any* literature has this capacity to compensate the conscious attitude, then we are most likely to see it in fantasy literature as fantasy is after all the most dreamlike of stories.

In effect, this means that the characteristics Manlove presents about Scottish fantasy could well be the opposite of people's experience of life in everyday Scotland. And this process would also hold true for English culture and fantasy. To simplify things I set out in table form (Table 3) the key elements of Manlove's conclusions about Scottish and English fantasy literature, and what I have so far presented in this book as the ordinary, everyday aspects of Scottish and English culture. Wherever possible I have used Manlove's precise words. The table shows that a 'compensation principle' *is* operating in these books in exactly

Table 3 Characteristics of Scottish and English fantasy literature v everyday culture of both countries

Scottish Culture	Scottish Fantasy Literature	English Culture	English Fantasy Literature
Future orientation stronger than harking back to the past.	'Always a sense of a pull backwards, or even downwards to one's roots.'	Veneration of the past; backward looking.	Emphasis on development.
Strong sense of possibilities and progress.	Heroes are 'often stripped of advances'; 'less sense of evolution and progression' than English fantasies. Often 'stasis or even decline or collapse'.	Emphasis on conserving the present; fear of change.	'Emphasis is not on loss as much as gain'; sense of evolution and progression.
Collectivity more important than the individual; social interaction valued and encouraged.	'Protagonist most frequently solitary.'	Individuality more important than collectivity.	Focus on community - e.g. *The Lord of the Rings* is 'about expanding relationships.'
Extravert world valued and emphasised.	'Inward search'; story is often 'an expression of the psyche of the central figure'.	Introvert world valued and emphasised; importance of privacy.	Concerned with 'other worlds.'
Notion of a collective quest or mission; strong sense of Utopian dream.	'Questioning and introspective analysis'; 'concerned to find something within'; 'No journeys in much Scots fantasy: one simply goes further within.'	No strong sense of collective mission or quest; dream of privacy.	'Outward quest.'
Emphasis on social cohesion and co-operation. Strong belief that our actions affect others.	'Destructive energy'; savagery and murder. Protagonist's deeds 'redound on themselves alone.'	Emphasis on the individual living his or her life. Emphasis on individual actions and rights.	Often describes a 'delightful, glorious world'. Group cohesion important for the quest; 'whole worlds or societies hang on the doings of individuals.'

Table 3 Characteristics of Scottish and English fantasy literature v everyday culture of both countries contd.

Scottish Culture	Scottish Fantasy Literature	English Culture	English Fantasy Literature
Outward looking; interested in other cultures.	'Exploring and transforming the familiar'; the focus is on 'the local' rather than the 'strange'.	Insular; Little Englander mentality.	'Journeys far from home'; investigating the strange.
Clear sense of acceptable behaviour; deviants criticised and censured.	Protagonists often 'social misfits', eccentrics or freaks.	Eccentricity not only encouraged but institutionalised.	Most 'deal with perfectly normal individuals.' They may be Hobbits but they are still normal chaps.
Rational, logical mind in control in the outer world.	Unconscious mind explored; 'certainties dislocated.'	Sensing, perceiving mind dominates in the introvert world.	Places value on order, control and structure.
Culture traditionally 'rich in fantasy'.	Less 'fantastic' than English fantasy; set more in 'everyday experience'; not visiting a 'magic realm.'	Weaker tradition of fantasy than Scotland.	More 'fantastic'; more of a sense of a division between everyday reality and a magical world.
Patriarchal culture; women play little public role.	Emphasises 'the power of women and worth of feminine values.'		(Manlove doesn't cover this for England.)
Strong sense of Scottish identity (even if simply based on the feeling of 'not being English'); strong sense of civil society.	Boundaries of self blurred; 'recurrent interest ... in questioning the self'; lots of contrasts and divisions, e.g. night and day; 'doppelgangers' and alter egos abound.	Hazy sense of what it means to be English; less clear sense of society and the civic realm.	'Any such dualities are overcome in the victory of good.'

the way Jung suggested. What Manlove describes as the characteristics of Scottish fantasy literature are the opposite of what pertains in Scottish life. As the table shows, if we take too literally the image of Scotland which emerges from this fantasy literature it is very easy to believe, as Scottish cultural analysts do, that the Scots must be pathological, anti-social basket cases. And this notion of the dark, brooding Jekyll and Hyde Scots is then sharpened even further by the contrast with the stories English writers create. While the lone psychopathic Scot, and his/her doppelganger, slinks about in dark alleys, murdering people, the English are out in the sunlight on a communal quest to fight evil. In short, the English seem to be 'normal' and the Scots seem to be 'sick'. In reality, however, it is the Scots who have a strong sense of community, national identity and a notion of social progress while the English struggle to see themselves as anything other than a nation of private individuals. Quite simply, our analysts have looked at the shadow of Scotland and mistaken it for the substance. Manlove is fairly circumspect in his comments, yet even he falls into this trap:

> Whether the repeated portrayal of the self under attack can be construed as a version of Scotland itself under threat - either through its own cultural self-divisions or in relation to the perceived rapacity of England - can only be aired, not answered here. But what Scottish fantasy seems to register is a fundamental lack of confidence *in the conscious or civil self*.[4]

When I was writing this book I felt intuitively that the conventional diagnosis of Scotland's culture is mistaken. As a Scot myself I have always been aware of having a very strong Scottish identity and I can see that holds true for most Scots. This does not mean that the Scots will always be able to tell you what being Scottish means or that they are happy with the political status quo. Nonetheless it does mean that Scottish identity and 'the conscious or civil self' is not the problem. Indeed the more I researched and reflected on Scotland the more I was convinced that the problem is, if anything, that we have too strong a sense of being Scottish. Too strong a belief system. Too strong a sense of an outer 'civil self'. In other words, being Scottish is very limiting and prescriptive for individual Scots. It undermines the sense of an inner, individual self and retards our personal development. So a major problem Stevenson, Hogg *et al* are pointing to is the difficulty with our identity as individuals, not our identity as Scots. This means that the problem as diagnosed by cultural analysts, such as Tom Nairn, needs to be stood on its head.

Analysts who advance the idea that there is something intrinsically divided about Scottish identity need to look again at Scotland's literature and assess what truly reflects outer Scottish society and what may be 'compensatory'. Indeed I suspect that much of the problem of cultural analysis in Scotland is that it mirrors the problem in wider Scottish society - it places too much emphasis on the social, outer world and not enough on the importance of individuals, individuality or psychological development. When I was undertaking research for this book I was struck by how much had been written over the years on Scottish history and politics; how much of the debate about Scottish literature has been influenced by political theories; and how little has been published in the past fifty years which really tries to explain how being Scottish affects our development as individuals.

I am not saying that it makes no sense to look at contemporary historical events or politics as a way to understand the motivations of writers - that would be absurd. Nor am I saying that politics and political solutions have no bearing on Scottish problems. What I am saying is that Scottish identity is *not* the big issue cultural analysts make it out to be. Indeed, as I showed in the previous chapter on Scotland's relationship with England, despite the warnings of Scottish Cassandras over the years, a distinctive sense of Scottishness has not withered - it has remained remarkably resilient. Instead a much bigger, but more subtle, problem for Scots is how Scottish culture constrains and limits individuality and how we are all rather tyrannised by public opinion. This is something which affects all Scots but Scottish writers are, by definition, more acutely aware of the problem.

Indeed Scottish writers are like canaries down pits - they are particularly vulnerable to constraints and slow suffocation and keel over earlier than the rest of the population.

It was Jung who came up with the idea that all societies force individuals into developing a 'persona' - an image, or mask, they create for themselves which gives them some amount of social acceptability.[5] At best this persona is an accommodation between who the person really feels themselves to be and who the society wants them to be - at worst it is a constricting corset (I'm resisting the term straitjacket, for obvious reasons!). A corset which doesn't allow an individual room to breathe, never mind the chance to realise much of his or her 'real' self. This is an issue in all societies, but for reasons I have set out in earlier chapters Scotland's history and preferences mean that the corset is likely to be more constricting and suffocating than in many other cultures.

So for me one of the main problems about Scotland is not that this corset is tartan, or has pictures of *Dr Finlay's Case Book* on it or is divided into two different parts and so can be likened to some 'Caledonian antisyzygy'. It's the fact that one-size fits all - that every single Scot is expected to squeeze or mould themselves into a fairly tight notion of right and proper behaviour and attitudes. I have little doubt that the corset which even modern (and often atheistic) Scots feel constrained by was designed centuries ago by John Knox and the members of the Kirk sessions. But I also believe that the corset was substantially re-laced for the modern Scot by socialist thinkers like Keir Hardie, John Maxton and more modern left-of-centre thinkers. So the issue in Scotland is tight conformity - not weak political or cultural identity. And surely this is why many acclaimed modern Scottish novels are about the 'search for self'. Indeed William McIlvanney's prize-winning novel *The Kiln* even starts with the lines 'It is as if ... who I thought I was has dried up like a well and I have to find again the source of who I am'.[6] In *Being Scottish* it is Kenyan-born Scot Mukami McCrum who seems most aware of the price of Scottish identity: 'Scotland made me almost lose "myself"'[7] is how she describes her experience.

We can also test the relevance of my contention that it is our individual self, not our political identity, which is most under threat in Scotland, if we go back and examine the kinds of issues which exercised the mind of the man who created Jekyll and Hyde-Robert Louis Stevenson.

Robert Louis Stevenson

It is very difficult to read the story of Stevenson's life in nineteenth-century Scotland and not be struck by how he was an extremely sensitive and imaginative individual who had to battle with his parents, and polite Edinburgh society, to get the chance to be himself. He was an only child. A sickly child of doting and rather conventional Presbyterian parents. His father and grandfather were celebrated engineers and his rather domineering father wanted him to follow this tradition. R. L. S. wanted to be a writer. A compromise was reached - he studied law. Fanny, the American woman he subsequently met and fell in love with, was ten years older than him. She was still married to another man and had two children. She planned to divorce her husband so she could marry Stevenson. This was in 1878, during Queen Victoria's reign, and so Stevenson's relationship with Fanny was not just shocking for his parents - even his fashionable friends were ruffled.

Stevenson was a sensitive man who did not enjoy hurting his parents. He found his constant battles with them, and the fact they not only disapproved of his behaviour but were also ashamed of him, deeply upsetting. He was also acutely aware of the difficult position Fanny was in as a result of their love affair. So trying to be true to himself and what he wanted, while living in a society with a very strict code of behaviour, was an enduring and very emotional issue in Stevenson's personal life. One insight into this emotion is apparent in a letter he sent to a friend after his father had asked him directly if he believed in God. Stevenson said 'no' and was later to write about how guilty he felt when he saw the effect this truth had on his mother and father. He even states: 'If it were not too late, I think I could almost find it in my heart to retract, but it is too late; and again, am I to live my whole life as one falsehood'?[8]

In his literary life too he was aware of the need to please and sometimes to toe the line. Francis Hart argues that Stevenson 'was extraordinarily susceptible to the aggressive influences of friends' and that his 'responses were chameleontic'.[9] Stevenson cared passionately about others' opinions of him but like Burns he valued 'his independent mind'. So he wanted others' approval but not so much that he would completely sacrifice himself to what they thought he should do. The subsequent quest for authenticity created a huge tension in his life.

If you read Stevenson's letters or essays it is impossible to miss how Scottish he felt. In July 1883 while on a visit to Suffolk he wrote to his mother about how 'good' he felt life in Scotland was, and then he continues:

> I cannot get over my astonishment - indeed it increases every day, at the hopeless gulph *(sic)* that there is between England and Scotland, and English and Scotch. Nothing is the same; and I feel as strange and outlandish here, as I do in France or Germany.[10]

Indeed I contend that Stevenson, much more than the average Scot, was acutely aware of the Scottish cultural characteristics which I have listed in Tables 1 and 3. In nineteenth-century Scotland there were marked differences between the Lowlands and the Highlands yet Stevenson still maintains that 'from his compatriot in the south the Lowlander stands consciously apart'. In short, he believed that urbanised Lowland Scots felt more affinity for Highlanders than for the English. And he goes on to describe the various ways Scotland and England differ, finishing with the very perceptive and memorable comment that even though the Scots have learned to speak English they 'will still have a strong Scots accent of the mind'.[11] So Stevenson certainly did not feel ambivalent or unsure about his Scottish identity and held definite views on how an individual's Scottish upbringing shaped his or her outlook on life. He even took S.R. Crockett to task for giving his address as 'North Britain'.[12]

But what is important here is not just that Stevenson's feelings of Scottishness were rock solid but that he harboured very intense feelings of warmth about Scottishness itself. Indeed it is impossible to read many of Stevenson's poems, essays and letters and not be struck by how positive he feels about Scotland:

> The happiest lot on earth is to be born a Scotsman. You must pay for it in many ways, as for all other advantages on earth. You have to learn the Paraphrases and the Shorter Catechism; you generally take to drink; your youth, as far as I can find out, is a time of louder war against society, of more outcry and tears and turmoil, than if you had been born, for instance, in England. But somehow life is warmer and closer; the hearth burns more redly; the lights of home shine softer on the rainy street; the very names, endeared in verse and music, cling nearer round our hearts.[13]

Of course, as an atheist and child of fairly strict Presbyterian parents, Stevenson did not like all aspects of Scottishness. He disliked intensely the emphasis on religion in Scotland as well as the nature of those religious beliefs. But, as the above passage shows, he was not only aware of but was also deeply touched by the Scottish emphasis on family and community. And at a conscious level he accepted that the price of a close-knit community is social conformity.

But below this conscious acceptance lurked his unconscious feelings. And Stevenson was only too aware that, in the artist's life at least, it is not often the conscious mind that is in the driving seat:

> What, then, is the object, what the method, of an art, and what the source of its power? The whole secret of it is that no art does 'compete with life'. Man's one method, whether he reasons or creates, is to half-shut his eyes against the dazzle or confusion of reality.[14]

In the case of *Dr Jekyll and Mr Hyde* Stevenson did not just 'half shut his eyes', he closed them completely; for the idea for this novel came to Stevenson in a dream. His American wife, Fanny, criticised it for being too simple and he then burned the original and rewrote it. It was Fanny who encouraged him to make his 'fine bogey tale' into 'allegory'. Stevenson then struggled to hold on to the atmosphere of the dream while trying to make it more complex to fit his wife's desire for something allegorical. It is astonishing that commentators make so little of the fact that Fanny, an American woman, was in large measure responsible for the creation of that great symbol for the divided nature of Scottish consciousness and identity - *Dr Jekyll and Mr Hyde*.

Given Stevenson's own comments on the story and his enduring interest in the negative impact of Calvinism, I have little doubt that the book can profitably be read as a commentary on the dangers of repression and hypocrisy; that the more we are forced to cut off from our true impulses the more they will wreak havoc in our lives. It can also be read as a generalised attack on the strictures of bourgeois respectability. But none of this gives support to those who believe it symbolises in any way the problematic nature of *Scottish* political identity. What's more I think there is another plausible reading of *Dr Jekyll and Mr Hyde*, both for Stevenson himself and for Scotland.

Jekyll and Hyde

Commentators continually portray Stevenson's Edinburgh as a town of sharp contrasts, dark alleys and Deacon Brodie's murderous intent. For example, Jenni Calder in her introduction to the Penguin edition of *Dr Jekyll and Mr Hyde* writes:

> The setting is London. But the ambience is without a doubt Edinburgh, the Edinburgh of the Old Town's dark wynds and closes, where the turn of a corner could, in Stevenson's day and even now, abruptly leave behind the world of surface respectability, and the lingering shades of Burke and Hare ... and Deacon Brodie ... still flavoured the atmosphere.[15]

Apart from the fact that such comments (minus the wynds, closes and specific personalities) could fit London, it is worth contrasting this image of Stevenson's Edinburgh with his own picture of the city. In his *Picturesque Notes* on Edinburgh, Stevenson mentions the wynds and the dark tales but his civic pride positively lights up most of the one hundred and twenty pages. Edinburgh is mainly portrayed as a light, airy city. Indeed he is so positive about the city it is hard to select one single quote to convey the extent of his appreciation. Let this suffice:

> For the country people to see Edinburgh on her hill-tops is one thing; it is another for the citizen, from the thick of his affairs, to overlook the country. It should be a genial and ameliorating influence in life; it should prompt good thoughts and remind him of Nature's unconcern: that he can watch from day to day, as he trots officeward, how the Spring green brightens in the wood or the field grows black under a moving ploughshare. ... If you could see as people are to see in heaven ... you might pause, in some business perplexity, in the midst of the city traffic, and perhaps catch the eye of a shepherd as he sat down to breathe upon a heathery shoulder of the Pentlands; or perhaps some urchin, clambering in a country elm, would put aside the leaves and show you his flushed and rustic visage; or a fisher racing seawards, with the tiller under his elbow, and the sail sounding in the wind, would fling you a salutation from between Anst'er and the May.[16]

For most of this book Stevenson writes with incredible warmth about the city and its people. His negative comments are reserved mainly for the weather - ' the vilest climates under heaven' - and for the Kirk and its history, which he refers to as 'much ado about nothing'. Towards the end of the book he views the city from the Pentland hills: 'The spiry habitable city, ships, the divided fields, and browsing herds, and the straight highways,' writes Stevenson, 'tell visibly of man's active and comfortable ways'. In short he finds in this view of Edinburgh 'pleasant reflections on the destiny of man'.[17]

At times, however, Stevenson overdoes the purple prose. He concentrates so much on the silver lining he does not even see the cloud. He is too appreciative. He even conveys in a lyrical light stories which could easily be viewed cynically and at one point is in danger of being, not just superficial, but gullible. For example, he describes how long ago a field at Swanston outside the city was bought by Edinburgh magistrates to collect spring water but then 'it occurred to them that the place was suitable for junketing'. He then describes in reverent detail how the garden was made by transporting materials from Edinburgh and how it matured into a beautiful dell:

> There, purple magistrates relaxed themselves from the pursuit of municipal ambition; cocked hats paraded soberly about the garden and in and out among the hollies; authoritative canes drew ciphering upon the path; and at night; from high upon the hills, a shepherd saw lighted windows through the foliage and heard the voice of dignitaries raised in song.[18]

Stevenson was a great optimist. Someone who passionately wanted to see the best in people and events. Indeed in the early part of his life Stevenson even referred to his 'own favourite gospel of cheerfulness'.[19] When he was thirty he wrote to a friend suggesting the words which should be inscribed on his tombstone. One of the sentences read: 'Can I make some one happier this day before I lay down to sleep?'[20] Recent biographers, such as Ian Bell, portray Fanny as a rather overbearing and manipulative woman and maintain that by the time Stevenson died his relationship with her was extremely strained. But four years into their marriage Stevenson was only able to lavish praise on Fanny, as this excerpt from a letter to his mother shows:

> I love her better than ever and admire her more; and I cannot think what I have done to deserve so good a gift ... my marriage has been the most successful in the world ... She is everything to me: wife, brother,

sister, daughter, and dear companion; and I would not change to get a goddess or a saint.[21]

So remembering Jung's injunction to ask of a dream 'what conscious attitude does it compensate?', let us look at how this question relates to Stevenson and his creation of *Jekyll and Hyde*. What is immediately apparent is that this dark tale could have served as a warning from Stevenson's unconscious not to be so ridiculously positive and optimistic - not to put so much faith in human beings and relationships. Stevenson's 'fine bogey tale', by showing him how dark motives could lurk below the surface, may well have been a warning from the deep recesses of his unconscious mind, not to trust people so much; that people may appear good when they are not. The dream also admirably illustrated how human beings are much more complicated than he thinks. And it may also have been a warning to him that his own identity was under threat if he kept trying to accommodate himself to other people. After all, one of the most quoted and memorable lines in the book is when Stevenson describes the transition from the good Dr Jekyll into Mr Hyde as 'a solution of the bonds of obligation',[22] indeed at one point Jekyll says:

> Yes, I preferred the elderly and discontented doctor, surrounded by friends and cherishing honest hopes; and bade a resolute farewell to the liberty, the comparative youth, the light step, leaping pulses and secret pleasures, that I had enjoyed in the disguise of Mr Hyde.[23]

I feel sure it is no coincidence that the dream came to Stevenson when his relationship with his oldest friend, W. E. Henley, was deeply strained as a result of their trying to write plays together, and when the fractures in his relationship with Fanny were first beginning to show. In short, when he felt troubled and burdened by his relationships. The fact that Stevenson burned his original story because Fanny criticised it and then, despite his acute illness, rewrote it along the lines she suggested is surely indicative of his own great need to please the people in his life. And events like these must have created a huge amount of turmoil in Stevenson's own mind. He must have felt simultaneously torn between his great need for approval and his overwhelming desire to be authentic and true to the man *hiding* within.

A final piece of evidence that *Jekyll and Hyde* resulted from a warning from Stevenson's unconscious about his own philosophy on life (carrying 'a pleasant face about to friends and neighbours'[24]) can be found in the dedication to the book. Stevenson dedicated it to his cousin Katharine De Mattos, who was part of his circle of friends, and then included the following lines adapted from two verses he had written for her the year before:

It's ill to loose the bands that God decreed to bind;
Still will we be the children of the heather and the wind;
Far away from home, O, it's still for you and me
That the broom is blowing bonnie in the north countrie.

Two years later his personal relationships with Katharine and Henley were so complex that he felt enmeshed and ground down by them. Henley accused Fanny of plagiarising a story of Katharine's, and Katharine tacitly accepted Henley's charge. As a result of this, Stevenson's relationship with Katharine became hopelessly strained and his close friendship with Henley almost irretrievably broken. R. L. S. wrote to his wife about 'these hobgoblin figures, once my friends'.[25] It is very possible that even before this incident Stevenson, albeit unconsciously, suspected that Katharine was closer to Henley than she was to him, hence the rather bizarre dedication, linking her with this dark novel in some way. Indeed this link is hinted at in his letter to Katharine informing her of the dedication when he writes ' it is sent to you by the one that loves you - Jekyll not Hyde.'[26]

James Hogg
Before turning to the Scottish significance of *Dr Jekyll and Mr Hyde,* let me say a few words about James Hogg, who wrote *The*

Confessions of a Justified Sinner - a novel which has been hailed as 'the most profound exploration of national psychology in our literature'[27] and which over the years has nourished the notion of Scottish consciousness itself being essentially divided. Reading about this nineteenth-century Scottish writer, it is clear that here was a man who was obsessed by his image and identity. Like Burns he came from fairly poor farming stock and wanted to become accepted by genteel Scottish society. He called himself 'the Ettrick Shepherd'. As with Burns, his whole life as a writer depended on how he was seen by others. And like Burns he was not averse to manipulating his image. He was a man who consciously created personas for himself and his characters. Like Stevenson, Hogg was heavily influenced by others and was very eager to please. It is also impossible to read about Hogg and not believe that here was a man with a strong sense of his *Scottish* identity. He was steeped in the Borders' ballad tradition and tales of fairies, kelpies and the like. As a Borderer he also had an acute sense of the differences between Scotland and England. Hogg's problem was how he could package and sell his writings, based on this heritage, to those in Edinburgh who defined what was artistically acceptable and interesting.[28]

Hogg, like Stevenson, was one of society's great optimists. Indeed his optimism even led him to speculate financially with his first literary earnings, and he lost the money. Thomas Crawford describes Hogg as 'a comic genius in life as well as in art, who appeared, when he first took Edinburgh by storm "singing his own ballads, and ... making himself and others uproariously merry."'[29] According to Crawford, Hogg was someone who never lost his temper and who, in the words of Thomas Carlyle, had 'almost the naiveté of a child'.[30] Much of Hogg's work reflects this optimism and he often portrays peasant communities in romantic and idealistic terms.

The criticism and indifference to his work, as expressed by Professor John Wilson and others, totally undermined Hogg's confidence. Round about the time he wrote, *The Confessions of a Justified Sinner* he declared: 'I am grown to have no confidence whatsoever in my own taste or discernment.'[31] And when his dark novel was published it did not bear his name as he was, rightly, scared it might offend. So, like Stevenson, Hogg needed a prompt from his unconscious to tell him to stop being so optimistic, trusting and positive about people. And again, as with Stevenson, Hogg also had to deal personally with issues of authenticity. He needed to stop living his life in the state Jean Paul Sartre described as 'a being for others' and start being true to himself.[32] Quite simply, if Hogg had not started to become more negative and pessimistic and had continued to be more and more appreciative, optimistic, humorous and positive, his personality would have been completely out of balance. He would have become even more of a caricature of himself.

A Balancing Act

Even a cursory inspection of the types of people who wrote the English fantasy fiction Manlove describes suggests that they had very different approaches to life from Stevenson and Hogg. For example, C.S. Lewis, who wrote the 'Narnia' books for children, was a reclusive Oxford don who found it difficult to relate to other people. J. R. R. Tolkein, author of *Lord of the Rings* was also an academic at Oxford University. The fantasies created by these men no doubt helped to compensate for their very individualistic and rather introverted lives.

A completely different challenge faced Stevenson and Hogg. They needed to toughen up and become more suspicious and cynical about other people. They needed to care less about others and their opinions and about the wider community. And in both cases the stories they created were an antidote to optimism, belief in progress and community values. As both these men were extremely negative about Calvinism it is unsurprising that it played a large part in the stories they created. And of course, both stories can profitably be read as a commentary and indictment of Calvinism. But to construe either story as saying something fundamental about the divided nature of *Scottish* identity and consciousness itself is to say the least, over-stretching the argument.

So what is the significance of these stories for Scottish culture? What is interesting about Stevenson and Hogg is that although they have a preference for feeling rather than thinking judgement, and so cannot be classed as archetypal, logical Scots, what they required as individuals to help bring them into balance was in many respects just what the Scots as a whole needed, and continue to need, to counterbalance conscious Scottish culture. In Scotland we are all encouraged to see others as more important than ourselves, thus all Scots are in danger of becoming 'a being for others' and find it difficult to develop an authentic individual identity.

So it is easy to see how in Scotland a necessary antidote or compensation to the everyday attitude are stories which encourage people to step back from an overwhelming sense of social obligation; stories which portray others as evil, unattractive or not to be trusted; which challenge the prevailing sense of social progress and force us to focus inwards on ourselves so that we can build a more robust, authentic and individual identity. In short Scotland needs stories which encourage people to reduce their sense of social obligations so that they can cultivate their individuality more. And if Manlove's descriptions are accurate, this is exactly what the creators of Scottish fantasy fiction provide.

NOTES

1 C. G. Jung, *Collected Works* 7 (Routledge: London, 1978), paragraph 330.

2 Again, these attitudes may not be conscious within the culture in the sense that they are openly acknowledged. A culture which is not self-aware - such as Scotland - may be unaware of these 'conscious attitudes'.

3 C. G. Jung, *Modern Man in Search of a Soul* (Ark Paperback: London, 1995), pp. 190 -191.

4 Colin Manlove, *Scottish Fantasy Literature: A Critical Survey* (Canongate Academic: Edinburgh, 1994), p. 246. My emphasis.

5 See C. G. Jung, *Collected Works* 6 (Routledge: London, 1978), paragraph 801.

6 William McIlvanney, *The Kiln* (Sceptre: London, 1996), p. 1.

7 Mukami McCrum in Tom Devine and Paddy Logue (eds), *Being Scottish* (Polygon: Edinburgh, 2002), p. 157.

8 *Selected Letters of Robert Louis Stevenson,* Ernest Mehew (ed.) (Yale Nota Bene: Yale, 2001), p. 29.

9 Francis R. Hart, 'Robert Louis Stevenson in Prose' in Douglas Gifford (ed.), *The History of Scottish Literature: Volume 3,* (Aberdeen University Press: Aberdeen, 1989), p. 292.

10 *Selected Letters of Robert Louis Stevenson,* Ernest Mehew (ed.), p. 37.

11 Robert Louis Stevenson, 'The Foreigner at Home' in *Memories and Portraits* (Heinemann: London, 1924).

12 *Selected Letters of Robert Louis Stevenson,* Ernest Mehew (ed.), p. 367.

13 Robert Louis Stevenson, *The Silverado Squatters* (The Folio Society: London, 1991) p. 165.

14 Quoted in Ian Bell, *Dreams of Exile: Robert Louis Stevenson - A Biography* (Mainstream Publishing: Edinburgh, 1992), p. 283.

15 Jenni Calder in the introduction to Robert Louis Stevenson, *Dr. Jekyll and Mr Hyde: and Other Stories* (Penguin Books Ltd.: London, 1979), p. 12.

16 Robert Louis Stevenson, *Edinburgh: Picturesque Notes* (Seeley & Co: London, 1903), pp 69 -70.

17 Ibid., p. 120.

18 Ibid., p. 115.

19 *Selected Letters of Robert Louis Stevenson,* Ernest Mehew (ed.), p. 59.

20 Ibid., p. 165.

21 Ibid., p. 257.

22 Robert Louis Stevenson, *Dr. Jekyll and Mr Hyde: And Other Stories* (Penguin Books Ltd.: London, 1979), p. 92.

23 Ibid., p. 90.

NOTES

24 *Selected Letters of Robert Louis Stevenson,* Ernest Mehew (ed.), p. 296.

25 Ibid., p. 366.

26 Ibid., p. 297.

27 Thomas Crawford, 'James Hogg: The Play of Region and Nation' in Douglas Gifford (ed.), *The History of Scottish Literature: Volume 3,* (Aberdeen University Press: Aberdeen, 1989), p. 103.

28 For more information on Hogg's work see Douglas Gifford, *James Hogg* (The Ramsay Head Press: Edinburgh, 1976).

29 Thomas Crawford, 'James Hogg: The Play of Region and Nation', p. 103.

30 Ibid., p. 103.

31 Quoted by Douglas Gifford in *James Hogg,* p. 136.

32 Jean Paul Sartre, *Being and Nothingness* (Routledge: London, 1969).

SECTION V

CONFIDENCE ISSUES IN CONTEMPORARY SCOTLAND

14

Never Good Enough

'Scotland ... has produced gallant soldiers, great philosophers, devoted missionaries, inspired inventors, scientists and engineers, even a few politicians of integrity. It is also the land of the maudlin drunk and the dangerous drunk, of the wife-batterer in the desolate housing scheme. ... We are bound together by a common fate which is not, much of the time, at all attractive. It is limited and limiting.'

Angus Calder, *Scotlands of the Mind*

'If I were chocolate, I'd eat myself.' That was how my parents would amusingly put my sister and myself down when we were young if we ever had the temerity to indulge in self-praise. Indeed, it is no exaggeration to say that, even today, farting in public is more acceptable in Scotland than speaking well of yourself. Americans are not boastful as such but they are able to tell you factually how they are good at this or that. But in Scotland no self-respecting Scot would make such pronouncements to the world. And it makes perfect sense. In a country which believes that people should see themselves as essentially the same as everyone else, it is extremely risky to say anything which sounds like you think much of yourself. There is nothing new about this. Even in the eighteenth century, David Hume wrote in the introduction to his brief autobiography: 'It is difficult for a man to write long of himself without vanity; therefore I will be short.'[1]

Unfortunately, the process which teaches children not to think too highly of themselves also minimises the likelihood that they will feel good about themselves. Indeed most of the Scottish beliefs I elaborated in earlier chapters have enormous implications not only for how the Scots see themselves but also for their personal self-confidence and the way they relate to others.

Over the years I have heard countless Scots say that when they were growing up they were not encouraged to think too much of themselves. In fact, any suggestion that they were becoming big headed or 'too big for their boots' would be met by a put-down of one type or another. Many people say they received little praise at home when they were young - presumably because parents fear 'spoiling' their children - and were then amazed when they grew up and were told by others how much their parents took pride in them and their achievements. People often recount sad stories of being told they were loved, or admired, only when a parent was literally on his or her death bed. Pamela Stephenson, in her biography of Billy Connolly, reports that Connolly's father William:

> ...verbally acknowledged his son's achievements only once in his whole life, when the Variety Club honoured him and gave him a statue ... On the way home in the limousine, Bill's father turned to him: 'You were very good.' That blew Billy away. He'd never said anything positive before.[2]

Far too many children in Scotland grow up in households, as Connelly did, where they are verbally and physically abused, and not getting praise is the least of their problems. But my argument is that even good, gentle parents believe it is better not to encourage their children to think too much of themselves. In other words, they keep their children's confidence in check not because they are nasty or deliberately undermining but because they think they are doing the best for their children. In a culture which detests self-praise, or people thinking too highly of themselves, adults are in a sense doing the right thing by children when they try to nip such behaviour in the bud and bring them up not to show off or think they are special. If the people I have spoken to over the past few years are anything to go by, such parental attitudes are beginning to soften. Parents now often say they think it is good to praise children and to help them feel special in some way and that they deliberately do this with their offspring. But the problem is that the desire to keep people in their place is endemic in Scottish culture - it is, as we shall see later, part of children's experience of school and common within social interaction. So it is difficult for the most encouraging parents to neutralise it effectively.

In America, the belief that everyone is of equal worth commonly translates into the notion that everyone is special; whereas in Scotland the belief that everyone is of equal worth feeds into the idea that no one is special. Of course, it is easy to poke fun at the American notion of everyone being special for, by definition, if everyone is special, nobody is special. But nonetheless in this respect it is a more generous and life-affirming ideology in the modern world than the Scots' belief, which can easily degenerate into the idea that everybody is worthless. Earlier I showed that there is a tendency in Calvinist thought to portray human beings as worthless and when this trait is coupled with a strong desire for redemption it can easily create a culture where everyone feels they are in competition with everyone else to prove themselves. Indeed despite the Scots' avowed respect for equality and belief in equality of worth, there is hardly a Scot alive who has not felt this need to prove themselves worthy in some way. Many psychologists and health professionals believe that the tendency to over-work in Scottish culture may well be the result of a deep cultural pressure to prove your worth. Even Scottish conversations often have a competitive edge, as people try to ensure they get the last word or are seen to be 'right'. Either way what is often important in Scotland is not to be outdone by other people. John Buchan sums this characteristic up so well when he recounts the story of a shepherd listening to a tourist enthusing about the beauties of a certain hill. '"Why from the top of it," said the tourist, "you can see Ireland." "Ye can see far further than that," said the shepherd, "you can see the mune."'[3]

Scottish humour too is often a type of competition where people make jokes at others' expense and put them in their place. Indeed it is common in Scotland for people to command respect or gain kudos in their peer group simply from their ability to put others down. Most foreigners in Scotland report being shocked by Scottish humour because it is so rude. It is also why psychologists working with young people talk about Scotland having a 'killer culture'. And there is nothing new about this. James Boswell, the eighteenth-century literary figure, detested 'the Scots strength of sarcasm which is peculiar to the North of Britain'.[4]

Another way in which the feeling of worthlessness commonly manifests itself is in the fear of being 'found out'. I was the first person in my family to attend university and I spent the first few months fearing that I would be ejected from the lecture theatre because there had been some mistake. Other Scots tell similar stories. Pamela Stephenson maintains that Billy Connolly, for all that he was exceptionally good at what he did, 'still felt like a fraud sometimes, a welder who hadn't been found out'.[5] Sometimes this type of fear relates specifically to how well a person can do things, or how clever they are. But often it is about whether they are a 'good' or 'worthwhile' person. According to Stephenson, Connolly started drinking, and ultimately required therapy, to help him cope with the general feelings of worthlessness engendered by his Glasgow boyhood:

> On the surface, Billy's life was quite jolly, but inside he was lost. When he made public appearances, he arrived to great fanfare. He would open shops and cut ribbons while pipe bands played. A little voice inside, however, kept nagging him. It sounded a bit like Mona (his aunt). 'Who do you think you are? You don't deserve this.'[6]

Harsh criticism can also contribute to feelings of worthlessness and low self-esteem. In the words of a Scots proverb - 'When I did well, I heard it never; when I did ill, I heard it ever.'[7] As Scots often cultivate logic at the expense of sensitivity and empathy, it is common for parents to criticise their children far too harshly. Instead of making a distinction between the child and his or her behaviour ('that was a naughty thing to do') parents often make a verbal assault which leaves the child feeling devastated and rejected. 'You are a bad boy', they'll say, or 'you are a selfish girl'. So instead of the specific behaviour being criticised, the whole child is damned, or at least this is how the child often feels. I remember my elder son, when he was about eight, responding to some of my very heavy-handed criticism of him by saying 'you think I'm the worst boy in the world. You think I'm the devil'.

I firmly believe that criticism can be helpful for an individual if delivered well as it gives people invaluable feedback on their performance and can accelerate the learning process. But in Scotland people's extremely negative experience of criticism in childhood means that they become overly sensitive to criticism. One of the great paradoxes is that Scotland has an extremely critical culture yet your average Scot loathes being criticised. Even being looked at the wrong way can provoke some Scots to aggression. Indeed many Scots become quite aggressive in conversation if they feel they are being slighted and over the years this has led to the common English observation that the Scots are 'chippy' - aggressively defensive if they have any reason to feel they are being put down. And it is not uncommon in Scotland for a person who is criticised to go immediately on the defensive ('well you are a fine one to talk, let me tell you ...') rather than listening to what is being said, deciding if it is of value and learning from it. Nowadays management consultants talk about a 'blame culture' existing in some organisations and such a culture certainly flourishes throughout Scottish life, as is well illustrated by the following extract from Douglas Fraser's contribution to *Being Scottish:*

> Something or somebody else must be to blame. The boss. The rich. The poor. The central belt. Lairds. Edinburgh lawyers. Subsidy junkies. Catholics. Protestants. The poll tax. The current Scotland football manager. Men. Wummin. Lanarkshire politicians. People who blame other people.[8]

If anything goes wrong the Scots are not likely to analyse the problem, learn from it and ensure that it does not happen again. Instead the hunt is on to find the 'eejit' who has made the mistake and rub his or her nose in it. In such an environment people are not likely to admit their mistakes and will often try to deflect the blame by saying 'it wasnae me'. In Scotland an unedifying stand-off inevitably follows when someone somewhere has messed up. Such punitive views of people's misdemeanours may even account for the fact that the Scots lock up a higher percentage of criminals than most European countries.

The defensiveness around criticism is also the legacy of one of the key aspects of Scottishness I have pointed out elsewhere in this book - the obsession with perfection.

It's Got to Be Perfect

'Too many people take second best but I won't take anything less. It's got to be perfect.' So says Scottish pop group 'Fairground Attraction' in their hit single 'Perfect'. And the quest for perfection is a recurrent theme, not only in Scottish culture, but also in the lives of individual Scots - a theme admirably summed up on a tee shirt I came across in Nova Scotia, Canada, which read 'Not only am I perfect. I am Scottish too'. Individual Scots often passionately believe that they should aim for perfection and when they do not attain it they are projected to the other end of the scale - they feel worthless. Perfect or worthless - that's the seesaw most individual Scots are on and it is not a comfortable way to live your life. Of course, there is nothing exclusively Scottish about this, but Scotland's religious past and the Scottish belief system mean that this mindset is more pronounced here than it is in other Western cultures. As rational beings, conscious of their own failings, the Scots do not seriously think they are perfect, but they think they should be and they do not like the feeling of worthlessness which descends upon them when they have to cope with the harsh realities of their own imperfections. This is why criticism must be avoided at all costs. If it happens, the criticism should be deflected as quickly as possible or denied. Whatever happens it must not stick, as that will only provide unwanted testimony of your imperfections. It is one thing for a Scot to feel worthless and aware of faults. It is quite another for him or her to let others know these imperfections. It is imperative to maintain the pretence of perfection at all costs.

In the pursuit of perfection Scots will avoid doing anything where they may make a mistake or not do well. In the words of an old Scots' saying: 'Better sit still than rise up and fa'.[9] This is partly why performing or speaking in public can be such an ordeal for many Scots. It is also why many adult Scots are extremely inhibited about trying their hand at anything artistic or creative. Overly concerned about getting it 'right', they simply cannot get into the mindset which encourages their creative juices to flow. The trouble with this approach to life is that it prevents people from growing and developing, for learning new skills or trying out anything new inevitably means making mistakes. Pamela Stephenson reports that Billy Connolly has a fear he 'won't master' things and that 'Any time when there's a fear that he won't be able to do something ... then he will slip back into that "You're stupid, you'll never amount to anything" stuff'.[10] It also helps explain why research undertaken on attitudes to entrepreneurship in Scotland shows that 'fear of failure' is one of the biggest barriers facing Scots. Research undertaken for the Global Entrepreneurship Monitor showed that more than 40 per cent of Scots agree with the statement that 'Fear of failure would deter you from starting a business'.[11] This figure is more than 10 per cent higher than either the rest of the UK or the average for small modern nations.

At the heart of the perfect/worthless dichotomy is the basic belief that we are not okay just as we are - that to be an acceptable human being we must be perfect, get everything right, excel or at least be much better than we are now. In short, the basic problem is self-acceptance. So long as we think we are only worthwhile if we can do x, y or z, or be respected by other people for our efforts we shall be trapped on the perfect/worthless seesaw. At times we desperately need to believe 'I am great' to feel good about ourselves, but as soon as we make a mistake we come crashing down to earth, engulfed by feelings of failure and worthlessness. So it is easy to see why the Scots have acquired a reputation for having an inferiority - superiority complex. This complex is usually attributed to Scotland's relationship with England and while I believe that Scotland's political status has contributed to its development, I do not think that it is the sole explanation as we can trace its roots back into the Scots' own cultural attitudes.

Glebe Street

Many of the aspects of Scottish life and culture I have addressed so far in this chapter, or elsewhere in the book, are clearly displayed in the chronicles of Scotland's most famous and 'happy family' - *The Broons* - a comic strip produced weekly in *The Sunday Post* and produced as an annual.[12] I chose a recent year at random (1997) and analysed the content of its stories. By far the most common storyline (thirty-eight stories out of ninety-seven) was about embarrassment. This was usually caused by someone trying to do something different or getting above themselves and then being caught out. The last picture usually shows the culprit 'black affronted' or with a right red face. Examples of such behaviour include Daphne (the fat, ugly daughter) having the cheek to think she could become a model, go cycling or sign up for a blind date. Hen gets his comeuppance for taking up bird watching, of all things, and trying to do his own car repairs. In many cases the story is simple: the character in question overestimates his or her ability to do something and ends up making a right mess of it, much to the amusement of the rest of the family. Sometimes a family member is supported by the others but more often they become the butt of jokes. When Paw sees Hen, Joe and Daphne dancing he says 'call that dancing? I thocht ye had midges in yer vests'. When Joe tries lifting weights even Maw puts him down by saying 'my washin' pooder's stronger'. A number of stories show how competitive the Broons are with one another. Paw and Granpaw regularly get the better of youngsters like Joe or Hen by beating them at football or water-skiing and giving them a right showing up.

I am not arguing that this type of humour is all there is in *The Broons* and that there are no moments of support or tenderness; no times when the family comes together to help one another or be loving - in their fashion at least. But the laughing at one another and putting each other down, particularly for doing anything different, is much stronger. Recently I overheard a conversation while picking raspberries in Stirlingshire which showed such attitudes are alive and well. A father was picking with his eight year old daughter. He just couldn't resist telling her how much better he was at it than she was and showing her his basket. After a while he then said 'Och you're quite good at picking really. You're good at picking your nose'. And then if that wasn't insulting enough he added 'ye've picked a right beauty there' and then had a good laugh at his own joke. No doubt he saw the hurt look on her face for he did change his tune and tried thereafter to be encouraging. But I doubt it mattered. The damage may already have been done. As the Scottish educational psychologist Alan McLean once told me, for some people 'self-esteem takes years to build but seconds to destroy.'

Personal Relationships

Which brings us on to how the Scots' way of seeing themselves affects their relationship with others. There is a deep-seated, almost unconscious belief in Scotland that people have better relationships with others if they do not think too highly of themselves: that self-esteem interferes with good relationships. And for me this is the biggest fallacy in the Scots view of the world. Of course, good relationships must be founded on positive regard for the other person and a sense of equality, but genuine self-esteem is another vital ingredient. If a person does not think well of him or herself and is extremely self-critical then he or she has two ways to view and relate to others. The first is to believe that others are better than they are. This viewpoint will intensify the person's negative feelings about themselves. Indeed when people take such a view it is easy for them to be abused by others or to play the victim. The alternative is for an individual to try to offset bad feelings about themselves by believing that others are no better than they are. In such a mindset people do not want to respect or admire others as this makes them feel worse about themselves. It also leads individuals to be very critical of others - to pick holes and find flaws in other people or what they are doing. And it is a mindset which is all too common in Scotland. It leads to the pleasure many Scots take in putting a spoke in other people's wheels or generally trying to cut them down to size. Such a viewpoint can lead Scots to be unduly negative about others and such negativity generally undermines, rather than builds, relationships. Another way that relationships in Scotland are often strained is through the constant competition I outlined earlier. And this competitiveness and insecurity can easily become aggression. It is also makes the Scots appear more individualistic than is actually the case.

Earlier I argued that the Scots have a tendency to black and white thinking and this creates an environment which is harsh and judgmental. Make the wrong move, say the wrong thing and you could be damned forever. This problem is intensified by the Scots' lack of empathy. Empathy is about understanding what it is like to be another person - it is trying to see the world through another person's eyes or, as native American Indians say, 'to walk a mile in another's moccasins'. Empathy is different from sympathy. To be sympathetic is to feel sorry for someone's plight, particularly if the person is down-trodden or victimised in some way. And many Scots can and do readily sympathise with others. But empathy is not something that most Scots find easy. Encouraged to develop and use logic and principles rather than feelings and values, we are much more likely to judge another's behaviour by our own principles or logical standards than to try to understand their mindset. What's more, we often do not have much understanding of our own thoughts, feelings and motivations, let alone the sensitivity to understand another's.

Self-awareness

It was the Greek philosopher Socrates who issued the injunction 'know thyself' and Aristotle who brilliantly elaborated the challenge: 'Anyone can become angry - that is easy. But to be angry with the right person, to the right degree, at the right time, for the right purpose, and in the right way - this is not easy'.[13] Despite these wise words on the importance of self-awareness for 'the good life', there is still a strong feeling in contemporary Scotland that it is self-indulgent to spend time analysing yourself in any way. And it shows in a generalised lack of self-awareness and a concomitant lack of understanding of what makes other people tick. Alastair Reid, the Scottish-born poet, translator and essayist has lived most of his life in foreign lands and is a keen observer of Scottish life. According to Reid, in an essay on growing up in the Borders, the Scots, in comparison with other peoples he has known, do not appear to have much inner emotional life and they display little understanding of other people:

> Ask who someone is, and you will be given a catalogue in reply, of family connection, of employment, of memorable feats, of external idiosyncrasies, but nothing more - nothing which might come from insight or observation or personal judgement. It is as though all the human characteristics we associate with 'personality' and an inner life just did not exist. In short, what perplexes me about the Scots as a vague generality, and about the Borders in overwhelming particularity, is the almost complete absence of the analytical dimension, the capacity to see into oneself and other people.[14]

Reid wrote these words in 1970 and though much has changed in Scotland in the intervening years the Scots are still a people who do not understand themselves, their emotions, or their behaviour very well. Fewer still are prepared to talk about their emotional life. And more's the pity. Indeed this inability to talk about such feelings may be costing lives. For example, the male suicide rate in Scotland used to be the same as England's - now the rate for young men is double England's. Many of these men would literally prefer to die than talk about their problems and get some help and advice.

The Roots of Scotland's Poor Health

Even a cursory inspection of data on health and social problems shows that Scotland has an appalling record on a whole range of indicators (see over).

Evidence of the Scots' poor physical and mental health

- Scotland has recently managed to cast off its reputation as the heart attack capital of the world but it still has the highest rates of heart disease for men and women in western Europe. It is estimated that half a million people across Scotland now have coronary heart disease. Fewer Scots now die as a result of heart disease but Scotland retains her poor position in the health tables because other countries are also reducing the number of deaths from the disease.

- Nearly half of people in Scotland's most deprived areas smoke and smoking rates for women in Scotland are among the highest in Europe. Given these figures it is hardly surprising that Scotland has one of the highest rates of tobacco related deaths in the world. Indeed women in Scotland have a 50% higher risk of developing lung cancer than the average for the UK as a whole. Lung cancer is now the commonest cause of cancer death in Scotland for both men and women.

- The typical Scottish diet not only lacks nutrition but also makes you fat. Twenty-two per cent of Scottish women and 19% of men are now classed as clinically obese. What is particularly worrying is that children are getting fatter - 7% of girls and 8% of boys are now classed as obese.

- An Office of National Statistics report published in 2001 showed that Scottish people take more sick days and are more likely to have a 'couch potato' lifestyle than the UK average. It is estimated that 6 out of 10 men and 7 out of 10 women in Scotland take below the recommended levels of exercise. The Scots also spend more money on junk food than the UK average.

- The Scots have one of the highest mortality rates in the UK. The 2001 Regional Trends Report found that the overall mortality rate in Scotland was 11.8 deaths per 1000 people whereas London had 8.5 deaths per 1000, the lowest rate in the UK.

- Scotland has one of the highest suicide rates for young people in the western world. The global average suicide rate for under 21s is 16 per 100,000. In Scotland the figure is 36 per 100,000 - more than double. In England and Wales it is just 14 per 100,000. Suicide now accounts for 20% of male deaths in Scotland in the 15-24 age group.

- It is estimated that there are 56,000 heroin users in Scotland - per capita this is three times the rate for Germany.

- Studies suggest that the number of annual deaths in Scotland linked to alcohol consumption is three times higher than deaths from illegal drugs. It is estimated that over 1000 people per year die as a direct result of drinking too much alcohol. Indeed Dr W. Stuart Hislop, a consultant gastroenterologist in Paisley, argues that drink is such a problem in Scotland that 'it might be appropriate to consider the nation itself to be like an alcoholic'.[15]

In June 2002 the Scottish Council Foundation published a report called 'Possible Scotland' based on research commissioned by two major public health bodies in Scotland - The Public Health Institute and the Health Education Board. In the introduction Phil Hanlon, the Institute's Director, explains that both organisations have come to see that 'significant change is necessary at a societal level' if Scotland's 'relatively poor health position is to improve'.[16] To help understand what these changes in attitudes might be, the report presents the views of eight diverse Scottish focus groups on a whole range of subjects. Much of this evidence corroborates the analysis presented so far in this book. For example, many of the responses suggest that the Scots are a people eager to envision a different future but with 'little practical sense' of how these changes might be achieved. According to the report's authors, participants also found it difficult to make 'connections between the steps they could take in their own lives to achieve personal goals'[17] and were much more likely to look to the government or other agencies to provide solutions. In other words, there was much evidence of a 'dependency culture'. The authors also state that 'a palpable sense of resignation' was evident in some of the interviews conducted - the 'cannae' as much as the 'canny' Scot[18] is how they described the attitude. And all but one of the twenty experts from government agencies and other organisations who were shown the results 'considered the level of ambition expressed by the public to be disappointing but not surprising'.[19] Some talked of how 'dispiriting' it is that 'ambitions are so limited' in Scotland.

According to the authors, the people who participated in the focus groups also had little understanding of 'the value of emotional and spiritual intelligence, or whether and how these could be fostered'.[20] From the arguments I have presented throughout the book about the ingrained preference in Scottish culture for objective, logical thinking it is not difficult to see why the Scots as a people should be particularly deficient in emotional intelligence. The important question is - does it matter?

EQ v. IQ

In 1995 the American psychologist and journalist Daniel Goleman published a groundbreaking book asserting the importance of what he termed 'emotional intelligence'. Goleman's book quickly became a best seller, not just in the United States but right round the world. It is a serious, academic book which cannot easily be dismissed as pop psychology or glib self-help. In it Goleman utilises the latest scientific research on the architecture of the brain to show that 'feelings are typically indispensable for rational decisions', and that 'the emotional brain is as involved in reasoning as the thinking brain'.[21] Goleman argues that academic intelligence - the type of intelligence valued by western, male-dominated culture and measured by IQ tests - plays little part in how happy an individual is or how well they relate to others. He also claims that it only makes a limited contribution to personal effectiveness and success. Indeed Goleman argues that all the research shows that 'at best IQ contributes about 20 per cent to the factors that determine life success, which leaves 80 per cent to other factors'.[22]

There's little doubt that emotional intelligence has always been an important, if unrecognised, factor in success for the simple reason that those who understand what motivates others, and who can manage their own emotions well, will always have an advantage over those who do not possess such 'people skills'. But there is also little doubt that, like confidence itself, EQ matters more than it used to. In the complex world in which we now live it has become increasingly difficult for one single individual to achieve much on his or her own. Indeed one of the reasons why organisations energetically promote team working is because there is a new-found awareness that individuals are likely to be more effective if they work with, and through, others.

Emotional intelligence - or emotional literacy as it is now sometimes called - does not just matter in the workplace but also in our personal lives. It affects our self-esteem, our relationships, our health and our happiness. Knowing yourself, valuing yourself, managing your moods and being able to empathise are fundamental in any personal relationship, particularly in parenting.

So without emotional intelligence, relationships are bound to be fraught and both adults and children will suffer. Leaving aside intimate personal relationships, those who are emotionally intelligent are less likely to be aggressive, bigoted or indulge in self-destructive behaviours such as drug taking or drinking. So this is why Scottish health professionals have started to use Goleman's concepts when talking about some of Scotland's appalling health and social problems.[23] It is also why we have to start taking the issue seriously in Scotland.

Dr Margaret Hannah, a health consultant in Fife and a prominent member of the Scottish Public Mental Health Alliance, is clear that the lack of emotional literacy in Scotland underlies many of Scotland's problems, including overwork, intravenous drug misuse, binge drinking and poor parenting. And like other Alliance members she believes that emotional literacy is such an important skill in the twenty-first century that it should be taught to young children:

> We need emotionally intelligent people. These skills can be taught at school. We should start valuing these skills in school. Children should get the recognition of their ability to empathise and communicate - this has to be tied to the curriculum.[24]

Which brings us on, conveniently, to consider the role that education plays in self-esteem.

The Best Years of Our Lives?

Over the years many commentators have pointed out that a country's implicit values and beliefs are inevitably embedded in its education system. While undertaking research for this book I had a meeting with Linda Kinney who is Head of Children's Services for Stirling Council. As we talked I learned from Linda that the Italians' love of children can be seen in their education system. Indeed one area of Italy called Reggio Emilia is internationally recognised as the world leader in pre-school education. Linda, like many educationalists, has been to this part of Italy to see how their approach is different from that pursued back home. She explained that the nursery teachers in Reggio Emilia are not there to 'do' things to children but simply to create the conditions *where the children themselves* can develop. The role of the nursery is to give children the opportunity to be creative, express themselves and develop a strong sense of self. To outsiders one of most striking features of these Italian nurseries is that they are full of mirrors and the children are encouraged to use these mirrors to build their sense of themselves as individuals. Linda and her team are now trying out some of these ideas in a few nurseries in their area. For example, they are trying out a process known as 'documentation' which puts the child at the centre of his or her learning. A few mirrors have also been included in these pilot nurseries. Many of the staff involved in the pilot projects have found this new approach challenging for the simple reason that it requires them to interact with children in different ways. Even though the initial assessment of these pilot projects is very positive, a potentially intractable problem remains: some of the teachers in the primary schools these children are going on to are finding that they are too assertive. In other words, this new approach means the children are not trained to 'fit in' with the demands and routines of the typical Scottish classroom.

Scotland's schools have traditionally evolved from a completely different set of assumptions and values from those at the heart of Italian pre-school education. James Scotland published a two-volume study of Scottish education in 1969. The author argues that one of the most important assumptions in Scottish education is that 'the training of the intellect should take priority over all other facets of the pupil's personality.'[25] So unlike Italy, which has put a great deal of emphasis on creativity and artistic expression, Scotland traditionally devised a school system to promote literacy and analytical skills. Historically the Scots were entitled to feel proud of their education system - not only was Scotland the first country to ensure that every child, no matter how poor, could read, she also developed university education earlier than her much more prosperous neighbour south of the border. Scotland also acquired a world-wide reputation for the brilliance of the thinkers such institutions produced. But from the twentieth century on, many Scots have questioned the quality of school education in Scotland claiming that it is too concerned with teaching facts, hinders creativity and imagination, and is obsessed by tests and examination results. Indeed one 1920s critic even described the Scottish education system as 'the gospel according to marks'.[26]

Another of James Scotland's observations on the Scottish education system is that it is teacher focused. 'The most important person in the school,' writes Scotland, 'no matter what the theorist say, is not the pupil but the (inadequately rewarded) teacher.'[27] Over the years there has been no shortage of critics who have pointed out that Scottish education is relentlessly hierarchical and authoritarian. And this view is best expressed by Alexander Scott in his poetic gem:

Scotch Education
I tell't ye
I tell't ye.[28]

But, before some negative Scots filter such comments through 'the dark glass' and use them as another rod to beat Scotland with, let me point out that there is nothing specifically Scottish about such views of education. Educators such as the American Paul Goodman, the Latin American Paulo Freire and European thinkers like Rudolf Steiner have criticised the education systems they were exposed to for similar reasons. And before we decide, in true Scottish style, that our teachers must come top of the class for being the most sadistic we must remember that countless Irish and English writers have exposed the savagery of the schools they had the misfortune to attend. What's more, when it comes to progressive ideas on education, Scots like A.S. Neill and R. F. MacKenzie of Summerhill fame, as well as educational theorists like John Anderson, have made an important contribution to the debate.

I do not intend to analyse here the nature of Scottish education and assess whether it was, and is, truly more authoritarian than other systems. I am simply going to argue that Scotland's school system is still important to the way children learn to know their place and that the system routinely fails to help children develop self-awareness or real self-esteem. I have formed this view as a result of the contact I have had with Scottish schools over the years. For example I have run many different types of courses for teachers and I have had various occasions to talk to pupils about the type of themes I've covered in this chapter. I also have two sons who are products of the Scottish education system. And, of course, I am also a product myself.

I believe that the whole ethos of Scottish education runs contrary to the development of healthy self-acceptance, and hence self-esteem, as it is too obsessed by academic performance and based on a standardised notion of how children should develop. Even though there is now more emphasis placed on personal and social development, to 'get on' at school a pupil must possess a fairly narrow set of academic skills. If you are not an academic type (and that covers most people) then the system is not designed to make you feel worthwhile or successful. What's more it doesn't do enough to help you develop the kind of EQ skills which are increasingly needed in the modern world.

Despite these rather critical remarks, I recognise that Scottish primary schools have changed radically since I was a pupil in the 1950s and that many of the worst practices have gone - the belt, the qualifying exam, the rote learning, the constant shouting, the pupils arranged in rows according to ability. The sheer joylessness of it all. Instead there are more teachers who believe that children should be encouraged, praised and supported and positive developments such as 'circle time' where children are able to talk about their feelings and solve problems more responsibly. Nowadays, it is possible to walk into many primary schools in Scotland and see children positively enthusiastic about learning and being taught by teachers who help them to feel good and positive about themselves. Sadly this is much less true in secondary schools. Of course, there have been some changes. The belt is forbidden. There are many more teachers with a benign attitude and much more taking place under the banner of 'personal and social development', yet somehow *the pupils' experience* of secondary school has not changed that much in the past fifty years. Many still leave school (with four highers or no highers) not feeling that good about themselves; more conscious of what they can't do right, of their failings, than with a strong sense of themselves as a worthwhile person and this affects not only how they communicate but also their inter-personal skills. And it is this lack of confidence and people skills that employers are particularly concerned about, as I explained in an earlier chapter.

Recently I was asked to take part in a Radio Scotland programme which was broadcast from a middle-class secondary school in Perth. I was part of a panel invited along to discuss the topic of self-confidence with an audience mainly comprising the most vocal pupils in the school. Members of the school management team valiantly tried to give the impression that this was a modern, forward-looking school which took such personal development issues seriously. The first-year pupils who spoke were positive about their experience as they had a teacher who encouraged and inspired them but just about every other pupil complained that the teachers did not like pupils to appear confident; that they were far happier telling you what you couldn't do well than encouraging you or inspiring you to do better. Many said they thought teachers just wanted pupils to know their place.

Any time I undertake assertiveness training with young people they immediately grasp the relevance to their own lives. After all, this is about them having the courage to say no for themselves (to sex, drugs or drink, for example). But, to a person, they hold the view that if the core of assertive behaviour is expressing yourself honestly, yet respectfully, they would be given a row for being assertive in school. 'We would be called "cheeky" if we were to voice our opinions,' is what most teenagers say. And they're right. Even well-meaning teachers often do not think they have to ask pupils for their views. Indeed I watched in disbelief as an assistant head teacher interrupted an assertiveness session I was undertaking with fifth and sixth year girls to shoo them into a photographic session without even asking them if they wanted to be in the picture. Young people, aged seventeen and eighteen, have told me how they feel humiliated at having to wear school uniform, or bring a note from their parents if they are ill.

If even the cream of Scottish pupils leave school feeling it did little to build their confidence and sense of themselves, imagine what it is like for those who leave with few academic qualifications or poor basic skills. A few years ago I ran some personal development courses at the Wise Group for trainees who had been unemployed for long periods of time. Many were not that literate and found it painful to talk about their experience of school. 'I don't think they always mean it but those teachers make you feel you're thick, a no hoper,' is how one man put it.

As the Scottish system has traditionally been teacher centred it has failed to give enough attention to motivation and to the fact that different types of people learn in different ways. Many types of pupils, possibly the majority, are turned off learning if it isn't interactive, fun or relevant to their perception of real life. In the past, the fear of authority in society at large meant that such children could be contained at school - if need be belted into submission. But nowadays unmotivated, undisciplined pupils often wreak havoc in the classroom, disrupting the learning of other pupils and making teachers' lives a misery.

I have no intention of dumping on teachers and holding them personally responsible for people's negative experiences of education - it is the system which is largely at fault. Much of the time teachers themselves are victims of a top-down process which simply tells them what to do, making them feel more junior and less professional. Of course, individual teachers have some room for manoeuvre. They can refrain from using sarcasm and belittling young people by telling them they are 'thick', for example. But much of the time teachers operate in a system which forces them, like it or not, into a way of behaving and relating to pupils which is not of their choosing and which they simply cannot change.

So, for a variety of reasons, teachers are carriers of many traditional attitudes in Scotland which keep people in their place and undermine the development of individual confidence. In recent years there have been some positive initiatives, such as the money now being spent on Young Enterprise. These projects, alongside some other changes currently taking place, may improve pupils' confidence and inter-personal skills to some extent. But I do not believe it is possible to graft on a few projects of this kind and expect it to deliver the substantial change in attitudes which Scotland needs to meet the challenges of the modern world. The Scottish education system requires much more radical changes at root and branch level. We need a new ethos and vision for Scottish schools. The Scottish people and their political and educational leaders must have the courage to grasp the thistle and start envisioning a new system - a system which fosters the kind of skills and attitudes needed in the new millennium and that includes academic and practical skills as well as self-confidence, interpersonal skills and emotional intelligence.

Achievement v Resignation

Throughout this and previous chapters we have seen how the typical Scot is subjected to two contradictory pressures - the first pressure is to be just like everyone else and leads to the fear of being different from others and censured by them. The second pressure is to 'prove' yourself; to achieve and be successful. And this pressure has undoubtedly provided the drive for many of Scotland's greatest sons. (I use the term sons deliberately because, as we have seen, historically there have been very few 'famous' Scotswomen.) For example, Hugh MacDiarmid was a Scottish figure with a great need to prove himself. According to Ann Edwards Boutelle, in her study of Hugh MacDiarmid's poetry, his 'lack of confidence coupled with a need to prove himself superior, has given us some of MacDiarmid's most interesting poetry'.[29] When we examine Scottish history we can see that when this need to prove yourself superior or worthy in some way has been coupled with some other strong Scottish traits such as seriousness and a sense of mission and purpose, it has led to some very fine Scottish achievements. But what is also clear is that the vast majority of Scotsmen and women have bowed to the first type of pressure. They have toed the line, conformed, kept their heads down. Resigned themselves to their fate.

So what is the answer to the Scots' problems with confidence? This is not the place to look in depth at the kind of health and education projects which might be needed so I shall confine myself to a few general remarks.

The sense of demoralisation and lack of confidence in Scotland is so strong that it is fairly natural for people to assume that the answer is to encourage more people to excel at what they do. At the school radio discussion I mentioned earlier, one seventeen year old boy argued that self-esteem is all about 'being the best'. Presumably concerned that he sounded elitist, however, the boy argued 'it doesn't matter if you are an astronaut or a bin man, what you need to do is be the best'. And not one of the hundred or so people present - either his peers or his teachers - questioned this view. In fact they nodded in agreement with him. Yet such a view simply does not make sense. Feeling you have to be the best to feel good about yourself is more likely to bleed confidence from people rather than build it. It means self-esteem is only within the grasp of the elite in any group and even then is short-lived as they are bound to be knocked off their pedestal at some point.

To get off the perfect/worthless seesaw and to start building genuine self-confidence in Scotland we have to understand that nobody is perfect and that it is human to have weaknesses and flaws; that it is okay not to excel at everything we do. We have to learn to like ourselves 'warts and all'. This is why Jungian typology, which illustrates so graphically that development is inevitably 'one sided' - that we can cultivate strengths only by simultaneously developing weaknesses - is so potentially liberating for the Scots. In short, Jung shows that perfection, and excellence across the board, is an illusion, not because we are mere, worthless mortals and only God is great, but because the human mind is constructed in such a way that we all develop some mental functions, and hence some skills, more than others.

Once we accept that we can never be perfect, and that we do not have to excel to be worthwhile people, life is not only more pleasant but we are then on the road to genuine personal development. Carl Rogers, a founding father of the personal development movement in the United States, once remarked: 'the curious paradox is that it is only when I accept myself just as I am that I can begin to grow and develop'.[30] Self-acceptance is therefore not the route to complacency but real development. Freed of the need to be perfect, or to excel, and liberated from the haunting fear of mistakes and criticism we would discover that 'anything that is worth doing is worth doing badly'. In other words, we would feel more encouraged to try new things. We would be less fearful of criticism and generally more open to learning and improvement. We would be prepared to take more responsibility for ourselves and stop being less dependent on others. Paradoxically, by being more accepting of ourselves and others, the achievements of the many, and not just the few, would be higher.

NOTES

1 David Hume, *My Own Life* (The Mill House Press, 1927), p. 1.

2 Pamela Stephenson, *Billy* (Harper Collins: London, 2001), p. 152.

3 John Buchan 'Some Scottish Characteristics' in W.A. Craigie, John Buchan, Peter Giles & J. M. Bulloch, *The Scottish Tongue* (Cassell & Company: London, 1924), p. 59.

4 Quoted by Janet Adam Smith, 'Some Eighteenth-Century Ideas on Scotland and the Scots' in N. T. Phillipson & Rosalind Mitchison (eds), *Scotland in the Age of Improvement* (Edinburgh University Press: Edinburgh, 1970), p. 113.

5 Pamela Stephenson, *Billy,* p. 175.

6 Ibid., p. 155.

7 Quoted in W. Gordon Smith, *This is my Country: A Personal Blend of the Purest Scotch* (Souvenir Press: London, 1976), p. 226.

8 Douglas Fraser in Tom Devine and Paddy Logue, Being Scottish (Polygon: Edinburgh, 2002), p. 77.

9 Ibid., p. 223.

10 Interview with Pamela Stevenson, *Sunday Herald Magazine,* 7 October 2001.

11 Dr Jonathon Levie and Dr Laura Steele, *Global Economic Monitor, Scotland 2001,* University of Strathclyde, p. 17.

12 *The Broons,* (D.C. Thomson, Dundee).

13 Aristotle, *Nicomachean Ethics* (Oxford University Press: Oxford, 1998).

14 Alastair Reid, 'Borderlines' in Karl Miller, *Memoirs of a Modern Scotland* (Faber and Faber: London, 1970), p. 160.

15 The Herald, 17 July, 2001.

16 *'Possible Scotland'* (Scottish Council Foundation: Edinburgh, 2002), p. 3.

17 Ibid., p. 27.

18 Ibid., p. 42.

19 Ibid., p. 29.

20 Ibid., p. 39

21 Daniel Goleman, *Emotional Intelligence* (Bloomsbury: London, 1996), p. 28.

22 Ibid., p. 34.

23 See, for example, 'With Health in Mind: Improving mental health and wellbeing in Scotland' produced by The Scottish Public Mental Health Alliance (Scottish Council Foundation: Edinburgh, 2002).

24 *The Sunday Herald,* 7 October 2001.

NOTES

25 James Scotland, *The History of Scottish Education,* Volume 2 (University of London Press: London, 1969), p. 275.

26 G. M. Thomson, Caledonia: Or *The Future of the Scots* (Kegan Paul, Trench, Trubner: London), p. 51.

27 James Scotland, *The History of Scottish Education,* Volume 2, p. 275.

28 *The Collected Poems of Alexander Scott,* David S. Robb (ed.), (Mercat Press: Edinburgh, 1994), p. 144.

29 Ann Edwards Boutelle, *Thistle and Rose - A Study of MacDiarmid's Poetry* (MacDonald's: Loanhead, 1980), p. 20.

30 Carl Rogers, *On Becoming a Person* (Houghton Mifflin: New York, 1995).

15

Towards a Confident Scotland

'We need to rediscover the can-do instincts that are too often unleashed only when Scots emigrate. If our politicians can't lead us on that journey, we need to start thinking about how we can do it for ourselves.'

Alf Young, *The Herald, January 2001*

There is no simple answer to the question - 'Why do the Scots lack confidence in themselves and their country?' Throughout the book I have outlined and explained the various beliefs and attitudes which, over the centuries, have militated against the development of Scottish self-confidence. I thought it would be useful for this concluding chapter if I put all the various factors in a pot and boiled them down to a few pithy statements which encapsulate the most important barriers to the development of Scottish self-confidence. I list below the ones which readily floated to the top:

- A strong tendency to criticise and focus on what is wrong with something rather than to praise, appreciate or be positive.
- An overwhelming sense that people's behaviour can be judged right or wrong, worthwhile or useless.
- A prevailing notion that if anyone makes a mistake or does anything wrong, no excuses will be permitted in their defense and that they should be blamed and criticised for their misdemeanors.
- An undeveloped sense of privacy: everything you do in life could be the focus of others' criticism and censure.
- A general belief that you are not okay just as you are and that you must compete and prove your worth.

- A strong set of egalitarian values which stress that no-one is more important than anyone else and a culture where people are routinely put down if they are seen to get above themselves.
- A prevailing belief that it is better if people do not like themselves too much.
- A strong sense that if you question Scottish values or step outside conventional behaviour or opinions your very right to call yourself 'Scottish' may be under threat.

There is nothing peculiarly Scottish about any of these individual beliefs, tendencies or attitudes. But there is something distinctly Scottish in the way they reinforce one another and are passed on through the culture. Over the years, such attitudes and beliefs have encouraged Scots to feel unduly fearful of doing anything different or making mistakes. They have also led to conformity and mediocrity and encouraged millions of the most able Scots to emigrate to other lands.

For decades there has been a general acceptance in Scotland that confidence is an issue facing the Scots yet little has been done to examine, let alone address the problem. Again, if we examine some common Scottish beliefs it is not difficult to see why. The Scots believe it is self-indulgent, and weak, to think about yourself, your emotions or your relationships. This means that while there is widespread agreement on the importance of the confidence gap, Scottish culture discourages people from the real introspection and self-analysis necessary to begin to understand the problem. The Scots are further discouraged from adequately analysing the confidence problem because there is an overwhelming tendency within the culture to see all problems as social or political. Just as all roads once led to Rome, all problems in Scotland lead back to politics or to the collective in some way. This point is admirably illustrated in Neal Ascherson's latest book, *Stone Voices*. Ascherson is aware that confidence is an issue in Scotland. Indeed at one point he claims that 'The Scottish trauma is to do with self-doubt (sometimes masked in unreal self-assertion) ... '.[1] But Ascherson mainly confines his analysis of the trauma, which he calls 'the St Andrews Fault', to the political domain. Thus he claims that 'above all, the trauma shows itself in a chronic mistrust of the public dimension.'[2] It is true that Ascherson argues that religion played its part in the creation of 'the Fault' but he still sees the solution to the problem as being largely political and constitutional and hence outside the immediate sphere of influence of individual Scots.

The idea that politics is the root-cause as well as the solution to Scotland's confidence problem is common within nationalist thinking. As I have shown at various points in this book, many nationalists believe the solution to Scotland's confidence problem is simple: independence. Socialists too frequently present a political answer, this time a fairer distribution of wealth, as the panacea to any Scottish problem you care to name. And for many policy makers in Scotland the solution to problems in their subject area often lies in strengthening Scottish identity, Scottish communities or feelings of citizenship. As I argued in Chapter 13, even among literary analysts there is an obsession with explaining literature with reference to writers' Scottish identity and the Scottish body politic. Of course, politics matter and many problems need to be solved collectively, but in Scotland the focus is so much on this collective world that the strength and psychological health of the individual gets lost.

Scotland will only begin to solve the growing crisis of confidence if alongside a belief in community and the collective there is a respect for, and encouragement of, individuality. Instead of a focus on 'citizenship' - a flagship policy for Scottish education unveiled in 2002 - Scottish schools must seriously begin to put the needs of the individual pupil at the centre of learning. We must learn to respect and value diversity. The arts and culture must be encouraged, not because they are politically or economically good for Scotland, but because they are worthwhile in their own right and symbolise a culture where individuals can express themselves. We also need to encourage individual creativity, flair and enterprise in whole areas of Scottish life. And I mean genuinely encourage rather than mouth the words and pay lip-service as is often the case in the current climate.

When I sat down to write this book I thought I would end by giving some suggestions for detailed policy initiatives to support the kind of changes which I think are necessary. But as I wrote I realised that the biggest challenge facing the Scots in raising confidence, or indeed in tackling any political problems, is not the quality or quantity of ideas, but about how we talk and engage with one another. Unless we begin to break out of some of the limiting and self-defeating beliefs I have outlined in the course of this book we shall be unable to create a more positive culture; one which nurtures and supports confidence rather than one which stifles it. So at the top of my list for the type of change needed to encourage greater confidence in Scotland is not detailed policy changes but how we individually see the world and how we talk to one another. Above all else we need to inject a healthy dose of wisdom into all areas of Scottish life.

The Problem of Wisdom
The mace lying in the Scottish Parliament bears four carefully chosen words which were broadcast to the world by Donald Dewar at the Opening Ceremony of the Scottish Parliament - wisdom, justice, compassion and integrity.

When it comes to realising important overarching principles or values, no society can afford to rest on its laurels. That being said, it is easy to see from the argument that I have presented in this book that integrity and justice go with the grain of Scottish culture and character. As a people we are deeply wedded to the idea of acting in a principled and moral fashion and of ensuring fair play and transparency in our decision making. From time to time there may be lapses, as was the case with Henry McLeish's 'Officegate' scandal. And, of course, there will be times when the Scottish justice system needs to be reinvigorated by new thinking and procedures to keep abreast of the modern world. But nonetheless, my basic point holds true: integrity and justice are important principles for the Scots and we should not find it too difficult to act in accordance with them. Look round the world and you will see that the same cannot be said of many other nations.

And what of wisdom? In 1961 Moray McLaren edited a book called *The Wisdom of the Scots* - an anthology of poetry, philosophy texts, extracts of historical documents and proverbs which McLaren thinks sum up Scottish wisdom.[3] Of course, there are wise words in these pages, such as John Barbour's plea for the importance of freedom and David Hume's defence of scepticism, but much of what McLaren chooses concerns the elucidation of 'first principles' - closely argued texts with many 'therefores' and 'if so' and 'if then' constructions. This is the type of thinking at which the Scots excel and it can be insightful, helpful and fiendishly clever but it is not necessarily wise. Indeed I would go so far as to say that one of the problems in Scotland is that Scottish culture does not encourage the development of wisdom.

What is wisdom? Most definitions of wisdom include two discernible elements. One is that it is a type of intelligence arising from a combination of different sources of information and mental processes. For example, the *Collins English Dictionary* defines it to be 'the ability or result of an ability to think and act utilizing knowledge, experience, understanding, common sense and insight'. So while a clever person may excel in one or two spheres such as knowledge of facts or the application of logical reasoning, the wise person blends different types of information and uses a number of mental processes. And this leads to a second, essential aspect of wisdom: it is based on 'accumulated knowledge, learning or enlightenment'. This means that wisdom is earned through experience and why it tends to increase with age.

So what is the kind of wisdom it would be helpful for the Scots to acquire? Increased self-awareness and a heightened sense of self would be helpful, for those who are wise know their strengths and weaknesses and use this knowledge to enhance their effectiveness and achieve their goals. They also know their imperfections but do not berate themselves unnecessarily for their mistakes or their faults. The wise also understand others. They are not out to blame and readily forgive others for their limitations. And it is this combination of being at peace with yourself, as well as being able to empathise with others, which means that wise people have positive and productive relationships. What's more, people who have acquired wisdom do things because they think they are of value and have little need to impress other people. In short, wise people have a developed sense of self and a strong notion of what they think constitutes 'the good life'.

Clearly, some individuals in Scotland have acquired wisdom but on the whole Scottish culture does not encourage us to learn the lessons which help us to become wise. To see more wisdom developing in Scotland we need to stop seeing things, people and events in such extreme either/or terms. As I have shown throughout this book, the Scots have a tendency to see everything as dualities - worthwhile/useless, good/bad, right/wrong, moral/immoral, saved/damned. But such thinking often simplifies the complexity of human existence. For example, things, such as the internet or television, can simultaneously have positive and negative effects. People can have a variety of motives for action and they can be a mixture of the altruistic and the self-serving. Tragic events can lead an individual both to despair and heightened spiritual and emotional awareness. In other words, to both positive and negative feelings. 'Good' things can become bad if overdone. Being a loving, caring parent is a good example of this - it is possible to be over-caring and smother the child, thus retarding development. Indeed in all areas of life it is difficult to judge behaviour as good or bad because it depends on the context. In other words, we must ask how 'appropriate' it is for someone to behave in one way or another. For example, it may be commendable for a lawyer to reason from first principles when arguing his or her client's case but completely inappropriate for a primary head teacher to use the same approach when running a school. Very rarely can we divorce something from its context, try to derive first principles and decide whether it is good or bad. Take honesty. For most people honesty is a fundamental human principle, but there are times when honesty is not the best policy. As William Blake once said, 'A truth that's told with bad intent/beats all the lies you can invent'. Life is much more complex than we Scots often allow. Rarely are things divisible into neat 'good' and 'bad' categories - it depends.

In today's complex and interconnected world it is exceedingly difficult to find political solutions to problems. If we had more wisdom we would refrain from denouncing as immoral people who hold views different from our own. More often than not the positions people adopt stem from their experience and their sense of priorities rather than from deep personal morality. So how helpful is it to cast people's opinions as immoral rather than misguided or mistaken? If a moralistic tone continues to characterise political debate in Scotland all it will do is engender ill-feeling and cynicism and make people afraid to make their opinions known in case they will be personally attacked. And, again as I've shown throughout this book, feeling that you have to conform to an accepted set of ideas is one thing we have to break free from if we are going to solve some of our pressing social problems.

It would also be helpful if we gave more weight in Scotland to the importance of human feelings and emotions - real wisdom is never just of the head but also of the heart. In other words, it gives weight not just to intellectual matters but to the emotional, feeling element as well. For example, if we gave more weight to human feelings in Scottish schools we would pay more attention to how pupils are motivated; how they feel about themselves; and how demoralised teachers feel at repeatedly being told what to do. Our decision makers would stop trying to implement educational change via control and regulation and would place more emphasis on motivation and inspiration. But it is also true to say that too much heart rather than head in public life can also be a problem, for an over concern for harmony and values can easily lead to complacency and paralysis. As is often the case in life, some kind of balance is required.

So am I saying that it is never good to argue from irreducible first principles; that morality has no place in life? Emphatically not. There are times when principles are of fundamental importance. There are times when issues are black and white and a moral stance should be taken. But, as I argued earlier - it depends. Context is everything. The American psychologist Abraham Maslow once remarked: 'If all we have in our tool box is a hammer, all the world will look like a nail'. In Scotland we need to have more mental tools and approaches at our disposal so that we don't keep using logic, either/or thinking and first principles to keep hammering home the same messages, for all we are doing is limiting everyone's room for manoeuvre. We need to be more flexible and learn to value difference. It is these types of changes which would also help us to realise the fourth value on the Scottish mace - compassion. It is by becoming wise that we shall become more empathetic and compassionate individuals.

An Optimistic Future

It is also important for us to counteract the strong pessimistic streak which bedevils discussion of Scottish issues. We are not doomed. We are not hopeless or powerless. As individuals and as a nation we have much more power and control over our own destiny than we often allow. So we need more optimism in Scotland. But not the optimism that is completely unrealistic; that encourages us to set our sights too high and then encourages cynicism to set in when we don't achieve our goals. A good example of such unrealistic, and ultimately unhelpful, optimism can be seen in Angus Calder's introduction to his recent book *Scotlands of the Mind* in which he encourages Scotland to 'recreate itself as a land without prejudice'.[4] Throughout the book Calder is critical of a number of ways the Scots behave and see the world, so why does he believe that somehow they are going to move to the other end of the spectrum? Has he asked himself whether such a land has ever existed and why Scotland, of all countries, should manage to recreate itself in this way?

As a typical Scot myself, I have perhaps dwelled too much in this book on the problems in the Scots view of the world, and the multifarious social and economic problems which confront the nation. Nonetheless I am optimistic about the opportunities for change. A huge number of Scots have a strong sense of mission and purpose and a passionate desire to make life better for other people. Unlike many Americans, for example, who see the world in such individualistic terms they often find it difficult to accept their responsibility to others, the Scots fully understand that all our lives are interconnected. Over the centuries Scotland has produced a large number of forward thinking, intelligent and innovative people and there is no reason why we cannot continue to do so. When we add into this pot of positive Scottish characteristics the Scots' reputation for being a people who act with integrity we have a formidable brew to sustain us in the modern world of constant change. And we can also take heart from the fact that Scotland is in a stronger political situation than she has been for centuries for she now has a good measure of Home Rule and a strong platform from which to campaign for more powers, or full independence, if that is what people want. In a hard-wired world, Scotland's isolation from the rest of Europe no longer matters the way it once did. And finally, Scotland could also capitalise on her size. Most political commentators these days admit that small countries are more able to respond to change quickly and so have definite advantages over their larger neighbours.

If the Scots could alter their mindset by even twenty per cent to embrace the type of attitudinal changes I have already outlined, we would be in an exceptionally strong position not only to make Scotland a better place to live but also to contribute to the type of thinking which is now needed in a global world of continuous change and uncertainty.

For Scotland to become the vibrant, confident nation most Scots aspire to, another change is needed. Alasdair Gray once wrote that 'the curse of Scotland' is 'the wee hard men who hammer Scotland down to the same dull level as themselves'. We can't take away their hammers or stop them thundering on about what's right and proper or 'truly Scottish' but we can stop paying attention to them and we can prevent them from fashioning Scotland in their own image. But we can only do this if we rebel against some cherished Scottish values. Instead of knowing our place we must begin to think well of ourselves, rather than fear drawing attention to ourselves we must stick our heads above the parapet. Instead of apologising for wanting to break out of restrictive Scottish beliefs and practices, we must start valuing our opinions and making our voices heard. Instead of toeing the line and playing safe, we need to start taking more risks and learning from mistakes. Of course, we should continue to honour some fundamental Scottish principles and basic beliefs but we should not feel obliged to cling to them so tightly that we sacrifice our feelings, emotions and personal values. We also need to stop policing each other's attitudes and behaviour and to start cultivating a greater sense of privacy and boundaries.

For Scotland to become a more confident nation and a better place to live we must cease the endless quest for Scottishness and renounce our previous obsession with Scottish identity. Almost three hundred years have elapsed since the Union and there is still a 'strong Scots accent of the mind' - we can afford to relax and take Scottishness more for granted. In place of the quest for Scottish identity we need a quest for individual identity. We need to encourage individual Scots to go forth and be themselves. We need to create the conditions where creativity flourishes, not conformity. Liberating this huge untapped potential would not just benefit individual Scots - Scottish society as a whole would be enriched. Such changes would not create a perfect Scotland but they would create a more vibrant, confident Scotland. A Scotland full of possibilities for people.

NOTES

1 Neal Ascherson, *Stone Voices: The Search for Scotland* (Granta: London, 2002), pp. 84 -85.

2 Ibid., p. 85.

3 Moray McLaren, *The Wisdom of the Scots* (Michael Joseph: London, 1961).

4 Angus Calder, *Scotlands of the Mind* (Luath Press: Edinburgh, 2002), p. xvi.

INDEX

INDEX

INDEX